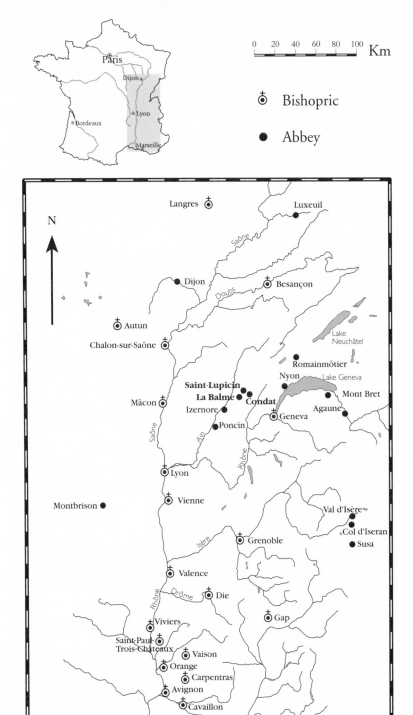

0   20   40   60   80   100 Km

⊚ Bishopric

● Abbey

N

Langres ⊚   Luxeuil ●

Saône

Dijon ●   ⊚ Besançon

Doubs

⊚ Autun

Lake
Neuchâtel

Chalon-sur-Saône ⊚

● Romainmôtier

Nyon   Lake Geneva

Saint-Lupicin ●   Mont Bret ●

La Balme ● **Condat** ●

Mâcon ⊚ Izernore ●   Agaune ●

Poncin ●   ⊚ Geneva

Saône *Ain* *Rhône*

⊚ Lyon

⊚ Vienne

Montbrison ●   Val d'Isère ●

Col d'Iseran ●

Isère   ⊚ Grenoble   Susa ●

⊚ Valence

Rhône *Drôme* ⊚ Die

⊚ Gap

⊚ Viviers

Saint-Paul-
Trois-Châteaux ⊚ ⊚ Vaison

⊚ Orange
⊚ Carpentras
⊚ Avignon
⊚ Cavaillon

⊚ Arles   *Durance*

Lérins ●

Agde ⊚   ⊚ Marseille

CISTERCIAN STUDIES SERIES:
NUMBER ONE HUNDRED SEVENTY-EIGHT

THE LIFE OF THE JURA FATHERS

Library of Congress Cataloging-in-Publication Data

Vies des pères du Jura. English. The life of the Jura fathers : the life and
rule of the holy fathers Romanus, Lupicinus, and Eugendus, abbots of the
monasteries in the Jura Mountains : with appendices, Avitus of Vienne, letter
XVIIII to Viventiolus—Eucherius of Lyon, The passion of the martyrs of
Agaune, Saint Maurice and his companions [and] In praise of the desert /
translated, with an introduction, by Tim Vivian, Kim Vivian, Jeffrey Burton
Russell, with the assistance of Charles Cummings ; preface by Terrence
Kardong ; foreword by Adalbert de Vogüé.
    p. cm.—(Cistercian studies series ; no. 178)
    Includes bibliographical references (p.) and indexes.
    ISBN 0-87907-678-X (alk. paper)—ISBN 0-87907-778-6 (pbk. : alk.
paper)
    1. Christian saints—Jura Mountains Region (France and Switzer
land)—Biography. 2. Romanus, Saint, 5th cent. 3. Lupicinus, Saint, 5th
cent. 4. Eugendus, Saint, d. 514. 5. Jura Mountains Region (France and
Switzerland)—Church history—Early church, ca. 30–600. I. Vivian, Tim.
II. Vivian, Kim. III. Russell, Jeffrey Burton. IV. Title. V. Series.
BR1710.V54 1999
274.4'4502—dc21   99–039501

CISTERCIAN STUDIES SERIES:
NUMBER ONE HUNDRED SEVENTY-EIGHT

the life of the jura fathers

THE LIFE AND RULE OF THE HOLY FATHERS ROMANUS, LUPICINUS, AND EUGENDUS, ABBOTS OF THE MONASTERIES IN THE JURA MOUNTAINS

With Appendices:

Avitus of Vienne
Letter XVIIII to Viventiolus

Eucherius of Lyon
*The Passion of the Martyrs of Agaune,
Saint Maurice and His Companions
In Praise of the Desert*

Translated, with an Introduction,
by
Tim Vivian
Kim Vivian
Jeffrey Burton Russell
with the assistance of Charles Cummings, ocso

Preface by Terrence Kardong, osb

Foreword by Adalbert de Vogüé, osb

Cistercian Publications
Kalamazoo, Michigan – Spencer, Massachusetts

This translation is based on the latin edition of
François Martine. *Vies des pères du Jura.*
Sources Chrétiennes 142. Paris. Les Éditions du Cerf, 1988.

THIS VOLUME WAS EDITED BY JOHN LEINENWEBER

CISTERCIAN PUBLICATIONS

Editorial Offices
Institute of Cistercian Studies
Western Michigan University
Kalamazoo, MI 49008
Cistercian Publications (Distribution)
Saint Joseph's Abbey
167 North Spencer Road
Spencer MA 01562-1233

Cistercian Publications (UK)
Mount Saint Bernard Abbey
Coalville, Leicester LE 67 5UL

The work of Cistercian Publications
is made possible in part by support from Western Michigan University
to The Institute of Cistercian Studies

Typeset by BookComp, Grand Rapids, Michigan
Printed in the United States of America

IN MEMORIAM

Jerrold M. Vivian
(1920–1978)

Leslie Paul Vivian
(1946–1983)

Louise S. Vivian
(1923–1996)

'I imagine the dead waking, dazed, into a shadowless light in which they know themselves altogether for the first time. It is a light that is merciless until they can accept its mercy; by it they are at once condemned and redeemed. It is Hell until it is Heaven. Seeing themselves in that light, if they are willing, they see how far they have failed the only justice of loving one another; it punishes them by their own judgment. And yet, in suffering that light's awful clarity, in seeing themselves within it, they see its forgiveness and its beauty, and are consoled. In it they are loved completely, even as they have been, and so are changed into what they could not have been but what, if they could have imagined it, they would wish to be.

'That light can come into this world only as love, and love can enter only by suffering. Not enough light has ever reached us here among the shadows, and yet I think it has never been entirely absent'.

Wendell Berry, *A World Lost*

and to
Sister Miriam of the Cross OCD

table of contents

preface

T HE APPEARANCE of an english translation of the *Life of the Jura Fathers*, the first published to my knowledge, gives me great satisfaction. For a benedictine monk like myself, a monastic account contemporary with Benedict's Rule cannot be without interest, especially when it comes not from the remote deserts of the east but from nearby Gaul. For many years I had seen references to the *Life of the Jura Fathers* and wondered what was in it, but no english translation was available. Finally my curiosity was so piqued that I began to translate it myself, but did not complete the job. Now the work is done, and the *Life* is accessible to all of us.

The *Life of the Jura Fathers* is an account of a monastic foundation in the rugged Jura Mountains of eastern France just before the time of Saint Benedict. This foundation, called Condat in French but Condadisco in Latin, had the good fortune to have not one but three great abbots among its founding fathers. Eventually they created other monasteries at nearby Lauconne (Lauconnus) and La Balme (Balma) but none of them have perdured to our time. The same cannot be said about the memory of the three great abbots, who are still venerated in the Jura today.

Although the account of their Life must be called hagiographic in that its aim is edification rather than historical information, nevertheless these three lives are recounted in a manner that not only conveys a good deal of the local color, but also manages to give us a fairly rounded picture of each saint. Romanus comes through as the aggressive, magnanimous missionary. Lupicinus is a harder character, but his courage often defends the weak and poor. Eugendus is a retiring mystic who still manages to function well as an administrator.

The *Life of the Jura Fathers* is not a mere string of miracle-stories as is sometimes the case with other hagiography of the period, not excluding Gregory's *Dialogues*. At least in some places, the anonymous author narrates an episode in such great detail and at such length that we get a good feel for late fifth-century monastic life and culture. This does not mean, of course, that the sensibility and spirituality of that time will be easily accessible to the modern reader. When Lupicinus gently rebukes an ascetic for ruining his health, for example, we wonder why he does not practice what he preaches. Nor does it mean that we learn all we would like to know about these monks. For instance, there is hardly a mention of the Divine Office in this document, nor do we learn much about the governance of the jura monasteries.

As one who has personally spent long hours battling the convoluted syntax and esoteric vocabulary of this latin text, I am very appreciative of the readable and accurate english version this team of translators has produced. This is not a mere paraphrase but a careful translation that tries to account for all the Latin. It is not easy to combine that aim with producing a graceful english sentence, but this translation does it.

The problem is not just the difficulty of the language but the obscurity of the history and spirituality of the merovingian period. No doubt all but the specialist will need the background help that is provided by an excellent introduction. This introduction and many of the helpful notes are based on the 1968 french version of François Martine (Sources chrétiennes 142) but the authors of the english work have enriched the data by observations from recent personal visits to Saint-Claude, Saint-Maurice, and other sites of the Jura.

Why is it important that these ancient monastic texts be translated in and for our times? Although they come from a very different time and place, nevertheless they do address many of the same problems we face today. The asceticism of the Jura Fathers attempts to counter the greed and lust and self-serving spirit that always threaten christian life. The dedication of these monk to christian community is a tonic for our individualistic times. Above all, their strenuous approach to christian discipleship is a good counterweight to our own culture of convenience.

Cistercian Publications is to be thanked once again for its long dedication to the project of disseminating serious studies of early monastic sources.

Terrence G. Kardong

February 28, 1996
Assumption Abbey
Richardton, North Dakota

fOREWORÒ

IRST, we will consider the brief legislation of Lérins, then the works of Caesarius of Arles, and finally the two extensive italian Rules of the sixth century.

THE RULES OF THE FATHERS (LERINSIAN TRADITION)

Toward the end of The *Life of the Jura Fathers* the monastery of Lérins is named twice, and each time by the adjective *lirinensis*. In the first passage (¶ 174) the hagiographer juxtaposes the observances of the Jura, which he has just outlined, with those described by four authors (or group of authors) brought together under the label 'eastern': Saint Basil; 'the holy fathers of Lérins'; 'Saint Pachomius, the ancient abbot of the Syrians [sic]', and finally 'the venerable Cassian', identified as the most recent.

Our interest in this catalogue is twofold. First of all we must note the inclusion of the 'fathers of Lérins' in a list of 'eastern' authors. Basil is correctly located in Cappadocia; the Copt Pachomius is erroneously placed in the syrian world; as for Cassian, it is well known he wrote in Gaul and for the Gauls, but in his *Institutes* and *Conferences* he constantly refers to palestinian and especially egyptian monasticism. These three writers certainly merit being considered as the spokesmen for monks of the East.

Consequently, it is clear that the 'fathers of Lérins', gallic like Cassian, have themselves something fundamentally 'eastern' that allows them to be compared with their three colleagues. Who then are these *sancti lirinensium patres*? In all likelihood

13

they are the authors of what is called the 'Rule of the Four Fathers', namely 'Serapion, Macarius, Paphnutius, and the second Macarius'. These abbots with egyptian names give an eastern flavor to a text written in Latin. This short Rule is probably the legislation which formed the basis of the monastery of Lérins, enacted around 400–410 by the founders of the community: Bishop Leontius of Fréjus, the aged monk Caprasius, and the first superior, Honoratus.

This testimony of the anonymous jura author is in fact one of the major pieces of evidence that allows us to identify with great certainty the primitive rule of that celebrated cenobitic institution. The same text, in addition to the conspicuous service it renders historiography, offers a remarkable feature: the 'fathers of Lérins' are connected there in a special way to Saint Pachomius. This link established between the lerinsian Rule and the pachomian Rule is in turn one part of the evidence that hints at situating in the Jura another document of latin cenobitism that in parallel fashion combines extracts from Pachomius and lerinsian texts: the 'Eastern Rule' (*Regula Orientalis*). But this new result appears only if we look at another passage of the *Vita* that mentions Lérins: the conclusion.

In this last paragraph, a kind of epilogue (179) the anonymous author says that the abbot-priest of Lérins, a certain Marinus, asked him to edit, for the use of the monastery of Agaune, some 'Institutions' that could help in the 'formation' of that very recent cenobitic institution. According to the rules of literary modesty observed by the ancients, this informative document— described as something 'exceptional'—can only be a joining of borrowed texts in which our author merely plays the role of compiler.

What then is this collection of *Instituta* that our monk from the Jura dispatched to Agaune with the *Vita*? The collection of ancient monastic Rules assembled by Benedict of Aniane around the year 800 contains an anonymous collection, the 'Eastern Rule', which could well be the document we are looking for. A first clue pointing in this direction is the title itself: the name 'Eastern' is reminiscent of the one our author gave above to the ensemble of Fathers he cited. But the 'Eastern Rule' is an anthology of pachomian texts combined with others, and in it we recognize a number of borrowings from the lerinsian 'Second Rule of the Fathers'. Probably edited at Lérins by Abbot Marinus personally, these non-pachomian texts of the 'Eastern Rule' are joined with extracts from Pachomius, exactly as the 'holy fathers of Lérins' were associated with 'Saint Pachomius, the ancient abbot of the Syrians', in the list of the 'eastern' authorities cited above.

The author of the *Life of the Jura Fathers* seems indeed to have composed the 'Eastern Rule' for the use of the monks of Agaune, to whom he sent it along with the *Life*. This hypothesis is confirmed by a passage of the *Life* that provides an account of two orders given by Abbot Eugendus to his monks: 'according to the Rule of the Fathers' no brother could have contact with lay visitors, even those belonging to his family, without permission; and each monk had to deliver to the abbot or the steward all gifts received from his kin. Indeed, these two prescriptions can be found, in the same order and in part in the same terms, at the heart of the Eastern Rule.

THE *LIFE* AND THE RULE OF CAESARIUS OF ARLES

The permanent confinement of nuns, such as the jura author describes (25–26) is the fundamental principle that Caesarius of Arles laid down at the very beginning of his *Rule for Virgins*. The burial of Romanus in the basilica of the sisters (61) is also reminiscent of Caesarius' interment in the church of Saint John at Arles, among his sisters.

Several other usages in the jura *Life* reappear at the monastery of Arles: the abbot or abbess eats with the community, not separately (170); the monks or nuns sleep in common quarters (170) while the sick have the right to separate quarters (171); all individual work is prohibited, as are any separate quarters and all personal property that one can lock up (173).

THE RULES OF THE MASTER AND OF BENEDICT

In the 'Rule of the Master', the abbot, like Romanus and Lupicinus (115 and 132) designates his successor without consulting

the community. In the case of Eugendus a ceremony of abbatial benediction is mentioned by the anonymous jura author
(135–137). We think here of an analogous rite that the Master
describes and that Benedict implies.

The communal dormitory instititued by Eugendus at Condat (170) was found not only at Arles, as we have just seen, but
also in central Italy, at the monasteries of the Master and of
Benedict. Only the *Life of the Jura Fathers* allows us to witness
the establishment of this new kind of habitation, substituted by
Eugendus for the primitive cells that cenobitism had preserved
from its anchoritic origins. In the Rules of the Master and of
Benedict the dormitory is already an established and unques-
tioned norm. One detail in particular links the benedictine Rule
and the *Life of the Jura Fathers*: an oil lamp illuminates the
dormitory throughout the night.

Benedict is again in accord with the jura author when he
writes to encourage his followers to work in the fields if need be:
'They are truly monks if they live from the work of their hands
like our Fathers and the Apostles'. In the same way, Romanus, at
the beginning, says 'as a true monk worked in order to provide
sustenance for himself' (10). It is not impossible that here the
Rule here may derive from the *Life*, as has been maintained.

In the same way we note that the word *scapulare*, designating
an outer garment, is found before the carolingian period solely
in the *Life of Eugendus* (127) and in the benedictine Rule. But
this common feature can hardly be a literary borrowing by
Benedict from the anonymous jura author. The two authors
simply attest to the existence of this garment in their respective
milieux, italian monasticism having been capable of borrowing
it from that of Gaul.

On two other points benedictine legislation particularly re-
sembles the jura *Life*. In both, from the very beginning, we
ascertain the presence of priests among the monks. This monastic sacerdotalism is not without its problems, as much in the
eyes of the hagiographer (18–21, 132, 151) as in Benedict's.
The latter, however, allows without hesitation the admission
of priests who become monks, and the ordination of monks

as priests or deacons, things the Master expressly excluded or did not even envisage. The monasteries of the Jura have priests (148, 163) and deacons (52–58) not to mention the abbot-priests of Condat (18–20) and Lérins (179).

Another common, much lesser feature, is the care taken in honoring poor seculars as well as rich (172). Here again the benedictine Rule has something in common with the *Life*, but without antecedent in the Rule of the Master.

These comparisonss, which I could multiply, allow a glimpse of the documentary richness of the *Vita Patrum Jurensium* and its importance to all research concerning western monasticism from the fifth and sixth centuries. Between the writings of Sulpicius Severus on Saint Martin and those of the two Gregorys—the bishop of Tours and the roman pope—there is no hagiographic text that reflects more clearly the world of monks. Only, perhaps, the *Life of Fulgentius of Ruspe* by Deacon Ferrand of Carthage, which is slightly later, offers testimony of a comparable quality. This biography of the bishop-monk contains, moreover, a feature that links it with the jura narrative: Ferrand twice depicts pairs of abbots on an equal footing, like Romanus and Lupicinus (17).

Ruspe and the Jura, Africa and Gaul: this is not the first time that the two regions, from one edge of the Mediterranean to the other, have been associated thus. Already the 'Rule of the Four Fathers', the charter of the foundation of Lérins, had followed closely the *Ordo monasterii* of Alypius and the *Praeceptum* of Augustine. But this time, the order is reversed: the great work of gallic monastic hagiography precedes that of its african sister. At an interval of a few years the two monastic milieux come together to celebrate the same evangelical ideal of renouncing the world for the love of Christ and of 'unanimity' in this common search for God.

Adalbert de Vogüé

Abbey of La Pierre-qui-Vire
Translated by Kim Vivian

authors' note

HE LATE THOMAS WILLIAMS, in his 'Author's Note' to his collected stories, said 'I think I know what I want to do—to populate an imaginary world with real people, and to cause the identification with others that is the best, the life-giving, talent of our race. I want to do this, and though I, too, am obviously haunted by theory, it is left behind at the moment when the white page is covered by shadows'.[1] The translators and authors of this book hope we have populated its imaginary world of fifth- and sixth-century Gaul—historically imagined, that is—with real people. One of our purposes has been to 'cause identification' with these monks who lived in such a different time and place from our own and who yet may offer 'a saving word' some fifteen hundred years later.

We have several purposes in offering this translation of the *Life of the Jura Fathers*, the first into English. We wanted to make this important work available to english-speaking readers who can not read the original Latin or the French of the Sources chrétiennes volume edited by François Martine in 1968. We wanted to make available to a larger audience both Martine's scholarship and the good scholarly work, much of it in French and German, done in the last thirty years. Most importantly, we wanted to make more widely available one of the fruits of the monastic desert tradition, a tradition which for many continues to produce life-giving fruit in our own day. One of the contributions we hope this translation makes is to draw more attention than Martine does, both in our introduction and in our notes to the translation, to sources in the desert monasticism of the fourth and fifth centuries.

---

[1] Thomas Williams, *Leah, New Hampshire: The Collected Stories of Thomas Williams* (New York: Morrow, 1992) 18.

We have endeavored, then, to make this book accessible to a general audience (if that phrase continues to have meaning) that has an interest in, and some knowledge of, church history, early monasticism, and christian spirituality. This book, therefore, is an introduction to the Jura Fathers and to the monastic way of life they represent; it does not attempt to answer in detail all the scholarly questions posed by the *Life of the Jura Fathers*, nor does it attempt to supplant Martine's fine edition. We have made every effort in the footnotes to supply interested readers with the necessary bibliographical information by which they may pursue their own interests and studies.

This translation of the *Life of the Jura Fathers* has been a work of fruitful and enjoyable collaboration every step of the way. Professor Russell and I have long served as readers for each other's work, but this is the first time we have worked together on a project; it is also the first time my brother and I have collaborated since our very different sort of efforts together thirty years ago on the high school basketball courts. I made a first translation of the *Life* which Professors Russell and Vivian then went over, offering their suggestions and corrections. For our translation of Eucherius' *In Praise of the Desert* (Appendix III), Professor Russell revised the translation of Charles Cummings, ocso, which was originally published in *Cistercian Studies Quarterly*; we wish to thank Father Charles, both as translator and now as editor of *Cistercian Studies Quarterly*, for his permission to update his excellent translation. Professor Russell and I together translated the letter from Bishop Avitus to Viventiolus (Appendix I), while I translated the *Passion of the Martyrs of Agaune* (Appendix II). Professor Vivian wrote parts I & V of the Introduction and supplied the map, while I wrote parts II-IV. Professor Russell then made suggestions for changes and improvements in the manuscript as a whole.

Translation is the fine (or not so fine) art of cutting your losses. The *Life of the Jura Fathers* sometimes offers rather difficult Latin. We often found Martine's french translation helpful. Even where we disagreed with him, he often pointed us in the right direction. We have tried to make our translation as idiomatic as possible while remaining as close to the Latin as we could; most of all, we have tried to make it readable and—dare we say?—even enjoyable.

With regard to place names, always a vexing problem when rendering an ancient text modern, we have decided to use both ancient and modern names. We have retained the ancient names of the three jura monasteries (as we have for the three saints themselves), but have used modern names for most cities, e.g., Lyon and Poncin. We have thus striven for consistency but not, to quote Emerson, 'a foolish consistency'. To assist the reader we have supplied a map, a chronological table, and a table of place names.

We wish to thank Father Terrence Kardong for his preface and Père Adalbert de Vogüé for his foreword. Father Terrence had already done his own translation of part of the *Life*, which he graciously set aside in deference to ours; my brother and I, along with our wives, were graciously received by Père Vogüé during the summer of 1997 at his hermitage where we had a delightful visit and an opportunity to compare notes on the Jura Fathers. We especially offer our grateful thanks to Professor Ralph Mathisen and Père Vogüé for reading the completed manuscript and offering many valuable suggestions and corrections; this book is much better because of their careful attention. We also wish to thank John Leinenweber for his editorial efforts. The authors, of course, are responsible for any remaining errors.

Professor Vivian wishes to thank Augustana College and the Faculty Research Committee for their generous financial support that enabled him to do on-site research in the Jura Mountains in France and at the abbeys of Romainmôtier and Saint-Maurice in Switzerland. He also thanks Sherrie Herbst and Donna Hill of the Interlibrary Loan Department at Augustana College for obtaining scores of hard-to-find books. I would like to add my similar thanks to Lorna Frost and the staff of the Document Delivery Department at California State University Bakersfield. Andreas Markloff came to my rescue when my computer malfunctioned just as I was getting ready to print a final copy of the manuscript.

As always, I wish to thank Dr. E. Rozanne Elder, Editorial Director at Cistercian Publications, for her encouragement, assistance, and friendly correspondence.

For Professor Russell and Professor Vivian,

Tim Vivian

Feast of the Transfiguration
6 August 1998

table of place names

Ancient Name	Modern Name(s)
Acaunus	Agaune, Saint-Maurice
Arelate	Arles
Augustodunum	Autun
Balma	La Balme
Condadisco	Condat; Saint-Claude
Gallia Sequanorum	———
Genua	Geneva
Isarnodurum	Izernore
Lauconnus	Saint-Lupicin
Lirinum	Lérins
Lugdunum	Lyon
Mons Brestus	Mount Bret
Noviodunum	Nyon
Pontianum	Poncin
Rhenus	The Rhone
Secundiacum	———
Sequania	———
Vesontio	Besançon
Vienna	Vienne

POLITICAL

Reign of Emperor Diocletian	284-305
Reign of Emperor Constantine	306-337
Invasion of Vandals, Alans, Sueves and Burgundians across the Rhine	406-7
Sack of Rome by Alaric and Visigoths	410
Burgundian defeat by roman army under Ætius	435
Resettlement of Burgundians in Gaul with Geneva as center	443
Invasion of Gaul by Attila; defeated by army of Romans, Burgundians and Visigoths	451
The removal of Emperor Avitus	456
Childeric, King of the Franks (d.481)	458
Reign of Euric, King of the Visigoths	466-484

ECCLESIASTICAL

Birth of Martin of Tours	316
Athanasius in exile in Gaul	335-7
Athanasius in exile in Italy and Gaul	339-46
Athanasius writes the Life of Antony	356
Martin withdraws to the island of Gallinaria	357
Birth of John Cassian	360
Birth of Sulpicius Severus	360
Martin founds monastery at Ligugé	360-1
Death of Martin of Tours	397-400
Sulpicius writes the Life of Saint Martin	397-400
Honoratus founds monastic community at Lérins	400-10
Eucherius is at Lérins possibly writes In Praise of the Desert	412-20
Cassian writes the Institutes	419-25
Death of Sulpicius Severus	420
Cassian writes the Conferences	425-6
Possible date for In Praise of the Desert by Eucherius of Lyon	427
Death of Augustine	430

THE JURA FATHERS

The birth of Romanus	400
Romanus at Monastery of the Confluence in Lyon	430-5

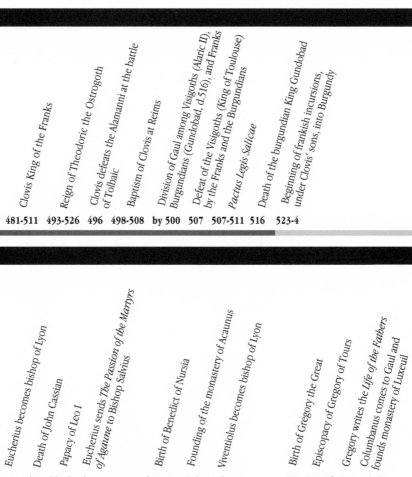

Clovis King of the Franks

Reign of Theodoric the Ostrogoth

Clovis defeats the Alamanni at the battle of Tolbiac

Baptism of Clovis at Reims

Division of Gaul among Visigoths (Alaric II), Burgundians (Gundobad, d.516), and Franks

Defeat of the Visigoths (King of Toulouse) by the Franks and the Burgundians

Pactus Legis Salicae

Death of the burgundian King Gundobad

Beginning of frankish incursions, under Clovis' sons, into Burgundy

481-511   493-526   496   498-508   by 500   507   507-511   516   523-4

Eucherius becomes bishop of Lyon

Death of John Cassian

Papacy of Leo I

Eucherius sends *The Passion of the Martyrs of Agaune* to Bishop Salvius

Birth of Benedict of Nursia

Founding of the monastery of Acaunus

Viventiolus becomes bishop of Lyon

Birth of Gregory the Great

Episcopacy of Gregory of Tours

Gregory writes the *Life of the Fathers*

Columbanus comes to Gaul and founds monastery of Luxeuil

427-31   435   440-61   450   480-90   514   514-15   538   573-94   580s   585

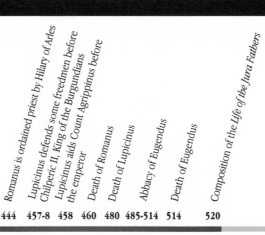

Romanus is ordained priest by Hilary of Arles

Chilperic II, King of the Burgundians

Lupicinus defends some freedmen before the emperor

Lupicinus aids Count Agrippinus before

Death of Romanus

Death of Lupicinus

Abbacy of Eugendus

Death of Eugendus

Composition of the *Life of the Jura Fathers*

444   457-8   458   460   480   485-514   514   520

introduction

a ROUND 50 BC Julius Caesar opened the narration of his gallic campaign, *De bello gallico*, with these words: 'Gaul is a whole divided into three parts, one of which is inhabited by the Belgae, another by the Aquitani, and a third by a people called in their own tongue Celtae, in the Latin Galli'.[1]

Had Caesar's soothsayer peered over his shoulder and read those words, he could have announced: 'Mighty Caesar, some six hundred years hence Gaul will be divided into one hundred twenty-seven *civitates*, all of which will bear a latin name'. Caesar might have smiled, re-read his words, and thought with some satisfaction about what he and the Roman Empire had set into motion.

Timing and expediency being of paramount importance in politics and soothsaying, Caesar's advisor would probably have left without telling the proconsul that those one hundred twenty-seven *civitates*, districts centered around a major city, would then become *dioceses*,[2] ecclesiastical precincts brought about by a religion that repudiated Caesar's, and that some, from the first century to the present, would name (or blame) as the reason for the collapse of the Roman Empire. And indeed the christian religion does constitute one of the three driving historical forces in eastern Gaul in the period

---

[1] Gallia est omnis divisa in partes tres, quarum unam incolunt Belgae, aliam Aquitani, tertiam qui ipsorum linguae Celtae, nostra Galli appelantur. H. J. Edwards, ed. and trans., *Bellum Gallicum* 1.1 (Cambridge, MA: Harvard UP, 1966) 3.

[2] As given in the *Notitia provinciarum et civitatum Galliae*, which remained essentially unchanged until the French Revolution.

covered in this book; the others being the movements and settlement of germanic peoples (traditionally called 'barbarian invasions') and the waning of roman power but the endurance of its culture.

Caesar noted further in *De bello gallico*: 'on another [side is] the Jura range, exceedingly high, lying between the Sequani and the Helvetii'.[3] The monasteries of the Jura Fathers fell within the bounds of the sixth-century *Civitas Belisensium*; this *civitas* in turn was part of the province of *Maxima Sequanorum* that made up a section of later historical Burgundy, the County of Burgundy (as distinct from the more western-lying Duchy of Burgundy) encompassing areas of the Jura Mountains and the Vaud region in Switzerland. The *Sequani* were a celtic people residing in the western part of the Juras; the *Helvetii* settled in the east (hence the name *Confederatio Helvetica* for Switzerland, and the—to foreigners confusing—abbreviation CH on swiss automobiles). Many names in the jura region have celtic origins, including Condadisco, the site of the first jura monastery.

The Romans established numerous settlements in southeastern Gaul or superimposed roman culture on previously existing ones. From the time of Caesar and Augustus date many of the magnificent monuments still to be seen in Arles, Nîmes, and Orange, to cite just a few examples. Even far to the north, in and around Izernore, the supposed birthplace of Eugendus, and Saint-Lupicin, the site of the second jura monastery, one can still see vestiges of roman culture; and the roman temple mentioned in the *Life of the Jura Fathers* (¶ 120) obviously fascinated our author.

As roman settlements prospered, aristocratic or wealthy families established *villae*, estates in the countryside, and roman culture flourished. Often the heads of these landed families came from the military: retired officers who may have married local women. By the time of Romanus' birth at the beginning of the fifth century, many of these families had become Christian.

---

[3] 1.2: altera ex parte monte Iura altissimo, qui est inter Sequanos et Helvetios.

It is likely that Romanus, Lupicinus, and their sister came from such a landed, possibly aristocratic, family (¶ 4).[4]

The indigenous 'barbarian' peoples the Romans initially encountered in the first century had been largely assimilated by the second century. At least since the reign of Constantius Chlorus (d. 306), the father of Constantine the Great, barbarian prisoners of war (*laeti*) had been granted land in Gaul in return for military service, and barbarian military units (*foederati*) stationed in or near large provincial cities came to play an ever more important role in the military. Throughout the fourth century, germanic soldiers from north of the Rhine served as roman allies in Gaul, Spain, and as far away as Egypt and Asia Minor. From the time of Constantine and his father, germanic tribes began filtering into Gaul. Not all migration occurred as the result of massive relocation of peoples.

In 376, the Huns invaded the area around the Black Sea, precipitating a movement of gothic peoples that would ultimately send them across Italy (where Alaric the Visigoth sacked Rome in 410), to Gaul, then to Spain, and finally back to southern Gaul where, in 418, some were settled as *foederati* in Aquitania. At the same time, Stilicho, the roman military commander in Gaul, for reasons of security moved the roman prefecture from Trier (on the Mosel, now in the far western part of Germany), long the imperial residence, to Arles, in Provence in southern France. Up to this time, the roman army along the Rhine had held the germanic tribes at bay, allowing into Gaul only those who served the Empire. Then, at the end of 406, around the time of Romanus' birth, other germanic tribes crossed the Rhine and entered Gaul: the Vandals, Alans, and Sueves.

In the first decades of the fifth century, another germanic people, the Burgundians, sought to move from the lower Rhine

---

[4] On the subject in general, see Jacques Fontaine, 'L'aristocratie occidentale devant le monachisme aux IVème et Vème siècles', *Rivista d'Istoria e Letteratura di Storia Religiosa* 15 (1979): 28–53, and Ralph W Mathisen, *Roman Aristocrats in Barbarian Gaul: Strategies for Survival in an Age of Transition* (Austin: University of Texas Press, 1993).

southward. In 435 or 436, around the time Romanus first
became an anchorite in the Juras, the roman commander Aetius
defeated them and resettled them as *hospites* to the south, in
Sapaudia, the modern region of Savoy. Like the Visigoths,
the Burgundians served as *foederati*. In the last half of the
fifth century the Burgundians profited from turmoil within the
empire to expand their territory to the south and west. From
this period comes Sidonius Apollinarius' description of the
Burgundians as being seven feet tall, wearing long hair scented
with rancid butter, and being fond of cooking with garlic and
onions.[5]

Although letters of Saint Jerome depict the terror of the
devastation wrought by the barbarian invasions of Italy, and
Ammianus Marcellinus describes the horrors of the hunnic
incursions,[6] contemporary sources in Gaul, such as the letters
of Paulinus of Bordeaux and the works of Sidonius, do not
hint at the imminent destruction of civilization at the hands
of barbarians. Indeed, in the mid-fifth century, Salvian, a monk
on the island of Lérins, equated the depravity of christian Gaul
with the barbarism of the germanic invaders and blamed the
downfall of the Empire on internal decadence, not incursions
from without.[7] Those with a classical roman education be-
moaned the decline of roman culture, and scholars have pointed
out the impoverishment of Latin as a literary language and the
near disappearance of the classical latin authors in Gaul before
the carolingian revival of the eighth and ninth centuries. Even
so, the wailings of these Gallo-Romans often have the ring of
a literary trope: one generation deriding the next.

---

[5] Sidonius, Carmen *XII, Ad V. C. Catullinum*; W. B. Anderson, ed., *Sidonius: Poems and Letters* I:212–213 (London 1965).
[6] Hieronymus, *Epistulae*, 123.16; *Patrologia Latina* 22.1057. Ammianus Marcellinus, *Works*, ed. and trans. by John Carew Rolfe (Cambridge, MA: Harvard UP, 1971–2) 3.382ff.
[7] *Concerning the Government of God*, cited in Jacques Le Goff, *Medieval Civilization* (Oxford: Blackwell, 1991) 11. Ralph Mathisen concludes: 'Away from the north, it now generally is accepted that the barbarian settlement was not as ruinous as once thought'. Mathisen, *Roman Aristocrats*, 28.

One must remember that the assaults of 'heathen' peoples like the Huns were relatively short-lived, and that the Visigoths and Burgundians, whose impact on Gaul was much greater and lasted much longer, practised the christian faith, albeit in arian form, and were known for their tolerance of orthodox Christianity.[8] To be sure, when the author of the *Life* describes how monks from the monastery were forced to travel to the Mediterranean to obtain salt because of the Alamanni to the north,[9] one senses the fear. Yet in a *vita* that covers eighty years in a tumultuous century, one is struck by the overall tranquillity of the *Life of the Jura Fathers*.[10] *Vitae* and letters composed centuries later during the invasions by the Saracens, Vikings (Northmen), and Magyars are far more chilling in their descriptions of the plundering, murdering hordes sweeping across a civilized Europe, and in their sense of the impending destruction of western religion and culture. Finally, a sense of 'gallic self-consciousness', a pride in Gaul, and a feeling that Gaul had been neglected or abandoned by imperial Rome, must have contributed something to a rapprochement with the new ruling germanic tribes.[11]

In Gaul, the end of the fifth century and the beginning of the sixth are marked by the struggle among the germanic tribes over who was to be heir to the dying Roman Empire, by the transference of power from roman authority into the hands of bishops (and, concomitantly, by the ever increasing importance

---

[8] 'For the first seven decades of the [fifth] century, the barbarian treatment of Gallic clerics and the Catholic church appears to have been exceptionally circumspect.' 'In the main, it would appear that the Arian beliefs of the Visigoths and Burgundians simply were not a primary cause for concern'. Mathisen, *Roman Aristocrats*, 32, 33.

[9] A story not without its problems; see ¶ 157.

[10] Perhaps the power and privileges of the gallo-roman aristocracy were the greatest losers during the barbarian settlement, as opposed to disruptions brought upon the common people and the Church. 'The arrival of the barbarians had a great effect upon the Gallo-Roman aristocratic lifestyle'. Mathisen, *Roman Aristocrats*, 35.

[11] See Mathisen, *Roman Aristocrats*, 26, and 17–26 in general.

of episcopal cities), and by the accelerating christianization of the countryside through the foundation of monasteries and the establishment of local parishes (hinted at in the *Life*, ¶ 16). The Franks, like many other germanic peoples, initially suffered defeat by the Romans, then gained power as *foederati* and allies of Rome, as happened when Childeric, father of Clovis, fought alongside the *patricius* Ægidius (who makes an unflattering appearance in the *Life*) against the Visigoths at the battle of Orléans in 463, about the year of Romanus' death. In 486, a few years after the probable date of Lupicinus' death, Clovis defeated Syagrius, 'king of the Romans', and in 507, about seven years before the death of Eugendus, defeated the Visigoths at the battle of Vouillé. Two decades later, near the time when the *Life of the Jura Fathers* was being written, Clovis' sons began the campaign that would lead to the defeat of the Burgundians in 534. The merovingian conquests in Burgundy probably had little effect on the jura monasteries; historically speaking, however, a new era had begun.

II. THE WAY OF THE DESERT

Around the year 435 a middle-aged man named Romanus, 'attracted by the solitudes of the desert . . . left his mother, sister, and brother and entered the forests of the Jura near his estate' (¶ 5).[12] He would soon be joined by his brother, Lupicinus; many years later, after the death of Lupicinus, their disciple Eugendus would become abbot. Together the three are known as the Jura Fathers. Romanus was, literally, a trailblazer; to his biographer, he was a latter-day Saint Antony. Yet archetypes dwell in real places: Antony and the desert fathers of Egypt inhabited a formidable desert; Romanus sojourned in a geographically far different wilderness, but spiritually his home and Antony's were the same. Wilderness is itself both geography and archetype:

---

[12] Middle-aged, that is, by medieval actuarial tables; Romanus was born around 400. He was, then, about 35, the same age as Antony when he set out for the desert; see *Life of Antony* 10–11. The latin word translated as 'desert' is *eremus*.

Moreover, if someone decided, with audacious daring, to cut across this roadless wilderness toward the territory of the Equestres, in addition to the dense forest and the heaps of fallen trees, he found high and lofty mountain ridges and steep valleys dividing the regions. There stags and broad-horned deer live. Even if the traveler were strong and lightly equipped, he would scarcely be able to cross it in a day, even the longest day of the year. Due to the distance and the difficulty of its natural inaccessibility no one could blaze a trail through this mountain range, to right or to left, from the regions of the Rhine and the raging of the north wind all the way to the farthest wooded regions (¶ 9).

For late antique and early medieval monastics, 'desert', as word, symbol, and location, had a number of meanings different from the modern understanding of 'desert' as a sandy waste. As far back as the late third century, a hundred and fifty years before Romanus' withdrawal, 'desert' referred to 'deserted' places outside the villages and cities of 'the world'. Distance from civilization and aridness were not the primary considerations; most importantly, a 'desert' needed to provide separation from the world. Romanus' 'desert', instead of being outside a city, lay just beyond his family estate.[13] In egyptian monastic tradition, 'desert' was the place where one confronted the Devil and the demons of the human heart. According to John Cassian (360–435) the desert was above all the dwelling place of anchorites; they, 'having perfectly overcome all their faults, in order to engage in the fiercest battles with the demons, enter the deepest recesses of the desert'.[14] As a result of this struggle, and the

---

[13] *Vicinas villae.* 'It was often to the marginal land, just within or beyond estate boundaries, that ascetics journeyed: this was their *desertum*'. Ian Wood, 'A Prelude to Columbanus: The Monastic Achievement in the Burgundian Territories', in H. B. Clarke and Mary Brennan, eds., *Columbanus and Merovingian Monasticism* (BAR Int. Ser. 113; Oxford: B.A.R., 1981) 3–32; the quotation is on p. 5.

[14] *Heremi profunda secreta. Institutes* 5.36; Michael Petschenig, ed., *Iohannis Cassiani: De Institutis Coenobiorum* (CSEL 17, Iohannis Cassiani Opera; Vienna: Tempsky, 1888) 108.

victory assured through Christ over the demons, 'desert' also came to have the connotation of 'holy desert', the holy ground where Moses, Elijah, John the Baptist, and Jesus had trod,[15] the place where holiness prospers. All of these meanings figure in the *Life of the Jura Fathers*.[16] Paradoxically (and this paradox goes back to the beginnings of monasticism), the desert of the Jura Fathers—wilderness, wasteland, uninhabited place— is both child and parent. It is the child of desert parents—that is, the monks of the egyptian desert and their descendants in Gaul: Cassian, Eucherius, and the monks of Lérins.[17] But the desert also becomes parent to community; the jura monasteries apparently grew to include several hundred male and female monks. To switch images, the jura monasteries had their roots deep in desert soil; to these monastic roots we now turn.

Romanus, 'before he embraced the religious life . . . had observed a certain venerable man, Sabinus by name, abbot of the Monastery of the Confluence in Lyon, his strenuous regulations, and the way of life of his monks' (¶ 11). Unfortunately, the precise location of this monastery is unknown, nor do other ancient sources mention an Abbot Sabinus.[18] Lyon, easily accessible on the Rhône River, was seventy-five kilometers (forty-seven miles) southwest from Romanus' home near Isarnodurum (modern Izernore) in Gallia Sequanorum, and one hundred twenty kilometers (seventy-five miles) from Condadisco (Condat), the site of his future monastery.[19] It was also, importantly,

---

[15] See note 139 below.

[16] Among a large bibliography on 'desert', see Jean Leclercq, '"Eremus" et "Eremita": pour l'histoire du vocabulaire de la vie solitaire', *Collectanea cisterciensia* 25 (1963): 8–30, and D. Fisher, 'Liminality: The Vocation of the Church (I). The Desert Image in Early Christian Tradition', *Cistercian Studies Quarterly* 24 (1989) 181–205.

[17] When two of the authors of the present volume visited Dom Adalbert de Vogüé at his monastery of La-Pierre-qui-Vire, he told us that the monastery's founder had, in the middle of the nineteenth century, sought 'the desert' deep in the forests of Burgundy. See also François Martine, ed. and trans., *Vie des pères du Jura* (SC 142; Paris: Cerf, 1968) 244 n. 3.

[18] For a full discussion, see Martine, 250–1, n 3.

[19] See the map. See ¶ 4 and note 18 there, and ¶ 120 of the *Life*.

the home of Eucherius, bishop of Lyon. Eucherius links Romanus to the desert.

Eucherius was bishop from at least 441, when he represented Lyon at the first Council of Orange, and he likely occupied his see by 431 and perhaps as early as 427.[20] More importantly, Eucherius was part of the early immigration to the monastic island of Lérins off the southern coast of Gaul; while there, sometime between 412 and 420, he may have composed his *Epistula de laude eremi, In Praise of the Desert.*[21] Like Cassian, Eucherius strongly connects western monasticism with the early desert monasticism of Egypt.[22] According to Cassian, Eucherius wanted to go to Egypt to learn about desert asceticism at its source; apparently he did not get there.[23] For Eucherius, the desert

[20] He died around 451. For the most thorough recent assessment of his dates, see Ralph W. Mathisen, 'Episcopal Hierarchy and Tenure in Office in Late Roman Gaul: A Method for Establishing Dates of Ordination', *Francia* 17:1 (1990) 125–38, and the table on 137–8. Mathisen suggests, 135, that Eucherius died between 450 and 455. See also S. Pricoco, 'Eucherius of Lyon', *Encyclopedia of the Early Church*, ed. Angelo Di Berardino (New York: Oxford University Press, 1992) I.295. Dom Pichery suggests that Eucherius became bishop 'around 435'; see Eugène Pichery, ed., *Jean Cassien: Conférences*, Sources chrétiennes 42, 54, & 64 (Paris: Cerf, 1955–9) 2.98, n. 1. Martine, 252–3, n. 1, recommends 434. Friedrich Prinz believes that Eucherius was bishop of Lyon when Romanus made his visit there; see Prinz, *Frühes Mönchtum im Frankenreich* (Munich & Vienna: R. Oldenbourg, 1965) 68.
[21] *In Praise of the Desert* may, however, be dated as late as 427, just before Eucherius became bishop of Lyon.
[22] Robert Markus, *The End of Ancient Christianity* (Cambridge: Cambridge UP, 1990) 160, says Eucherius provides the 'finest Western statement' of the monastery 'constructed in the image of the Desert'. Markus contrasts *In Praise of the Desert*, with its image of the monastery as desert, with 'Augustine's model of the monastery, built in the image of the City'. On Eucherius and Lérins, see Salvatore Pricoco, *L'isola dei santi: Il cenobio di Lerino e le origini del monachesimo gallico* (Rome: Edizioni dell'Ateneo & Bizzarri, 1978) 44–46, 144–53, 192–203. See Appendix III for a translation of *In Praise of the Desert*.
[23] Cassian, *Conferences* 11, Praefatio (Pichery, ed, 2:98). Eucherius took his wife and children with him to Lérins; his family may have been the reason for his not making it to Egypt.

deserves to be called a temple of our God without walls. Since it is clear that God dwells in silence, we must believe that he loves the solitary expanses of the desert. Very often he has let himself be seen there by his saints; he willingly meets with people in favorable places such as the desert. In the desert Moses gazed upon God until his face shone with glory. In the desert Elijah covered his face for fear of seeing God. Although God is present everywhere, and regards the whole world as his domain, we may believe that his preferred place is the solitudes of heaven and of the desert.[24]

For Eucherius, to possess the desert is 'to possess God himself'.[25]

We do not know whether Romanus met Eucherius, but Eucherius was certainly bishop and undoubtedly a very important person in the church of Lyon at the time of Romanus' visit sometime before 435. If Romanus went to Lyon to learn the monastic life, it certainly seems probable that he would have encountered *In Praise of the Desert* and the monastic tradition of Lérins as embodied by Eucherius.[26] The *Life of the Jura Fathers*, written some fifty to sixty years after Romanus' death in 460, acknowledges the importance of the monastic island: at the end of the *Life*, the author tells us that Abbot Marinus of Lérins requested 'the institutes regarding the rules and regulations of . . . the community of Agaune' (¶ 179).

How much of this history and tradition was known by the author of the *Life* is not clear. There is no doubt, however, that he knew about, or at least sensed, the tradition at the jura monasteries that connected them with desert monasticism, with the Egypt Cassian made famous and Eucherius longed to visit, and with monasticism's honored founder, Antony of

---

[24] Eucherius, *In Praise of the Desert* 3; Appendix III, p. 199 below.

[25] *In Praise of the Desert* 41; Appendix III, p. 213.

[26] One might object that the author of the *Life* would certainly have proclaimed the fact if he had known that Romanus had met Eucherius, but his knowledge of the facts of Romanus' life is sketchy; his silence, therefore, is not definitive.

Egypt.[27] Before Antony, according to his *Life*, 'there were not yet monasteries in Egypt neighboring on one another, and no monk at all knew the remote desert; each one who wished to watch over himself spiritually would practice ascetic discipline by himself not far from his own village';[28] similarly, 'before Romanus, not a single monk had dedicated himself to the religious life in this province, either to solitude or to communal observance' (¶ 5). When Romanus went to Lyon (¶ 11) he observed Abbot Sabinus, just as Antony sought out 'zealous persons' for emulation. This emulation—Antony and Romanus of their monastic elders, Romanus of Antony, and the *Life of Romanus* of the *Life of Antony*—is captured in the *Life* by a single image: Romanus, according to his biographer, is 'like a honeybee that goes from flower to flower; after gathering from each the small flowers of perfection, Romanus returned home' (¶ 11). Antony, less ornately, searches out the zealous 'like the wise bee' (*Life of Antony* 3).[29] In paragraph 12 our author makes the metaphor explicit: Romanus is 'the imitator of the venerable Antony'.

Explicitly and implicitly, then, in history and tradition, the monasteries of the Jura belong to the desert. When Romanus left the monastery at Lyon he took with him 'the book *The Life of the Holy Fathers* and the admirable *Institutes of the Abbots*' (¶ 11).[30]

---

[27] Saint Antony was considered the founder of monasticism in monastic and Church tradition, although we know now that monasticism pre-dates Antony and seems to have arisen simultaneously in Egypt, Palestine, and Syria.

[28] *Life of Antony* 32; translations from the greek *Life of Antony* are from Tim Vivian and Apostolos N. Athanassakis, trans., *The Life of Antony* (Kalamazoo: Cistercian Publications, forthcoming) based on the new text edited by G. J. M. Bartelink, *Vie D'Antoine*, Sources Chrétiennes 400 (Paris: Cerf, 1994) 123–377.

[29] Not only does our author delight in expanding the image of the peripatetic bee, he also probably puns on the dual meaning of *flosculus*, 'flower', which may also suggest *froccus*, 'cowl' or 'habit.' See ¶ 11.

[30] *Librum vitae sanctorum patrum eximiasque institutiones abbatum*; Martine, 252.

It is not certain what these books were, but the titles undoubtedly point to the desert tradition: the *Life of Antony*, the
Life of Paul by Jerome, the *Rule of Pachomius*, and the *Institutes*
and *Conferences* of Cassian.[31] Cassian, who wrote his *Conferences*
around 425–6, dedicated Conferences 11–17 to two people:
one was Eucherius, who may still have been at the monastic
island of Lérins; the other was Honoratus, the founding father
of Lérins.[32] Honoratus—later bishop of Arles—founded the
monastic community at Lérins (Lirinum) sometime between
400 and 410, around the time of Romanus' birth. Lérins represents the 'second phase' of gallic monasticism.[33] The founder of
monasticism in Gaul was Saint Martin of Tours. He and Antony
of Egypt are the patron saints of the *Life of the Jura Fathers*: for
Eugendus, according to his disciple and biographer, 'the deeds
of blessed Antony and Martin and their way of life never slipped
away from his spirit' (¶ 168).[34]

Martin had been a hermit near Milan when, because of arian
pressures, he withdrew to the island of Gallinaria off the Riviera
around the year 357, just after Antony's death and around the
time of the composition of the *Life of Antony*. After Hilary of
Poitiers returned from exile in 360, Martin lived in a hermitage
near that city, possibly at the site of the later monastery of
Ligugé, the first monastery in Gaul.[35] Like Romanus at a later

[31] See Martine, 252–3, n 1; Martine also notes, from Vogüé, that *patrum instituta* could be a collective or generic phrase.

[32] In *Conferences* XI, Praefatio (Pichery, ed., II. 98), Cassian exclaims, 'O sancti fratres Honorate et Eucheri. . . .'

[33] The phrase is Karl Baus'; Karl Baus, et al., *The Imperial Church from Constantine to the Early Middle Ages*, vol. II of *History of the Church* ed. by Hubert Jedin and John Dolan (London: Burns and Oates, 1980) 381.

[34] On Martin's influence see especially the *Life of Eugendus* ¶¶ 141–46, 152, and 157–64.

[35] Jacques Fontaine, 'L'ascétisme chrétien dans la littérature gallo-romaine d'Hilaire à Cassien', *La Gallia romana* (Rome: Academia Nazionale dei Lincei, 1973) 87–115, makes the case for christian asceticism in Gaul before Saint Martin, an asceticism influenced by Hilary of Poitiers and deriving ultimately from Cyprian and Tertullian in North Africa.

date, and like Antony and the *abbas* of the egyptian desert, Martin attracted disciples, and a community of anchorites gathered around him. After becoming bishop of Tours in 371 Martin worked to develop communal monasticism at Marmoutier;[36] Marmoutier was 'so sheltered and remote that it could have been a desert solitude'.[37] Martin, in fact, may have been indirectly influenced by the desert fathers.[38] Sulpicius Severus, Martin's friend and biographer, in his *Life of Saint Martin* and *Dialogues* presents Martin as a healer and wonderworker; it is this Martin who appears in the *Life of the Jura Fathers* as a patron to the monks of the jura monasteries.[39]

Within a few years of Martin's death in 397, Honoratus was at Lérins. He and his brother Venantius had left their family estate (as Romanus and Lupicinus would do), and toured the monasteries of the Mediterranean. Honoratus eventually settled on the island of Lérins.[40] By 425, according to Cassian, Lérins was an 'enormous community of brothers'.[41] The Rule of Lérins has not survived, a fact that has led to a great deal of speculation regarding the monastic way of life there.[42] What is

[36] Baus, 380.

[37] Edward James, 'Archaeology and the Merovingian Monastery', in H. B. Clarke and Mary Brennan, eds., *Columbanus and Merovingian Monasticism* (BAR Int. Ser. 113; Oxford: B.A.R., 1981) 33–55; the quotation is on p. 36.

[38] Fontaine, 'L'ascétisme', 93–96. The 'monastic family tree' might have run from Eusebius of Vercelli to Hilary of Poitiers to Martin.

[39] For Sulpicius' works, see 'Primary Sources in English Translation' in the Bibliography. On Martin and his legacy, see especially Clare Stancliffe, *Saint Martin and his Hagiographer* (Oxford: Clarendon, 1983); for the chronology, see Stancliffe, 112–13. On Sulpicius' presentation of Martin, see Philip Rousseau, *Ascetics, Authority, and the Church in the Age of Jerome and Cassian* (Oxford: Oxford University Press, 1978) 143–65.

[40] See Pricoco, *L'isola*, especially chapters 1–2.

[41] *Conferences* 11, Praefatio: *ingenti fratrum coenobio* (Pichery, ed, II.98).

[42] For example, Pierre Riché, 'Columbanus, his Followers and the Merovingian Church', in H. B. Clarke and Mary Brennan, eds., *Columbanus and Merovingian Monasticism* (BAR Int. Ser. 113; Oxford: B.A.R., 1981) 65: 'The rule of Lérins, whose text we no longer possess, must have been inspired by Eastern customs that had been adapted on Cassian's advice to conditions in the West'.

clear is that Lérins became 'a center of spirituality and learning and, equally important, . . . a source of leaders for the church'.[43] What was the inspiration and source of this spirituality? Egypt. The desert.[44] But Egypt and the desert as mediated by Cassian, Basil—and Augustine.[45]

Although Cassian extolled the solitary, anchoritic life as the ideal, he traced cenobitic monasticism back to the apostolic community of the primitive Church.[46] For Augustine, obedience 'constituted the unity of the community', while for Cassian obedience was 'the monk's first step on the way to perfection'.[47] Apparently quite early at Lérins there was an emphasis on obedience, but by the end of the fifth century charity had come to be equally important.[48] During the fifth century there was another, equally important, shift in monastic spirituality in the West: from an emphasis on individual asceticism to an emphasis on the communal.[49] The lives of the Jura Fathers precisely illustrate this shift: Romanus withdrew to the Juras as a hermit early in the fifth century; by the end of that century (and undoubtedly before) individual asceticism had clearly shifted to community life. The 'small dwellings', that is, cells (¶ 13), that the first monks used gave way in Eugendus' day to a common dormi-

---

The definitive work is Adalbert de Vogüé, *Les Règles des saints pères* (Sources chrétiennes 297–8; Paris: Cerf, 1982); he suggests that the Rule of Lérins is probably the 'Rule of the Four Fathers' (see the Foreword to this volume).

[43] William E. Klingshirn, *Caesarius of Arles: The Making of a Christian Community in Late Antique Gaul* (Cambridge Studies in Medieval Life and Thought; Cambridge: Cambridge UP, 1994) 20.

[44] See Riché, 105; Baus, 382.

[45] According to R. A. Markus, *The End*, 164, Lérins combined 'a veneration for Augustine with a spirituality of markedly Cassianic stamp'.

[46] *Conferences* 18.5.2–3 (Pichery, 3:14–15). On the subject of the apostolic origins of monasticism, and the implications for modern christian spirituality, see Adalbert de Vogüé, *Théologie de la vie monastique* (Paris: Aubier, 1961) 213–40, English trans. in 'Monasticism and the Church in the Writings of Cassian', *Monastic Studies* 3 (1965): 19–51.

[47] Markus, 214.

[48] Klingshirn, 24 and 28.

[49] See Markus, 196. Markus, 77, sees Augustine 'abandoning' 'the pursuit of perfection through self-denial'.

tory (¶ 170). Eugendus, who became abbot in 480, embodies this change.

For Augustine, who died about the time Romanus withdrew to the Juras, 'the creation of a perfect community rather than the pursuit of individual perfection came to be the keynote of his theology of the monastic life'.[50] The *Life of the Jura Fathers* depicts this communal theology made flesh: it does not mention solitaries. Lupicinus, a strict ascetic himself, heals a severe ascetic whose practices are harming himself and apparently the community. His biographer comments that by means of this 'clear and divine example, Lupicinus clearly taught that no one, once he has embraced the monastic precepts, ought to walk along the steep path to the right nor along the slopes to the left, but ought to undertake the middle course of monastic discipline that is "the royal path"' (¶ 77). Eugendus 'had everyone sleep with him in a common *xenodochium* so that a common building, with only the beds being private, might also encompass those whom a common room enclosed for the common meal' (¶ 170). Thus, rather than the monasticism of the anchoritic and semi-anchoritic *abbas* of the egyptian desert, the *Life of the Jura Fathers* stresses the cenobitic monasticism of Pachomius and Basil—both of whom are acknowledged at its conclusion (¶ 174)—as mediated by Cassian.[51] The desert tradition none the less remains vitally important: the *Life* upholds a belief in withdrawal from society (Eugendus never leaves the monastery) and in the necessity of waging unrelenting war against the Devil.

If the roots of the jura monasteries lie deep in desert soil, what of the stock and, more importantly, the fruit-bearing branches? A chief characteristic of fifth-century monasticism in Gaul is its individuality;[52] yet even so, one eminent scholar believes that 'the Jura monks were still exceptional. An authentic

---

[50] Markus, 158.

[51] See Markus, 188: Cassian, in the course of the *Conferences*, had come to prefer cenobitic practices over hermitism; see 182–5 and references there to the *Conferences*.

[52] Markus, 'From Caesarius to Boniface: Christianity and Paganism in Gaul', in Jacques Fontaine and J. N. Hillgarth, eds., *Le Septième siècle: Changements et*

manifestation of the fifth-century Gallic Church, they were not characteristic of it'.[53] The desert tradition has been seen—rightly—as both a 'permanent challenge to the Church' and as 'a break with the organized societies of Roman city life'—themes still important today for Church, monastery, and society:

> To enter the Desert was to assert one's freedom to extricate oneself from the suffocating bonds of that society, from the claims of property relationships, of power and domination, of marriage and family, and to re-create a life of primal freedom, whether in solitude or in an alternative and freely chosen social grouping.[54]

One scholar has put the matter even more bluntly: the Jura Fathers 'were not merely opting out of the life of civilization (a point their biographer insists on); they were actively hostile to it'.[55]

But the *Life of the Jura Fathers* does not support easy dichotomies. One could say that Romanus' withdrawal is proof enough, but his biographer sees no hostility in his actions. Romanus, in fact, became a priest (¶ 18), an honor Eugendus resolutely refused (¶¶ 132–4). In describing Romanus' ordination, however, his biographer, undoubtedly influenced by Eugendus, does take the opportunity to aim attacks at both the 'illicit usurpation of power' by bishops (¶ 19) and the 'mad ambition' of priests (¶ 21).[56] Nevertheless, when Eugendus declined ordination, the reasons he gave his biographer are

---

continuités, 154–72 (London: The Warburg Institute/University of London, 1992) 156.

[53] John M. Wallace-Hadrill, *The Frankish Church* (Oxford: Clarendon, 1983) 9. The jura monasteries 'flourished at the time in a nearer approach to a real desert than anything Eucher[ius] had known' (8).

[54] Markus, *The End of Ancient Christianity*, 165 and 167.

[55] Wallace-Hadrill, 8

[56] R. W. Mathisen observes: 'Here, as is often the case in such denunciations, one perhaps can detect a bit of personal animus on the part of the author: was he himself one of the *seniores* who resented the advancement of more aggressive juniors?' See *Roman Aristocrats*, 96.

practical and administrative rather than anti-clerical (¶ 133). Elsewhere in the *Life* clergy are spoken of with respect (¶¶ 140 and 151) and the *Life* takes it for granted that monks from the monastery have gone on to preside as priests in parishes.[57] Not long after the death of Eugendus in 514, Viventiolus, a jura monk, chose to become bishop of Lyon rather than abbot.[58]

The attitudes of the *Life* toward society are equally ambivalent—perhaps 'complex' or 'nuanced' would be better words. A good portion of the *Life of Lupicinus* is concerned with Lupicinus' dealings with civil authorities (¶¶ 92–110). It is true that those in power—or in the city—do not come off well in these paragraphs. One person, 'puffed up by the prestige of being at court', is an 'oppressor'; a much more powerful figure, the *patricius* Ægidius, tries to have a rival unlawfully executed (¶¶ 96–110). Lupicinus, through prayer, defeats both representatives of 'the world'. But the *Life* is both realistic and honest about life away from the world: it forthrightly acknowledges that Eugendus had enemies 'swelled up with burning hatred for the blessed man' (¶ 138), and there are several examples of disgruntled monks (¶¶ 36–40, 81, 138). Life inside the monastery is not automatically more prayerful or holier than life outside.[59]

Perhaps the most damning charge that the *Life* levels against society is the fickleness and mob-mentality of its members (¶¶ 101 and 109); the most chilling is captured by a single, indelible, image: the Vatican is 'that most famous place, where on one

---

[57] ¶¶ 16 and 32, if these are historically reliable. The enthusiastic—and rather vague—language makes one wonder: 'The venerable swarms of fathers, impelled by the Holy Spirit, then began to spread from there like a beehive filled with bees; they spread so far that not only the more remote parts of the province of Sequania, but also many regions far and wide in different regions of the earth, were filled with monasteries and churches by means of the grace spread abroad by that godly group of people'.

[58] See Appendix I for a translation of the letter from Avitus, Bishop of Vienne, to Viventiolus.

[59] Martine drily observes, 387, n 2, that the *Life* 'montre à diverses reprises que les moines du Jura ne sont pas toujours faciles à conduire'.

side of the public porticos small shelters have now been pieced together for the sick' (¶ 104).[60] Regrettably, one has only to think of any modern city with its abandoned sick and poor. By contrast, the monastery is the place where 'people tormented by demons and by other spirits of the Devil, along with the insane and paralyzed', come for consolation and healing. The author of the *Life* is quick to contrast the 'sweet fragrance' and healing renown of Romanus and Lupicinus with 'the horror and stench of worldly life' (¶¶ 14–15). On one level the *Life of the Jura Fathers* gives the impression that the world is corrupt and that salvation lies only in the monastery; but more deeply— perhaps inadvertently—it acknowledges that the *whole* world is fallen, both society and monastery, and the whole needs healing and repair.

The dividing line between Desert and City/Church is not absolute in the *Life of the Jura Fathers*. Clearer is the divide between the gallic monasticism of the fifth century and that of the sixth, and even more so between it and the merovingian monasticism of the seventh and eighth centuries. By the year 500, the time of Eugendus' abbacy, gallic aristocrats, both Visigoths and Burgundians, had been roman landowners for several generations, with roman senators as their neighbors.[61] Romanus and Lupicinus left their family estate for the solitudes of the wilderness; in this sense—and this sense only—the jura monasteries were 'aristocratic'. But a huge gulf separates the jura monasteries from even those of the sixth century, still more

---

[60] As Peter Brown graphically puts it: 'For the great basilicas could be grim places. A human refuse tip was piled up against their walls. These were the incurable cripples who had not even come for cures: they had just been dumped there by their families so that they could at least have a chance of begging enough to eat from the visitors'. Brown, 'Relics and Social Status in the Age of Gregory of Tours', in Peter Brown, *Society and the Holy in Late Antiquity*, 22–50 (Berkeley & Los Angeles: University of California Press, 1982) 22.

[61] See Edward James, *The Origins of France: From Clovis to the Capetians, 500–1000* (London: Macmillan, 1982) 127. On the subject in general, see Mathisen, *Roman Aristocrats in Barbarian Gaul*.

those of the seventh and eighth centuries. The monastery of Acaunus (Agaune), for example, was founded around the time of Eugendus' death (514) by Sigismund, a royal patron with no personal interest in following the ascetic life.[62]

The Franks conquered Burgundy in 534, fourteen years after the composition of the *Life of the Jura Fathers*. Monasticism in the frankish Church was to be different. For the frankish royalty, 'monasteries ensured perpetual intercession with the spiritual world for the security of rulers . . . . it was the founder and his or her kin and other benefactors who reaped the reward of intercession'.[63] The *Life* has numerous examples of intercession, but none of benefactors and royal patronage.[64] In fact, the section where Romanus deals with a too-exclusive monk may be more opposed to class distinctions than it is to augustinian predestination (¶¶ 27–34). Not unnaturally, such a divide finds representation in the monastic writings themselves.

The *Life of the Jura Fathers* belongs to 'the old Gallic hagiography' of the sixth century, with its emphases on 'the poverty of the living-quarters, the primitiveness of the clothing and utensils, the contempt in which these monks held the world and its civilizations'.[65] These are characteristics of the desert tradition of eastern monasticism; the *Life* borrows heavily from the most important literary work of that tradition, the *Life of Antony*. In the seventh and eighth centuries, by contrast, 'aristocratic hagiography' came into prominence, emphasizing richness and beauty rather than simplicity and austerity'.[66]

---

[62] Wood, 'A Prelude', 15, characterizes Sigismund's foundation an 'act of state'.

[63] Wallace-Hadrill, 58–9.

[64] On the 'Gallo-Roman senator class', see Friedrich Prinz, 'Aristocracy and Christianity in Merovingian Gaul. An Essay', in Karl Bosl, ed., *Gesellschaft, Kultur, Literatur: Beiträge L. Wallach gewidmet* (Stuttgart: Anton Hiersemann, 1975) 155–9.

[65] Prinz, 162.

[66] Prinz, 162. James, 'Archaeology and the Merovingian Monastery', 38, comments on the differences in architectural description between the fifth and sixth centuries and the seventh and eighth.

Given this dramatic change, can the Jura Fathers be seen as a 'Gallo-Roman prelude' to the Franks?[67] Sadly, we know very little about the jura monasteries beyond the early sixth century, and it is likely that at least some of them—probably Balma—were abandoned at this time.[68] In that sense, the Juras are a prelude, both to Columbanus, who came to Gaul from Ireland around 585 and founded Luxeuil in Burgundy, and to frankish monasticism. But in another, stronger, sense, the Juras are an important establishment on the road of monastic development that leads from Augustine to Benedict.[69] That image, though, will not suffice. It might suggest that the beginning and the end of the road—Augustine and Benedict—are what matter and that the jura monasteries are merely a rest stop on the way. But in the spiritual life the journey matters as much as the destination. In that sense, the spirituality of the Jura Fathers matters as much as Augustine's or Benedict's. That spirituality leads from Antony of Egypt and the fathers of the egyptian desert—and from them back to the apostles and Jesus—through Cassian and Pachomius and Basil and the monks of Lérins to today.

---

[67] Wallace-Hadrill, 8–9.

[68] The 'Chronique de Saint-Claude' provides a list of the abbots of Condadisco/St-Claude up to around 1150. See Ulysse Robert, 'Chronique de Saint-Claude', *Bibliothèque de l'École des chartes* 41 (1880) 561–9. This Chronicle supplies some interesting information: it omits Lupicinus (p. 565) while the list of abbots in the *Gallia christiana* includes him (p. 562). 'Romanus', the Chronicle says, 'was abbot 100 years. He lived, moreover, 135 years. He first entered the Juras in the year 384 from the incarnation of the Lord, that is, in the third year of Emperor Gratian'. These figures are impossible on a number of counts. Minausius is listed as the second abbot; he held office for 50 years, also an impossible number. The Chronicle continues a bit more accurately, if still vaguely: Eugendus was abbot '13 years, 6 months. He is reported to have been here in the 10th year after the death of Clodovic [Clovis]'. Clovis died in 511; Eugendus was abbot from about 485–514.

[69] See R. Lorenz, 'Die Anfänge des abendländischen Mönchtums im 4. Jahrhundert', *Zeitschrift für Kirchengeschichte* 77 (1966): 61, and Markus, *The End of Ancient Christianity*, 78, 196.

III. THE LIVES OF THE JURA FATHERS

Some people have asked us whether we should say the *vita* [life] or *vitae* [lives] of the saints. A. Gellius and several other philosophers have said *vitae*. But the writer Pliny in the third book of the *Art of Grammar* says, 'The ancients have said "the lives" of each of us; but grammarians did not believe that the word *vita* has a plural'. From which it is clear that it is better to speak of the 'Life of the Fathers' rather than the 'Lives of the Fathers', the more so since there is a diversity of merits and virtues among them, but the one life of the body sustains them all in this world.[70]

This passage from the Preface to the *Life of the Fathers* by Gregory of Tours is interesting for a number of reasons. Gregory's desire for a classical precedent gets him bogged down in an arcane grammatical discussion that obscures his real reason for gathering together the twenty Lives in his book into a single Life: 'there is a diversity of merits and virtues among them, but the one life of the body sustains them all in this world'. As Gregory's recent translator notes, 'His use of the singular "Life", rather than "Lives", has much more to do with his wish to point out that those who were deemed holy by God all lived the same kind of life, the life of a true Christian—all saints have the one life in Christ'.[71] If the saints are united in Christ they are, *ipso facto*, a sacred community: 'the author for sacred biography is the community, and consequently the experience presented by the narrative voice is collective'.[72]

Gregory wrote his *Life of the Fathers* in the 580s, some sixty years after the composition of the *Life of the Jura Fathers*.[73] Our

---

[70] Edward James, trans., *Gregory of Tours: Life of the Fathers* (Translated Texts for Historians 1; Liverpool: Liverpool UP, 2nd ed., 1991) 2.

[71] James, xiv.

[72] Thomas J. Heffernan, *Sacred Biography: Saints and their Biographers in the Middle Ages* (New York & Oxford: Oxford University Press, 1988) 19.

[73] James, xii; Martine, 71, dates the *Life of the Fathers* 'without a doubt' to 585–90, while Heffernan, 3, prefers 591.

author, therefore, did not have recourse to Gregory's grammatical arguments; it is doubtful whether he had access to A. Gellius or Pliny either. But the author of the *Life of the Jura Fathers* did share Gregory's theological presupposition: many lives, one life in Christ: 'I shall put myself forward for your benefit as the trinal narrator of the life of the three abbots of the Jura Mountains' (¶ 2). Instead of seeking classical precedent, as Gregory does, he locates the justification for his method in the scriptures: he offers the Lives of Romanus, Lupicinus, and Eugendus as 'loaves of bread' (¶ 2). These 'loaves of the Trinity' (¶ 1)—three in one—are the loaves that the insistent neighbor asks for in the dead of night in Jesus' parable (Luke 11:5–8). Mystically interpreted, our author says, those three loaves in the Gospel represent the three Lives of the Jura Fathers; like the Trinity, these three Lives are also one and indivisible. Gregory's pedantic grammatical reference pales by comparison.

1. *The Author*

The historian must always probe and question how much a biographer has shaped the life of his subject.[74] As one historian has trenchantly put it: 'How is it possible to compose a biography which conflates the subject's life with the lives of others [i.e., Christ, the saints] and still expect it to be a record of that subject's life? Whose life is recorded when such a work is finished?'[75] This question becomes acute in hagiography when the biographer/hagiographer forces his saint into

---

[74] For a recent searching examination of the relationship between biographer and biographical subject—and the biographer's agenda(s)—see David Brakke, *Athanasius and the Politics of Asceticism* (Oxford Early Christian Studies; Oxford: Clarendon, 1995). Since one of the themes of Brakke's book is how Athanasius 'shaped' the image of Antony, and since Antony is a patron saint of our author, Brakke's study is of interest here. A striking wall painting from early monastic Egypt depicts Athanasius enthroned with Antony and Pachomius on his right and left hand.

[75] Heffernan, 12.

a preconceived mold.[76] If our author had a mold, however, Romanus, Lupicinus, and Eugendus broke it. Even with their shared characteristics, they are surprisingly distinct—even individual. In writing about his saints, the author of the *Life of the Jura Fathers*, however, had an advantage that Gregory did not: he knew one of them, Eugendus, personally, and lived in close physical, communal, and spiritual proximity with the other two.[77] In this regard he is like Theodoret of Cyrrhus and his *History of the Monks of Syria*.[78]

The author of the *Life of the Jura Fathers* says very little directly about himself; he is, in fact, anonymous. Early on in his narrative we learn that he himself was at Condadisco: 'I shall now therefore endeavor to reproduce faithfully in the name of Christ—according to what I saw there with my own eyes or received from the tradition of the elders—the deeds, the way of life, and the Rule of the esteemed fathers of the Jura Mountains' (¶ 4). In the *Life of Eugendus* he tells us that Eugendus himself told him of the details of a vision he had had as a child (¶ 124); the details of the vision he reports (¶¶ 121–3) confirm that he had them from Eugendus—either that or he had a *very* active imagination. Later in the *Life of Eugendus* (¶¶

---

[76] This is especially true for Saint Martin of Tours who, in the course of the fifth century, was transformed from a monk into a bishop. During the sixth century he appeared to someone 'clothed in a bishop's robe'. See Raymond Van Dam, *Saints and Their Miracles in Late Antique Gaul* (Princeton: Princeton UP, 1993) 19. Our author refers to Martin as 'Bishop Martin' (¶ 152). On the 'cult of Saint Martin', see Van Dam, 13–27. Friedrich Prinz, 'Aristocracy and Christianity in Merovingian Gaul', 14, believes that already in the late fourth and early fifth centuries Sulpicius Severus was modifying the image of Saint Martin 'in accordance with his own aristocratic outlook. . . . Sulpicius' conception of the saint . . . corresponded closely with the values of the aristocratic life-style in which he himself had been trained'.

[77] On the renewed emphasis on the importance of testimony in historical study, see Rick Kennedy, 'Miracles in the Dock: A Critique of the Historical Profession's Special Treatment of Alleged Spiritual Events', *Fides et Historia* 26.2 (1994) 7–22.

[78] See R. M. Price, trans., *A History of the Monks of Syria* (Kalamazoo: Cistercian Publications, 1985) xi–xiii.

135–7) he reports in detail another, even more striking, vision. In this vision Eugendus foresees, literally, his future investiture as abbot. Elders, ancients of days from the time of Romanus and Lupicinus, surround him carrying 'candles and lighted lamps'. In a startling image, a portent of troubles to come, 'they all, after one had begun to do so, immediately dashed the bright and comforting lights against the wall, snuffing and extinguishing them' (¶ 136). What is most telling here is that neither Eugendus nor his biographer flinches from evil or tries to cover up the fact that Eugendus had enemies (¶ 138). The account rings true.

If our author knew well the facts of Eugendus' life, he knew Romanus only by 'tradition', that is, the traditions handed down by older monks at the monastery. Undoubtedly, he gathered much of his information from Eugendus (¶ 42). He says that he was 'a young child' during the abbacy of Lupicinus (¶ 78) but whether he was at the monastery at this time is not clear. Our author knows the precise whereabouts of Eugendus' birthplace (¶ 120) but is vague about that of Romanus, giving only the province in which he was born (¶ 4). The author of the *Life* probably entered the monastery before the end of the fifth century; at that time there were undoubtedly monks still living who had known Lupicinus and even Romanus.[79]

What more can we say about him?[80] Although the Latin of the *Life of the Jura Fathers* can be cumbersome and even exasperating, it seems clear that its author was a practised writer.[81] He had read and had access to the *Life of Antony*, the *Life of Saint Martin*, the *Life of Paul the Hermit* by Saint Jerome,

---

[79] Martine, 82.

[80] Wood, 27 n 118, following Moyse, says that it is 'plausible' that the author of the *Life* is Viventiolus, the priest at Condadisco who became bishop of Lyon and to whom Bishop Avitus wrote (see Appendix I). Wood's hypothesis is predicated on an early date for the *Life* (see n. 82 below) and is impossible to prove.

[81] See Martine, 51. For an exhaustive study of the Latin of the *Life of the Jura Fathers*, see P.-W. Hoogterp, 'Les Vies des Pères du Jura: Étude sur la langue'. *Bulletin du Cange: archivum latinitatis medii aevi* 9 (1934) 129–251.

and the *Dialogues* of Sulpicius Severus. He probably knew, at least in excerpted form, the writings of Cassian, Basil, and Pachomius. He has an understanding of—and preference for—the 'mystical' interpretation of scripture (¶¶ 1–3). Romanus, as we have seen, brought books with him to the Juras, and Eugendus may have known how to read both Latin and Greek (¶ 126).[82] Since the author of the *Life* was a disciple of Eugendus, it is reasonable to suggest that he learned his skills from the abbot.[83] In fact, the respect for reading and *lectio* that the *Life of Eugendus* demonstrates (¶¶ 126 and 169) must have come down from the days of Romanus, probably through the authority of the abbots: 'Asceticism could now be read about and no longer depended on oral transmission. It could be taught by an abbot, the monks' intermediary with God, himself the supreme abbot of the elect. Gallic monks were hereby encouraged to read books; and they could write them'.[84]

The author of the *Life of the Jura Fathers* addresses his work to two monks at Acaunus (Agaune), John and Armentarius; perhaps, like Romanus (¶ 44) he had traveled there. He probably wrote the *Life* around 520, just a few years after the death of Eugendus.[85] Abbot Marinus of Lérins had requested the 'Institutes' written by the author of the *Life* for the monks of

---

[82] If Eugendus and the author of the *Life* did indeed know how to read Greek, it may have been because they were heirs of the classical learning apparently taught at Lérins; see P. Courcelle, 'Nouveaux aspects de la culture lérinienne', *Revue des études latines* 46 (1968) 379–409, and *Late Latin Writers and Their Greek Sources*, trans. Harry E. Wedeck (Cambridge, Mass.: Harvard UP, 1969) esp. 261–62. By contrast, Pierre Riché, *Education and Culture in the Barbarian West, Sixth through Eighth Centuries* (Columbia, SC: South Carolina UP, 1976) 119 n. 30, believes that it is 'hardly probable that Eugendus, who entered the monastery at age seven, knew Greek in a period when it was forgotten. . . . He undoubtedly read translations of the Greek Fathers'. Martine, 374–5, n. 2, says that such ability would have been 'exceptional'. See his note for further references.
[83] Riché, 119.
[84] Wallace-Hadrill, *The Frankish Church*, 7.
[85] See Martine, 53–7; Wallace-Hadrill, *The Frankish Church*, 8, dates the *Life* to 525. Wood, 20 n. 10, following Masai, places the *Life* 'earlier than

Acaunus (¶ 179). All in all, he seems to have been a person of some learning and prominence in the community, with perhaps some embarrassment over the 'rustic nature' of the saints he is portraying (¶ 59).[86] His *Life of the Jura Fathers* has received high praise from modern scholars as 'an excellent biography' and 'the most interesting of the "Burgundian" saints' Lives'.[87]

2. The Lives

The author of the *Life of the Jura Fathers* seems to know—or care—little about the birthplace and origins of Saint Romanus. He says vaguely that Romanus was from Gallia Sequanorum and that he 'came from a not insignificant family' (¶ 4). Such vague and stereotyped wording should be regarded with considerable wariness.[88] Suspicion—at least historical suspicion—is warranted here: the events of Romanus' pre-monastic life would have lain in the dim past for his biographer; he came to the monastery probably thirty years after Romanus' death. More important than chronology, though, is intent: there is a hint that Romanus' 'not insignificant family' is modeled on the 'noble' family of Saint Antony in Evagrius' latin translation of the *Life of Antony*.[89]

---

the foundation of Agaune (September 515). Thus a date of 512/4–515 is demanded', but it is not clear why this must be so.

[86] See Martine's appreciation, 67.

[87] Wallace-Hadrill, *The Frankish Church*, 8, and Wood, 'A Prelude to Columbanus', 4. The authenticity of the *Life* is now completely accepted. For a thorough discussion of the question, see Martine, 14–44. As L. Duchesne long ago concluded: 'The biographer is older than Gregory [of Tours]. Nothing argues against his having lived at the beginning of the sixth century as he claims. He wrote at Condat; he knew Saint Eugendus; he tells us, doubtless with great accuracy, what people were saying in the Jura monasteries in his time, about the saints of the preceding generation, the founding saints, Romanus and Lupicinus'. L. Duchesne, 'La Vie des Pères du Jura', *Mélanges d'archéologie et d'histoire publiés par l'École française de Rome* 18 (1898) 1–16; 16.

[88] See Wood, 4.

[89] PL 73:427A.

Suspicion turns to conviction in the next paragraph when inference becomes proclamation: Romanus is the gallic Antony.[90] Like Antony and the communion of ascetics long before him, Romanus is 'attracted by the solitudes of the desert'. We now know that our author's purpose is not to praise Romanus, or even to describe his life for that life's sake, but to praise the desert—or, rather, the way of the desert, the way of detachment from the world and attachment to God. For the author of the *Life*, this way stretches far beyond the Jura mountains in both time and distance. This is why one must also speak of the *lives* of the Jura Fathers, because within the *Life* are different lives. Not merely the lives of Romanus, Lupicinus, and Eugendus, but lives within lives. Lives appear—or, better, surface—from within the sacred Life (or hagiography) which is the life, or way, of the desert.

These lives intersect, or intertwine, throughout the *Life of the Jura Fathers*. According to his biographer, Romanus was soon joined in the Juras by his brother and, later, his sister. Such reunion is 'a standard feature of Merovingian hagiography. . . . Saints, who had begun by dissociating themselves entirely from their families, came into closer contact with their relatives once sanctity was achieved'.[91] Since there can be no doubt that Romanus' brother and sister did in fact join him, this 'standard feature', however it was later employed in merovingian hagiography, clearly reflects and results from a historical social pattern.

Another social reality that the *Life* indirectly pictures is power. As the monastic community in the Juras grew and there were two monasteries, Condadisco and Lauconnus, Romanus and Lupicinus 'were abbots of both monasteries'. But such shared power appears to have been in name only: Romanus was clearly associated with Condadisco, the monastery he founded; Lupicinus 'stayed especially at Lauconnus' (¶¶ 36–39). Lupicinus' affection for his monastery is evident; he was

[90] See ¶ 5 of the *Life* and the notes there for references to the *Life of Antony*.
[91] Wood, 8.

buried there (¶ 117).[92] Romanus was buried not at Condadisco
but at Balma, the third jura monastery; this house for women
was founded by the brothers, and their sister was its first abbess.
Sole rule of Condadisco eventually passed to Lupicinus; just
before his death, Romanus commended 'the entire community
of brothers' to Lupicinus, 'to be ruled with pastoral love' (¶ 61).
Lupicinus apparently retained sole rule of the monasteries; just
before he died he first chose 'a father for Condadisco, the older
monastery. Then, with his death now imminent, he appointed
an abbot for the monastery of Lauconnus' (¶ 115).[93]

Another clear theme in the *Life* is a unity modeled on the
primitive community in Acts (see, for example, ¶ 111), and the
co-abbacy of Romanus and Lupicinus suggests a harmony that
may be more authorial than actual, as if pebbles on the seashore
had started out round and smooth. Personality, however, has a
way of stressing individuality over real or imagined homogene-
ity, reminding us of corners and sharp edges. The *Life of the Jura
Fathers*, in the persons of Romanus and Lupicinus, has plenty
of personality.

Romanus and Lupicinus, although brothers, were apparently
very different. As different, we might say, as night and day;
the author of the *Life* would probably have preferred to say 'as
different as *the divine offices* for night and day'. That is, although
some offices are said in light and some in darkness, they are

---

[92] In 1689 a funerary inscription was discovered at the church of Saint-
Lupicin: hic reqviesci beatvs lvppicinvs abbas ('Here rests the blessed abbot
Lupicinus') engraved on a small lead plaque 90 mm x 35 mm. Martine
suggests, 79, that the plaque dates from the eighth century at the latest but 'can
very easily date back to the end of the fifth century and be contemporaneous
with the *depositio*' of Saint Lupicinus around 480. It is more likely, though,
that the plaque was engraved at the time of the transfer of the relics to the
small tomb under the altar than at the time of the first inhumation of Saint
Lupicinus; unfortunately, Martine notes, we do not know the date of this
translation.
[93] ¶ 111 might suggest that there was a co-abbacy after Romanus' death;
Martine takes it this way (132 n. 4). But ¶ 111 may in fact be synchronic
rather than diachronic and may be referring to the time of the co-abbacy of
Romanus and Lupicinus.

two parts of the same intention: praise of God. Our author, therefore, sees the differences between the two brothers as 'the requisite and complementary skills of ruling and governing' (¶ 17). In making a virtue out of differences, he may very well be right. But those differences, freely acknowledged, are nevertheless striking:

> Blessed Romanus was very loving towards everyone and perfectly tranquil, while his brother was more severe, both towards others, correcting and ruling them, and especially towards himself. Romanus, even when pardon was not to be expected, was eager to forgive those who had done harm; Lupicinus, on the other hand, afraid that repeated light punishment would have no effect, rebuked people very severely. Romanus, in laying privations on the brothers, would order only those that their will and spirit could bear; Lupicinus, offering himself as an example to everyone, did not allow anyone to refuse what is possible with God's help (¶ 17).

One story in particular forcefully displays the different personalities of the brothers (¶¶ 36–40). 'Certain brothers', it seems (we do not know how many),[94] turned gluttonous after an abundant harvest. Ignoring the Rule, they showed 'disrespect and contempt for their abbot'. Romanus 'rebuked' the brothers, but, apparently because he was 'the gentlest of souls', they ignored him and became 'even more wanton'. Faced with such disrespect, and possibly even revolt, 'Romanus, whose staff was truly gentle and easy, had to seek out the rod of his brother's severity'. Lupicinus arrived and promptly took charge. After he cleverly exposed the monks' gluttony, all but one of them left the monastery, apparently for good, "not to serve Christ, but [each] his own belly" (see Rom 16:18). Lupicinus' response was 'good riddance'. 'Now that the chaff has been tossed out and scattered by the wind, keep the wheat; now that the jackdaws

---

[94] Gregory of Tours, in his version of the story, says twelve; *Life of the Fathers* 3 (James, trans., 6–8). On Gregory see pp. 58–59 below.

and ravens have flown away, peacefully feed the gentle doves of Christ'.

Although Gregory of Tours, when he tells this story, supplies a happy ending to this episode—the twelve repent and found twelve monasteries!—he preserves the differences between Romanus and Lupicinus, and even intensifies the conflict: after the departure of the gluttonous brothers, Romanus accuses Lupicinus of 'driving the monks away' and exclaims, 'It would have been better if you had stayed behind!' Lupicinus, in character, responds, 'Do not be angry over what has happened, dearest brother. Know that the threshing floor of the Lord has been purified, and that the wheat alone remains for placing in the granary: the chaff has been thrown away'. Romanus, less rigid, weeps and prays for the brothers, and 'the Lord did indeed touch their hearts with remorse'.[95] Even time's erosions and the requirements of hagiography cannot efface the very human natures of Romanus and Lupicinus. Their co-abbacy may have been a trial to both of them.

Paradoxically, the *Life of Eugendus*, whom our author knew personally, is in some ways the most hagiographical of the three: at a tender age Eugendus had a vision that prophesied his future (his prophetic forebears are Abraham and Samuel) (¶¶ 121–4); he was famous as a healer and wonderworker (¶¶ 139–48); he held conversations with the apostles and Saint Martin (¶¶ 152–60). The author of the *Life* clearly sees his hero's life through the twin lenses of Antony and Martin (¶¶ 157–60, 167–8). And yet Eugendus too comes across as very human. Our author acknowledges that the abbot could get 'perhaps a little too gruff over some offense (as often happened)' (¶ 151). And the setting for one of Eugendus' visions is delightfully specific: 'on a summer's day he was outside the monastery resting beneath his favorite tree beside the road that crosses over the mountains and runs to Geneva' (¶ 153).

In the *Life of Eugendus* even healings, about which we moderns are far too skeptical and dismissive, are very particular and

---

[95] Gregory of Tours, *Life of the Fathers* 3; James, trans., 7- 8.

very human. One woman, 'seized by a horrible demon', not only was 'locked away, but was even restrained by iron chains. As is the custom, in order to heal her a number of people tied written formulas of exorcism around her neck as she lay all tied up' (¶ 141). The townspeople 'ran with absolute faith to the blessed man' (¶ 143) and Eugendus healed the woman with a letter of exorcism. Similarly, a woman (Syagria, known historically as a person of nobility and philanthropy from Lyon) asked Eugendus for a letter of healing; when she held it to her eyes and gripped it in her teeth while praying, she was healed (¶¶ 145–6). Scholarship has shown that these sorts of appeals to christian holy men date back at least to the fourth century; papyri letters have shown that a certain Paphnutius was receiving letters in Egypt similar to those sent to Eugendus at a later date in Gaul.[96] From the fourth century on, the monastic communities of Egypt, Palestine, Syria, and Europe had holy men (and women) such as Paphnutius and Eugendus. Some of their names have come down to us; many more undoubtedly have not.

Toward the end of the fifth century, Gennadius of Marseilles wrote his *De ecclesiasticis scriptoribus* (*De viris illustribus*). Modeled on Jerome's book of the same name, it is a collection of some one hundred brief lives of christian authors that provides a good window into the intellectual and spiritual life of fifth-century Gaul.[97] Romanus, Lupicinus, and Eugendus, because they were not writers, are not included. About a hundred years later, Gregory of Tours wrote his *Life of the Fathers*, the first two chapters of which are devoted to Romanus and Lupicinus (Eugendus does not appear). Outside of the *Life of the Jura Fathers*,

---

[96] James E. Goehring and Robert F. Boughner, 'Letters to Paphnutius', in Vincent L. Wimbush, ed., *Ascetic Behavior in Greco-Roman Antiquity: A Sourcebook* (Minneapolis: Fortress, 1990) 459–62. 'Their direct documentary evidence of this popular appeal to the authority of the early ascetics corroborates the more literary evidence of the *Apophthegmata Patrum*' (p. 458).

[97] Gennadius apparently did not write all 101 lives; some were added by later editors.

Gregory offers the only contemporary or near-contemporary account of the Jura Fathers .[98]

That account is not very reliable, at least if we are thinking in terms of historical accuracy. Gregory provides hardly any details about the first monasteries in the Jura or about the material and spiritual life of the community.[99] Where his stories can be compared to similar accounts in the *Life of the Jura Fathers*, the comparison does not favor Gregory.[100] Gregory probably did not know the *Life of the Jura Fathers*;[101] 'at the most we may admit that Gregory of Tours used a very poor and unreliable summary of [the *Life of the Jura Fathers*], or else that the two authors had access to the same old and brief account of the two monastic founders'.[102] But Gregory did not seek verisimilitude: 'the sacred biographer's *primary* mission in writing the life is not to render a chronological record of the subject's life, Xenophon's *praxeis*, but rather to facilitate the growth of the cult'.[103] Gregory does not want to bestow knowledge on his readers; he seeks emulation.[104]

All of this raises important questions for the *Life of the Jura Fathers* and for the individual Lives of Romanus, Lupicinus,

---

[98] Sidonius Apollinaris, bishop of Clermont, in a letter to his friend Domnulus around 470, during the abbacy of Lupicinus, refers to Domnulus' frequent trips to the monastery: 'And now, unless the monasteries of the Jura keep you, where you love to ascend as if in foretaste of a celestial habitation, this letter ought to reach you'. O. M. Dalton, *The Letters of Sidonius* (Oxford: Oxford UP, 1915) Book IV, 25; Martine, 68–9. The *Martyrology* of Florus of Lyon (around 837) includes brief notices about Romanus, Lupicinus, and Eugendus.

[99] Martine, 81.

[100] As the story of the gluttonous monks, described on pp. 55–56 , shows.

[101] James, 4; Martine, 72.

[102] Martine, 73. James notes, 7 n. 8, that both authors in the story of the gluttonous monks (see above, p. 00) use variants of the unusual word *cothurnus* to denote haughtiness or pridefulness, which would suggest that they shared a similar source. Both also use the image of the wheat and the chaff. See *Life of Romanus* 35 and note 94 and ¶ 21, note 60.

[103] Heffernan, *Sacred Biography*, 35. Heffernan prefers to use 'sacred biography' rather than 'hagiography'; see 15–18.

[104] Heffernan, 3: 'the life of the saints not only opens up their intentions but also excites the minds of listeners to emulate them'.

and Eugendus. There is no doubt that for our author Saints
Martin and Antony are heroic forefathers worthy of emulation.
To borrow one of his own images (¶ 129), he does sometimes
shape the gallic wooden clog into a desert sandal. (Our author
can be apologetic and deferential about gallic 'weakness' and yet
display a fierce gallic pride for his region's monastic customs.)
And yet the *Life of the Jura Fathers* has a richness, a texture,
a heft that is lacking in Gregory's treatment of Romanus and
Lupicinus. For contemporary readers of the *Life* this may have
been due to the very resemblance these saints bore to Antony
and Martin and the desert fathers; for us it may be *in spite of*
these resemblances.

It may be a question of what we see when we look at the
picture offered us of the Jura Fathers, whether we see individuals and their lives, or whether we see saints whose *life* is
worthy of emulation. Or, more deeply, it may be a question of
the Jura Fathers not as a picture but as a mirror. Huston Smith
has suggested that early Christians felt 'that three intolerable
burdens had suddenly and dramatically been lifted from their
shoulders'. The third of these was 'the cramping confines of
the ego'.[105] Contemporaries of the author of the *Life of the
Jura Fathers* would look into the mirror of the *Life* and see
not individuals, but saints; as saints themselves in communion
with the saints of old, they could escape the confinements of
the self.

For us today, this mirror can still be of great—even inestim-
able—value; but in the spirit of our global awareness of other
faiths, which the early medievals did not have, we need perhaps
to add to the communion of saints the image of the zen mirror.
Thomas Merton, himself a christian monk, offers that image
to us in the West:

> The mirror is thoroughly egoless and mindless. If a flower
> comes it reflects a flower, if a bird comes it reflects a bird. It

---

[105] Huston Smith, *The World's Religions: Our Great Wisdom Traditions* (San
Francisco: Harper San Francisco, 1991) 333. The other two burdens are fear
(including fear of death) and guilt.

shows a beautiful object as beautiful, an ugly object as ugly. Everything is revealed as it is. There is no discriminating mind or self-consciousness on the part of the mirror. If something comes, the mirror reflects; if it disappears the mirror just lets it disappear . . . no traces of anything are left behind.[106]

The object of zen consciousness (if there is an object!) is to free ourselves from our cramping confines. Merton goes on, using Meister Eckhart, to show that for the Christian such freedom is the way to God:

Here it is essential to remember that for a Christian 'the word of the Cross' is nothing theoretical, but a stark and existential experience of union with Christ in His death in order to share in His resurrection. To fully 'hear' and 'receive' the word of the Cross means much more than simple assent to the dogmatic proposition that Christ died for our sins. It means to be 'nailed to the Cross with Christ', so that the ego-self is no longer the principle of our deepest actions, which now proceed from Christ living in us.[107]

The Jura Fathers may be just such a mirror for us: like our early medieval ancestors, we see not ourselves but the saints when we look into the mirror; we free our egos in them. But Merton— and Eckhart, and Zen—urge that we need to go further. After not seeing ourselves, we need to not see the saints; finally, we need to not see God—that is, our conception of God, which is, after all, a projection of our own egos. These saints, through their lives—their *life*—can point us in such a direction.[108]

---

[106] Zenkei Shibayma, *On Zazen Wasan* (Kyoto, 1967) 28, quoted by Thomas Merton, *Zen and the Birds of Appetite* (New York: New Directions, 1968) 6.

[107] Merton, 55–56.

[108] 'What then? Is there some new possibility, some other opening for the Christian consciousness today? If there is, it will doubtless have to meet the following great needs of man: *First*; His need for community, for a genuine relationship of authentic love with his fellow man . . . I might suggest a *fourth* need of modern man which is precisely liberation from his inordinate

IV. SPIRITUALITY AND WAY OF LIFE[109]

The author of the *Life of the Jura Fathers* says surprisingly little—almost nothing—about three central parts of monastic life: *lectio divina*; the Divine Office, the regularly appointed times of prayer and worship during the day; and work.[110] This is in spite of the fact that he promises in several places 'to reproduce faithfully in the name of Christ . . . the deeds, the way of life, and the Rule of the esteemed fathers of the Jura Mountains' (¶ 4).[111] Nevertheless, he does say a good deal—indirectly and unsystematically—about the way of life and the spirituality of the Jura Fathers. There are, really, *three* ways of life in the *Life of the Jura Fathers*. Despite our author's intention to see the lives of Romanus, Lupicinus, and Eugendus as one life (see above, pp. 47–48) each of the lives is distinct, and dramatically different. In an image our author would favor, the three ways of life are like the three persons of the Trinity, each a distinct reality, but reflecting one final Reality.

1. *Romanus*

Romanus is an earth-figure. Our author, with inherited christian dread of the chthonic practices of the pagans, would undoubtedly not have appreciated this characterization. But from his own description, Romanus is a man of rocky mountains, fir trees, icy cold streams of water, and 'the burning heat of summer days and the freezing rains of winter' (¶¶ 7–8). Some of this description is stereotypically hagiographical, modeled on

---

self-consciousness, his monumental self-awareness, his obsession with self-affirmation, so that he may enjoy the freedom from concern that goes with being simply what he is and accepting things as they are in order to work with them as he can' (Merton, 30–31).

[109] For a sympathetic discussion of the spirituality of the Jura Fathers, see Martine, 86–95, 'La Spiritualité de Condat'.

[110] Though he does explicitly refer to 'nocturnes and matins', *nocturnis matutinisque* (¶ 129).

[111] By contrast, the *Rule of Saint Benedict* devotes chapters 8–19 to worship and chapter 48 to work.

the *Life of Paul the Hermit* and the *Life of Antony*. Nevertheless, Romanus *was* the first person to seek out the monastic life in the dense and nearly impassable jura forests; except for an occasional hunter (¶ 12) he was alone.

After finding a tillable spot (¶ 6) Romanus discovered a place to live: 'When the new arrival was seeking an appropriate place to live, he found to the east, at the foot of a rocky mountain, a dense fir tree whose branches, spread out in a circle, were covered with an abundance of leaves' (¶ 7). The fir tree under which Romanus lived is emblematic for our author, reminding him of the palm tree that sheltered Paul the hermit in the first desert: 'owing to the merits of the saint, it enjoyed a truly perpetual spring' (¶ 8). Fir trees are evergreens by nature, one might snidely retort, but miss the point: date palms in the egyptian desert, contrary to horticultural reality, gave fruit year round to the holy ones.[112] Romanus has regained Paradise.

We need the imagination necessary to realize that Romanus undoubtedly did sleep under a tree at first. That fir tree, and the spring beside it, are emblems of the hermit life.[113] Modeled on the lives of the desert fathers, Romanus lived the hermit life of work, prayer, and reading (¶ 10).[114] That life did not last

---

[112] For the theme of the recovery of Paradise in egyptian monasticism, see Tim Vivian, trans., *Paphnutius: Histories of the Monks of Upper Egypt and the Life of Onnophrius* (Kalamazoo: Cistercian Publications, 1993) 155, 161–2. For the modern economic application of this theme, see M. Francis Mannion, 'Benedictine Economics and the Challenge of Modernity', *Amercian Benedictine Review* 47.1 (March 1996) 14–36: 'The way of life into which the monk is initiated is designed to reverse the disruptive economy of Adam and to restore the economy established by God at the creation of the world. Indeed, it is instructive in this regard to invoke the motif in the monastic tradition that conceives of monastic life as an anticipation of paradisal existence . . . . We cannot understand monastic economics except as a reversal of Adamic economics and a restoration of the economy of God's Kingdom' (19–20).

[113] As caves and springs are for judean desert hermits in the early byzantine period. See Yizhar Hirschfeld, *The Judean Desert Monasteries in the Byzantine Period* (New Haven: Yale UP, 1992) 215–16.

[114] The summary of the eremitic life in ¶ 10 is a literary construct, clearly modeled on monastic life in the Egyptian desert. By no means, however,

long; soon Romanus had a community around him. It is not coincidental that as jura monasticism moves from eremitic to cenobitic, both the fir tree and an awed appreciation of nature disappear from the *Life*. European and western monasticism, as we have seen, was to be decidedly communal rather than eremitic. But the anchoritic musings of a late-twentieth century american monk remind us what the 'wildness' of solitude preserves for us in our technological and industrial society:

> I came up here from the monastery last night, sloshing through the cornfield, said Vespers, and put some oatmeal on the Coleman stove for supper. It boiled over while I was listening to the rain and toasting a piece of bread at the log fire. The night became very dark. The rain surrounded the whole cabin with its enormous virginal myth, a whole world of meaning, of secrecy, of silence, of rumor. Think of it: all that speech pouring down, selling nothing, judging nobody, drenching the thick mulch of dead leaves, soaking the trees, filling the gullies and crannies of the wood with water, washing out the places where men have stripped the hillside! What a thing it is to sit absolutely alone, in the forest, at night, cherished by this wonderful, unintelligible, perfectly innocent speech, the most comforting speech in the world, the talk that rain makes by itself all over the ridges, and the talk of the watercourses everywhere in the hollows![115]

Romanus' biographer, living in a community with perhaps a hundred other monks and writing some seventy-five years after the saint's withdrawal to the forests of the Jura, emphasized that

---

should it therefore be seen as a fabrication or creation by our author. Romanus learned of the desert tradition at the monastery of the Confluence in Lyon and brought that tradition with him to the Juras.

[115] Thomas Merton, 'Rain and the Rhinoceros', in *Raids on the Unspeakable* (New York: New Directions, 1966) 9–10. For a good interdisciplinary appreciation of the positive attitude of the early desert monks toward wilderness and nature, see Susan Power Bratton, 'The Original Desert Solitaire: Early Christian Monasticism and Wilderness', *Environmental Ethics* 10.1 (1988) 31–53.

Romanus' solitary spring now feeds a *monastery*: 'even today its waters, channeled with wooden pipes to the distant monastery, are placed at the disposal of Romanus' heirs as a pledge of the inheritance that was to come' (¶ 7). Channels and wooden pipes: the desert has become a city.[116] Perhaps our author, now a 'city-dweller', had stood quietly at that source—both of water and the monastic life—watched its waters, and wondered. The image, both its depth and its beauty, is powerful. The entire history of the monastery can be seen there.

Romanus was soon joined by his brother, Lupicinus, then by two young clerics from the city of Noviodunum (Nyon); monastic life in the Juras changed from the eremitic, to the semi-eremitic, the 'lauritic' in judean monasticism, where the monks lived separately but gathered together for work and prayer:

> Since that birthplace of the saints (if I may speak this way about it) could now scarcely contain their increased numbers, they took up residence not far from the tree, on a small hill with a gentle slope, where the oratory reserved for private prayer now stands to their memory. Once the wood had been hewn and planed with the utmost care, they constructed small dwellings for themselves and prepared others for those who would come in the future (¶ 13).

Soon, according to our author, 'throngs of believers' were coming to the monastery. One wonders what Romanus thought of this. The evangelist in him must have rejoiced, but the solitary must surely have felt some loss. For the monastery was now, whether its founder liked it or not, a social institution. Now the monks and their monastery were known for their healing. In contrast with the egyptian desert tradition, the author of the

---

[116] The image is Athanasius', *Life of Antony* 14.7, repeated by Cyril of Scythopolis in his *Life of Sabas* 6.90.8–10. Derwas Chitty used the image to entitle his famous study of early egyptian and palestinian monasticism, *The Desert a City*. That the metaphor was not universally admired is apparent from the coptic translation of the *Life of Antony*, which drops it.

Life associates healing with communal, not solitary, monasticism. Healings led to converts (¶ 15). The Juras now became something of a boom town, and the narrative has some of the breathless quality of a promotional brochure; there were now two monasteries: Condadisco, associated with Romanus, and Lauconnus, closely connected with Lupicinus (¶ 24). Soon (¶¶ 26–27) there was also a monastery named Balma for women—an exceptional institution at this time in this part of Gaul.[117]

Renown and building programs had a way of coming to the attention of bishops, whether in Egypt or Gaul: Hilary of Arles summoned Romanus to Besançon and made him a priest (¶ 18).[118] Now the snake enters the garden. The image is deliberate, for our author, clearly mindful of Genesis 3, evokes the possibility of ruin in Paradise:

> While these things were being accomplished because of the admirable way of life of the monks, the Devil, the enemy of the very name of Christian, was indignant that the monastic life was increasing for so many by daily renunciations of the world. He dared to assault blessed Romanus, under pretense of offering him good counsel, with the ancient weapon of envy (¶ 27).

The rest of the *Life of Romanus* is about the assault—and defeat—of the Devil: Romanus bests a prideful monk who, spurred on by the Devil, is judgmental and exclusive (¶¶ 27–34); the Devil 'overwhelms' some monks with gluttony and Romanus has to summon Lupicinus to restore order (¶¶ 35–40); Romanus, 'protected as he was by divine grace . . . worked to repel unclean spirits', agents of Satan (¶¶ 41–51). So intent, in fact, is our author on this theme of the Devil's assaults that he leaves Romanus and relates 'how the Enemy attacked one

---

117 Wood, 'A Prelude', 5. In the southern cities during the time of the Jura Fathers, convents were common; but it was Burgundofara, a follower of Columbanus, who started convents in the north.

118 On gallo-roman bishops, see Markus, *The End of Ancient Christianity*, 199–211, and Wallace-Hadrill, *The Frankish Church*, 42–3.

of the brothers there [the deacon Sabinianus] in order to show more readily, to those who desire to know, the steadfastness of all the others at that time' (¶ 51). Except for the conclusion, the final eight paragraphs of the *Life of Romanus* are about the warfare Sabinianus wages against evil (¶¶ 52–58).[119]

At first, the *Life of Romanus*, unlike the other two *Lives*, does not really seem to be about spirituality or way of life; there is no exposition of a daily regimen of prayer or presentation of the prayed life. But the *Life of Romanus* does establish a way of life—the monastic way of life in the desert: prayer, work, and reading, though not dwelt upon, are important parts of that life. So are healings and the miracles of the saints. The spiritual understanding in the *Life* is that God gives these gifts to his holy ones; such gifts are necessary and important because the Devil is abroad and active. He is envious, and is constantly seeking to destroy the good works of God's servants. The author of the *Life of the Jura Fathers* will elaborate these two themes—of a holy way of life, and the diabolical threats upon it—in the *Lives* of Lupicinus and Eugendus.[120]

2. Lupicinus

The *Life of the Jura Fathers* provides very few details about Romanus' daily way of life, perhaps because its author knew very little—or perhaps he was reserving his discussion of the monastic life for Lupicinus, who for him is the model ascetic, the man of the desert.[121] Ironically, of the three Jura Fathers

---

[119] Similarly, of 94 chapters in the *Life of Antony*, 28 (chs. 16–43) 'record' Antony's speech to the monks concerning Satan and his minions, while many of the rest are concerned with Antony's contests with the Devil.

[120] On the Devil and demons, see Clare Stancliffe, 'From Town to Country: The Christianisation of the Touraine, 370–600', in Derek Baker, ed., *The Church in Town and Countryside* (Oxford: Blackwell, 1979) 228–33. For a survey of the Devil in Late Antiquity and the Middle Ages, see Jeffrey Burton Russell, *Satan: The Early Christian Tradition* (Ithaca & London: Cornell UP, 1981) and *Lucifer: The Devil in the Middle Ages* (Ithaca & London: Cornell UP, 1984).

[121] On 'The Egyptian Ascetic Background', see Stancliffe, 233- 41.

Lupicinus is the one most embroiled in political matters, the things of this world. About a third of the *Life of Lupicinus* is devoted to Lupicinus' dealings with the world. Most of Lupicinus' *Life*, however, is about his role as abbot. Our author does not connect these themes; apparently he did not see—or did not wish to make—the connection between ascetic practice, political involvement and abbatial duties. There is, to be sure, some overlap: when Lupicinus defends the poor at court, he does so with an 'authority' that was undoubtedly founded as much on his office as it was (according to our author) on his 'sincerity of conscience' (¶ 92).[122] On one level, the *Life of Lupicinus* seems to be two *Lives*: the life of the ascetic and wonderworker (¶¶ 63–70) and the life of the abbot: healer, reconciler, conciliator, defender of the poor and misused (¶¶ 71–111); these lives come together at the end in the account of the venerable abbot's last days (¶¶ 115–17). Yet on a deeper level these lives converge as one *Life*: they are united by the struggle against the Devil.[123]

It is clear from the outset of the *Life of Lupicinus* that its author is intent on giving the details of Lupicinus' way of life: 'let me reveal right from the start how mean his clothing was, with what frugality he was accustomed to eat and, finally, his extraordinary and inimitable conduct in the religious life' (¶ 62). The inspiration for this description, and some of its details, comes once again from the *Life of Antony* and the *Life of Martin*:

Therefore, to protect himself against the frosts of that extremely cold land and to wear down the wantonness of the

---

[122] See ¶ 92 and n. 29 there.

[123] As Stancliffe observes, 234, 'The ascetic's struggle to subject his own body and to ward off demonic attacks are two aspects of the same thing' As Philip Rousseau has wisely observed: 'The imaginative vigor of any ascesis that involves, among other elements, a demonology is likely to awaken the scientific suspicions of a modern student, but the last thing we are thereby entitled to doubt is that consistency, purpose, and indeed perception lay behind it'. See his *Pachomius: The Making of a Community in Fourth-Century Egypt* (Berkeley: University of California Press, 1985) 135.

body, he always used a tunic made out of hide and fur which for the sake of humility was patched or sewn together from various animal hides; not only was it shaggy and hideous, it was also soiled and made in a kind of variegated ugliness. His cowl, equally ugly, protected him only from the rain, and was of little use in warding off the bitter cold of that place, of which I have spoken. As for his shoes, he wore them only when he happened to leave the monastery to go to the court in order to intercede on behalf of this or that person (¶ 63).

Once again, as with the *Life of Romanus*, it is difficult to separate the exigencies of hagiographical tradition from what we would prefer to call historical detail. Are the two, however, so easily separated?[124] If the desert tradition handed down from Egypt suggested or dictated certain practices, could Lupicinus not have adapted his own practices to inherited ones? That certain descriptions of Lupicinus' practices have analogues in previous desert tradition does not mean that these practices are the hagiographical overlay of our author. Our author could be accurately describing *tradition*—the tradition that Lupicinus inherited and lived—rather than imposing iconic details of that tradition from literary models.[125]

Our author is well aware of 'the excellence of the monks of Egypt and the east' (¶ 65) and strives mightily to have his hero(es) outdo the desert saints of old: 'In fasting and keeping vigils [Lupicinus] was so mighty that gallic nature defeated even the excellence of the monks of Egypt and the east' (¶ 65).

---

[124] One of the most striking things about modern coptic monasticism is its refusal to compartmentalize history, myth, legend, and tradition. It does not even entertain the possibility of doing so. See Tim Vivian, 'The Monasteries of the Wadi Natrun, Egypt: A Personal and Monastic Journey', *American Benedictine Review* 49.1 (1998): 3–32.

[125] The same question applies to Martin of Tours: Edward James observes, 'Archaeology and the Merovingian Monastery', 36, that the description of the architecture of Saint Martin's monastery at Marmoutier is 'an obvious imitation here of an Egyptian monastery', and says that J. Fontaine 'is surely right to suggest that the imitation may be as much literary as architectural'.

This might suggest that his description of Lupicinus' way of life is purely literary; there is, however, enough 'local color' to urge that our author's account is based on life as well as literature. For example, in ¶ 64 we see both: Lupicinus 'never used bedding or a bed', thus outdoing Antony, who usually slept on the ground but occasionally used a rush mat (*Life of Antony* 7). When Lupicinus 'went some distance to work in the fields', however, he did so as a native of Gaul: 'he would take with him only wooden clogs, which they commonly call *socci* in the monasteries of Gaul' (¶ 64). Lupicinus' ingenious defense against the cold is strikingly idiosyncratic:

> If harsh and powerful cold assailed him, he had a bag shaped like a cradle, measured to fit his size, made from bark stripped from an oak and closed off at each end by pieces sewn together from the same bark. After he had privately and lengthily warmed up the part of the bag that was open toward the coals, he either rested in it, enjoying the warmth for a bit, or he immediately carried the bag under his arm, while it was still warm, into the oratory in order to sleep there (¶ 65).

These examples are representative of the details of Lupicinus' way of life: at this distance it is impossible to disentangle completely the various traditions, local and literary, within the ascetic life—a situation that probably obtained in the author's own day.

While the author of the *Life of the Jura Fathers* does not connect Lupicinus' ascetic practices with either his miracles or his duties as abbot, he rather blandly leaps from his description of the saint's way of life to his miracles (¶ 68). He does, however, know what is important: 'Lupicinus, fearlessly trusting in the Lord, lifted up his soul and the eyes of his heart to the living bread that came down from heaven' (¶ 68). As our author concludes, 'Thus the man of God, trusting in faith, delivered both the community of brothers and the multitude of lay people from the danger of famine' (¶ 70). The result of such faith, such calling on the Lord, was that 'if someone placed a sick person' on the bed of a monk whom Lupicinus had healed, 'the illness was driven completely away and the person was immediately fully restored to his former good health' (¶ 78).

Lupicinus' faith apparently blessed him with deep sensitivity and compassion; these are the two qualities that shine forth from his *Life*. This seems surprising, given the picture of Lupicinus in the *Life of Romanus* as a rather severe and unforgiving perfectionist. In the *Life of Lupicinus* he is, by contrast, gentle, moderate, forgiving, and even courageous in his advocacy for the oppressed. The story of Lupicinus' healing of a severe ascetic is vivid and memorable (¶¶ 71–78):

> At that time a certain monk had, by the severity of intense abstinence, caused his poor body to be shriveled up with a kind of mange and with extreme emaciation. Half alive and knotted up like a paralytic, he could neither straighten his spine, nor control his walking, nor bend or extend his arms in order to use them. Except for the weak breathing that still sustained his body, you could have almost believed that he had departed this life.

Lupicinus, recognizing the danger of such extreme asceticism both to the monk and the community, goes to extraordinary lengths to heal him: he carries the monk out into the warm sun of the garden, fixes him food, massages his limbs, and exhorts him to 'lay aside' his 'willful severity'.

Lupicinus' compassion may in fact have been of secondary importance to our author: the ascetic's overly severe privations, he makes clear through Lupicinus' words, are against the Rule of the monastery (¶ 75) and Lupicinus' moderate views exemplify 'the middle course of monastic discipline that is "the royal path"' (¶ 77). One may suspect the story of being a construct, a vehicle for our author's views on the importance of the monastic *via media*, but Lupicinus' character continues to give a very personal stamp to the theme of moderation. When two monks plot to leave the monastery in the middle of the night, they are surprised by Lupicinus in the chapel and fall sobbing on their faces. 'But Lupicinus called each of them by name and, slowly putting forth his hand, took each of them by the chin; gently caressing each one, he warmly kissed them. With no further discussion, he knelt down, and with paternal love, took up the weapons of prayer' (¶ 81). The monks repent, Lupicinus keeps their secret and, twenty years later, addressing the community, presents a very balanced and sensible pastoral and monastic outlook:

> Just as the contumacious and proud, therefore, ought to be rebuked more severely,[126] those who feel remorse through humility of conscience should be treated with mild medicine. Who among you does not know that in the administration of this community that has been entrusted to me I must preserve a treatment in accord with the art, just as medicine is administered by skilled doctors to each patient in accordance with the nature of his wounds or the cause of his infirmity?
>
> I must not put him under the surgeon's knife or cauterize him with burning instruments; often he should be treated with poultices and warmed with plasters lest, through hasty treatment or treatment inconsistent with fevers, the doctors not bring healing to the person but instead, through untimely and inopportune practice, weaken him (¶¶ 85–86).[127]

This moderation is even more striking—and impressive—when we realize that Lupicinus maintains it in the face of unrelenting assaults by the Devil. The author of the *Life* makes clear that it is the Devil who is attacking these monks—and the monastic way of life (¶¶ 81 and 87). Lupicinus, rather than becoming rigid and restrictive in the face of diabolic assaults, demonstrates an admirable openness and trust. This trust, our author emphasizes, is grounded, deeply rooted, in faith in God.

Lupicinus' public efforts (¶¶ 92–5, 96–110) are extensions of this trusting faith; they are the way of the monastery (seen

---

[126] This belief is in keeping with Lupicinus' treatment of the gluttonous monks in ¶¶ 36–40 of the *Life of Romanus*.

[127] Such moderation also applied under Eugendus to those who were literally sick, who received special consideration; see ¶ 171.

ideally, perhaps) taken into the world.[128] Satan does not make an appearance in the 'public sections' of the *Life of Lupicinus* (¶¶ 92–110). Perhaps our author assumes that 'the world' is the Devil's domain; the evils, and evil men, in these paragraphs are obvious, and the monastery should be immune from the assaults of the Devil. But as Antony and the egyptian ascetics quickly realized, the Devil may be more visible precisely among those who are trying most diligently to live in conformity with God's will.[129]

'Conformity' does not have a good reputation in our individualistic, even solipsistic, culture. But to our author, conformity had a 'sweet scent' about it because it defines a time when 'deceitful envy' and 'consuming jealousy' did not have a hold on the community: 'Everyone, I say, was one because everyone belonged to the One' (¶ 111). This vision is based on Luke's depiction of the primitive christian community in Acts 4: 'Absolutely no one, in accordance with the law laid down by the apostles, said that anything was his own. One person differed from another only in the ownership of his name, and not with respect to possessions or reputation' (¶ 112).

Undoubtedly this is an idealization—as was Luke's; deceitfulness and jealousy had probably not been banished from the monastery out into the wilderness. In a consumerist society such as our own, where we are told hundreds of times a day that we are what we possess, such communion—and community—as our author depicts is scarcely imaginable. Yet if the picture our author presents is ideal, its results, as the *Life of Lupicinus* demonstrates, were very concrete:

---

[128] As R. A. Markus comments with regard to Lupicinus' political efforts: 'The ascetic ideology had moved from the fringes of society to its centre. From institutionalized alienation the monastery had turned into focused representation of the community's social ideal'. See Markus, *The End of Ancient Christianity*, 214.

[129] Derwas Chitty observed that as early as the *Life of Antony* 'the desert is represented as the natural domain of the demons, to which they have retreated on being driven out of the cities by the triumph of the Church, and into which the heroes of the faith will pursue them.' See Derwas J. Chitty, *The Desert a City* (Crestwood, NY: Saint, Vladimir's, n.d.) 6.

So content with nakedness were they, so fervently of one heart and mind in charity and faith, that if a brother, say, were ordered for some necessary reason to go somewhere out in the cold, and if, say, he returned soaked by the winter rains, each monk eagerly, of his own volition, removed his drier and more comfortable clothes and took off his shoes and hastened to warm and comfort his brother's body rather than his own (¶ 113).

It would take a hardened heart not to be moved by this passage; it would take a cynical person to dismiss it as merely an idealization, or wishful thinking. The community envisioned—and, apparently, lived—in the *Life of the Jura Fathers* forms a vital part of the desert tradition. Pachomius 'sought for a community built upon mutual respect and mutual support'; he 'seems to have in mind an asceticism closely bound up with a sense of obligation toward other people'.[130]

Communion is not easy to maintain. The successive generations of egyptian monks looked back longingly to a golden beginning; it is one of the recurring themes in the *Apophthegmata*. Our author does the same; the times are now evil, and monastic institutions have fallen into disrepair:

Up to that time no brother, sent out of the monastery by the abbot for some reason or other (and it provokes shame to refer to this or speak about it now that the monastic ordinances are everywhere thwarted), had himself, a creature

---

130 Rousseau, *Pachomius*, 66 and 64. One might contrast this with Karl Barth's bleak assessment of secular community: 'the civil community as such is spiritually blind and ignorant. It has neither faith nor hope nor love. It has no creed and no gospel. Prayer is not part of its life and its members are not brothers and sisters'. Karl Barth, *Community, State and Church*, cited by Andrew W. McThenia, 'An Uneasy Relationship with the Law', in Andrew W. McThenia, Jr., ed., *Radical Christian and Exemplary Lawyer: Honoring William Stringfellow* (Grand Rapids, MI: Eerdmans, 1995) 173. For a recent strong contrast between monastic spirituality and modern secular culture, see Archimandrite Boniface (Luykx), *Eastern Monasticism and the Future of the Church* (Redwood Valley, Calif.: Holy Transfiguration Monastery; Stamford, CT: Basileos Press, 1993).

of two legs endowed with reason, conveyed by a horse, a creature with four legs. Rather, each person was satisfied with the support of a walking stick, just as he made do with the coarse and substantial wheat bread of the monastery (¶ 113).

Is the Lupicinus of the *Life of Romanus* the 'real' Lupicinus, while the Lupicinus who compassionately looks out from his own *Life* represents for our author the hopes and dreams of the monastic life, shored up against the very ruins of that life? This falling away is an old, old theme—in world history, religious history, and monastic history. Later disrepair makes us wonder if things were ever in real repair. Our author undoubtedly believes that things were once whole. Whole, and yet under assault. His longing for wholeness is saved from nostalgia (which is self-delusion, whether personal or communal) by the very real and present figure of the Devil and by the saint. Nostalgia builds a perfect dream home in the past; for our author, the saint continues to dwell very much in the present: 'Lupicinus would for the time being furnish the monastery of Lauconnus with his powers, imbue it with his example, adorn it with his patronage, and aid it continuously with his prayers' (¶ 117).

3. *Eugendus*

If the publisher of the *Life of the Jura Fathers* had wanted a summary of the *Life of Eugendus* for the book's dust jacket, our author probably would have chosen the subtitle 'The Rule of Saint Eugendus'.[131] In the *Life of Romanus* he declares: 'since I promised that I would at the same time set down the Rule of these same fathers, know that I am reserving that for the third book. To produce this in the *Life* of blessed Eugendus who, inspired by the Lord, more artfully arranged these same regulations, is more proper' (¶ 59). Toward the end of the *Life of Eugendus* he concludes, apparently with some satisfaction, that he has fulfilled his promise: 'My discourse has caused me to

---

[131] See Wood, 4.

touch upon some of the institutions of the fathers as they were imitated by blessed Eugendus. According to the promise that I made above, that I would reserve this for the third section of my work (as Christ inspires my memory), I am making known as of first importance the initial steps of those who renounce the world' (¶ 174). The only problem is he does not keep his promise, at least not in any kind of straightforward manner.[132]

The *Life of Eugendus* is for all intents and purposes not a Rule but rather the life of a visionary (literally) and wonderworker. Eugendus' two remarkable visions take up almost half of its first twenty paragraphs (¶¶ 121–4, 135–8). More importantly, these visions establish a tone of 'signs and wonders' for the *Life*; after reading them, one does not doubt our author's assertion that Divine Compassion watched over its servant Eugendus (¶ 139). Eugendus—unlike Romanus and Lupicinus—holds conversations with the apostles and Saint Martin (¶¶ 152–60); in this third *Life*, Saint Martin in fact becomes a kind of guardian angel for Eugendus and the monastery (¶¶ 161–4). Wonders build upon wonders: the saint heals a possessed woman with a letter of exorcism (¶¶ 141–4); another of his letters heals the noblewoman Syagria (¶¶ 145–6); the sick, not surprisingly, flock to the monastery (¶¶ 147–8); like Saint Antony, Eugendus possesses the divine gifts of foresight and discernment of spirits (¶¶ 165–8).[133] The *Life of Eugendus*, which promises to be a Rule, is in fact the most hagiographical of the three *Lives*. Eugendus, reminiscent of Christ, is 'the holy child' (¶ 121).[134]

---

[132] Perhaps our author's presentation of the 'institutions' of Eugendus is missing. Martine believes there is 'an important lacuna' at this point in the text (427 n.2); see his discussion, 31–33.

[133] On the holy man in sixth-century Gaul, see Wallace-Hadrill, *The Frankish Church*, 40–41. In commenting on Gregory of Tours, Wallace-Hadrill, curiously, sees a society 'suffused with the miraculous' as one that 'is in some ways a nightmare-society, living in fear' (p. 42).

[134] Wood suggests, 4, that the main purpose of the *Life of the Jura Fathers*, unlike most hagiography, is not to describe the wonderworker, but to set down the monastic routine as 'laid down by the founders'. The visions and

Paragraphs 169–174 of the *Life of Eugendus* do nevertheless make up a kind of customary providing at least some of the rules and practices of the jura monasteries during the abbacy of Eugendus and at the time of the writing of the *Life of the Jura Fathers*. This 'customary', combined with other suggestions scattered through the *Life*, provides us with a valuable look at the spirituality of the Jura Fathers. The description of Eugendus' way of life (¶¶ 126–7, 129–31) serves as a prologue to the customary. Eugendus, like Lupicinus, dressed simply and rustically (¶¶ 127 and 129); as Jesus commanded (Lk 9:3), he did not have a change of clothing (¶ 127). His dress habits seem to be modeled on those of Antony and Martin so once again it is impossible to separate practice from hagiography.

The *Life of the Jura Fathers* offers no explicit rules or institutions for either private or communal prayer; what 'customs' we have must be gleaned from the individual practices of the three saints.[135] Eugendus devoted himself to *lectio*, the reading of scripture or the Fathers, 'day and night' (¶ 126). His habits of prayer are striking:

> No one ever saw him leave either the daytime or nighttime gathering before it was finished. Just as he entered the oratory at night a long time before the others in order to pray privately and at length, so after everyone had left he was spiritually nourished no less by a long prayer of set words

---

miracles of Eugendus, however, and the unsystematic presentation of any kind of Rule, do not support this.

[135] Pierre Riché argues that there is nothing in the institutional organization of columbanian monasticism (as taken from the *Life of Columbanus*) that fundamentally differs from the practices at the jura monasteries: 'the chapters of the Rule tell us nothing about the relations between abbot and *praepositus*, the liturgical *horarium*, the times of meals, and so on. What matters is obedience, fasting, chastity, mortification, and penance'. J. Gaudemet's observation on the Rule of Columbanus, cited by Riché, applies also to the Juras: 'It was little concerned with juridical formulae and more a guide to austerity than a Rule for communal living'. See Riché, 'Columbanus, His Followers and the Merovingian Church', 67.

that he recited lying down on a bench. He would leave there at whatever hour it was and approach the brothers with a glad and joyful face, just as other men, once their ambitions have been satisfied, are accustomed to showing faces awash with laughter and good cheer (¶ 130).

Eugendus' practice was probably not the norm, although Lupicinus also apparently at times kept nightly vigils in the oratory. When the two monks mentioned earlier plotted to forsake the monastery, they decided that the safest place for their nocturnal and clandestine rendezvous was the oratory (¶ 79)—obviously not a highly frequented place!

For our author one of the chief purposes of the 'customary' in paragraphs 169–74 is to describe the changes instituted at the monasteries by Eugendus. Earlier he noted that *lectio*, divine reading, was so important to Eugendus, that he spent all his spare time at it; he now says that reading 'so refreshed him that, while being read to during meals, he was often overcome by thoughts of the future as though he had fallen into ecstasy, and he forgot about what had been set before him'. Personal practice led to institution: 'He it was at Condadisco who, following the ancient fathers, properly introduced the practice of reading [in the refectory]' (¶ 169).

While Eugendus followed the ancient fathers in instituting reading, he refused to follow their sleeping arrangements. After a great fire destroyed the monastery (see ¶¶ 161–2), Eugendus had the monks sleep together, not in individual cells but in a common dormitory. Our author commends this practice as fostering community—he uses 'common' four times in a single sentence,[136] and even emphasizes that a *single* candle lit the sleeping hall!—and goes on to praise Eugendus for sharing the same food and table as the other monks—a practice, he laments, that is now breached. This allows him to re-emphasize one of the chief themes of the *Life*: 'Everything belonged to everyone in every way' (¶ 170).

---

[136] *Cunctos, unitae, una, una.*

All the rules of the monastery—so far as we are able to discern them—seem to have as their purpose the fostering of communal, religiously communistic, living: no one was to receive personal gifts (¶ 172) or have 'a private cell, closet, or box: no one was given the smallest opportunity to work for his own personal needs. Down to the simplest needle, even to woolen thread for sewing and mending, all things were held in common by the community' (¶ 173).[137] These rules demonstrate a deliberate effort to make the monastery different from the outside world and like the primitive, apostolic Church (see Acts 4). The very specific rules of enclosure for the female monks at Balma, the most explicit rules in the *Life*, confirm this separation and, though it is assumed rather than stated, dedication. Once the women entered the monastery they were not to leave it, 'unless they were being carried on their final journey to the cemetery'. If a sister had a relative at Lauconnus, the two were not to communicate with each other: 'each of them considered the other already buried, so that the bonds of monastic profession would not be worn down little by little by a kind of softening due to memories of things of the flesh' (¶ 26).

The *Life* evinces an honest realism concerning a difficult life: 'All the brothers know what I am saying: in the cenobium the most powerful opportunities for backsliding and falling into sin are never lacking' (¶ 173). That is, perhaps, to put it negatively, if realistically. But our author also sees the positive implications of the Rule: 'Among all the occupations, the only ones that allowed for personal profit were reading and prayer' (¶ 173). The goal of equality in the monastery was not, as in american society, individual self-fulfillment; it was humility. Humility is an important theme in each of the *Lives*: Romanus, although a priest, strives to show 'himself to be a monk among monks' (¶ 20); Lupicinus addresses the monks on 'humility of conscience' (¶ 85); Eugendus insists that no brother is above

---

[137] Although ¶¶ 79, 88, and 90 interestingly suggest that the monks had possession of their own tools—unless the miscreants in these passages are stealing the implements.

another (¶ 134). Humility is one of the clearest inheritances from desert spirituality in the *Life*.

The privations of the Jura Fathers—difficult for moderns to understand or even stomach—are also, finally, in the service of humility. It is a humility assumed rather than theologized: the *Life* makes no mention of the *kenosis* (emptying) of Christ or the abasements of the Suffering Servant. Humility is not belabored, defined, or defended; it is lived. It is simply what has long been done, expressed in the humblest of images: 'Blessed Eugendus wore sturdy country shoes in the manner of the ancient fathers' (¶ 129). The spiritual goal of the Jura Fathers as presented in their *Life* is not explicitly life in Christ, or life modeled on Christ. Christ is rarely mentioned in the *Life*, and quotations of Scripture are relatively infrequent.[138] It is Antony and Martin and the Desert Fathers to whom our author looks.

The Desert Fathers understood that they were following in the footsteps of Elijah and the prophets, John the Baptist, the apostles, and Christ;[139] what the desert forebears understood, the *Life* assumes. When we look at the desert tradition, we are inclined to see numerous desert footprints; where these steps seem to merge or run together, modern scholarship painstakingly attempts to separate them. Where we point out differences and conflicts, the ancients saw identity and unanimity (*unus animus*). Our ways are not our author's ways: instead of seeing three sets of footprints—those of Romanus, Lupicinus, and Eugendus—or thinking historically and seeing the

---

[138] In this regard the *Life* is more like the *Apophthegmata Patrum* (where Scripture is more implicit than explicit) than the *Life of Antony*; by way of contrast, see Eucherius' *In Praise of the Desert*, with its multitude of scriptural allusions, in Appendix III

[139] For example, see *In Praise of the Desert* (Appendix III below) where Eucherius lists the desert forefathers: 7–16 (Moses); 17 (David); 18 (Elijah); 19 (Elisha); 20 (the descendants of Elijah and Elisha); 21 (John the Baptist); 22–26 (Christ). Saint Jerome stresses the importance of Moses: 'that you may leave the bricks and straw of Egypt and follow Him, the true Moses, through the wilderness and enter the land of promise'. *Ad Eustochium* 22.24 (PL 22.410A); Wright, trans., 106–7.

thousands of footsteps of the monks who had gone before them in the desert, he sees one.[140] That is why, for our author, there is really only one *Life*:

> A condition of complete simplicity
> (Costing not less than everything)
> And all shall be well and
> All manner of thing shall be well
> When the tongues of flame are in-folded
> Into the crowned knot of fire
> And the fire and the rose are one.[141]

V. IN THE FOOTSTEPS OF THE JURA FATHERS

The modern traveler will look in vain for Saint Martin's monastery and the *mons excelsus* outside Tours, described by Sulpicius Severus, and will thus be led to consider Sulpicius' description, at least in part, a literary topos drawn from the *Lives of the Desert Fathers*.[142] By contrast, the author of the *Life of the Jura Fathers* gives a realistic, sometimes detailed, account of the Jura region, one that can often be followed *in situ* today. This is not to say that there are not geographical flights of fantasy in his account, but on the whole the author's description of, and obvious interest in, the area is a rarity in early medieval *Lives*. From roman ruins to monastic buildings (though obviously much altered), from rivers and creeks to precipitous crags and deeply furrowed valleys, readers of the *Life of the Jura Fathers* who visit the region even today will have the feeling that they are indeed walking in the footsteps of Romanus, Lupicinus, and Eugendus.

---

[140] As Wallace-Hadrill, *The Frankish Church*, 79, puts it: 'But the pattern [of the saint's *Life*] did not change . . . It was the same God intervening in the same way through his chosen medium, the saint. Sameness, in a word, is proof of authenticity'.

[141] T. S. Eliot, 'Little Gidding', *Four Quartets*, in *The Complete Poems and Plays 1909–1950* (New York: Harcourt, Brace & World, 1971) 145.

[142] J. Fontaine, ed., *Sulpice Sévère: Vie de saint Martin*, Sources chrétiennes 133–35 (Paris: Cerf, 1967–9) vol. 133:274–5, vol. 134:667ff.

Lovers of romanesque church architecture who revel in the sites of the Cluny/Mâcon region of southeast Burgundy will find the less-visited region of the Jura Fathers only a morning's drive away. In the summer of 1995 we left Bourg-en-Bresse and the secularized flamboyant gothic church in Brou, and driving along highway D979, quickly moved into a very different geographical region. Gone were the verdant plains and vineyards of Burgundy; before us stretched the Gorges de l'Ain and terraces of pines and firs. If we had followed the Ain river along back roads north to where it empties into Lac de Vouglans, we would have been only a few kilometers west of Saint-Lupicin, one of our central sites. Instead, we turned north onto D18 so we could pass through Izernore, the birthplace of Saint Eugendus, and the province where Romanus and Lupicinus were also born (¶ 120). To the north of the village, along the road, lay gallo-roman ruins; here we were literally back to the time of the Jura Fathers, for they may have known these buildings, if indeed they were not born in one or another of them.

Anxious to reach Saint-Claude, the Condat/Condadisco of the *Life of the Jura Fathers*, we turned onto D436 outside Oyonnax and wound our way north/northeast on a fairly narrow road. To our right was the Bois de la Balme, and here we were not far from the site of the convent of Balma founded by Romanus for his sister (unnamed in the *Life*, but called Yole in french tradition) (¶ 25). Along the road lay the village of Vaux-lès-Saint-Claude, one of the many places in the region named after the Jura Fathers or a site of their activity. Soon we saw the Bienne river, which flows through Saint-Claude, and we were only a few kilometers from the former monastery of Condadisco.

Today it is difficult to imagine what it must have been like for Romanus as he wandered north from his home near Izernore in search of a suitable site for his hermitage. We can look at the cliffs and ravines and think how hard it must have been to traverse this terrain on foot, especially in winter. But only in isolated places can we picture what Romanus must have experienced as he first gazed into the valley where the Bienne

Figure 1

Saint-Pierre Cathedral, Saint-Claude

and Tacon flow, near whose junction he would establish his first rude habitation under a fir tree (¶¶ 6–9).

Although the Michelin *Green Guide* bestows two stars (out of a possible three) on Saint-Claude, the city of some 15,000 inhabitants offers a dreary view from a distance. Industrial strips, supermarkets, and gas stations unexpectedly appeared

Figure 2

Drawing of wooden choir stalls showing SS. Romanus and Lupicinus. From
D. P. Benoit, *Histoire de l'Abbaye et de la Terre de Saint-Claude (1890)*.

before us; high-rises in the unfortunate style of the 1950s, a bleak, east-bloc architecture, lined the hills surrounding Saint-Claude. One can only imagine what Romanus might think if he were to stand now on the hills overlooking his 'desert'.

The view in Saint-Claude is not much better. The main road wraps around the cathedral of Saint-Pierre, making access to the site of the former abbey no easy task, to say nothing of the concomitant noise and pollution. The cathedral of Saint Peter is built over the former abbey of Condadisco founded by Romanus, but dates from the fourteenth and fifteenth centuries with eighteenth-century neo-classical additions, particularly on the exterior. The façade itself is an attractive admixture of Gothic and Neoclassical in lovely indigenous stone; the spired apse is noteworthy, though not easy to see because of the crowded setting.

Inside, we were struck by the vastness and the sobriety of style. The main attraction of the cathedral is the ornate fifteenth-century choir stalls by the genevan master Jehan de Vitry. Sculpted in wood are scenes from the history of the abbey, including depictions of Saints Romanus and Lupicinus.[143] To the right of the choir, in a chapel, we saw the ornate reliquary of Saint Claude, the twelfth abbot of Condadisco, and in a chapel to the left the reliquary of Saint Romanus, its first abbot.[144]

---

[143] Unfortunately, the choir stalls were undergoing renovation, and we could see them only from the arcade level, thanks to the generosity of the parish priest. D. P. Benoit's study has a number of drawings of scenes from the choir stalls: *Histoire de l'abbaye et de la terre de Saint-Claude* (Montreuil-sur-Mer: Imprimerie de la Chartreuse de Notre-Dame des Prés, 1890) 62, 78, 106.

[144] According to Gregory of Tours (*Life of the Fathers* 16) Lupicinus asked the dying Romanus where he would like his tomb, so that later the two could rest together. Romanus must have known that his brother wanted to be buried at his monastery of Lauconnus, for he stated that he did not want a sepulcher where women were excluded. Gregory goes on to say that Romanus was buried 'ten miles from the monastery' of Condadisco, 'on a small hill' (*Life of the Fathers*, trans. Edward James, 10). The *Rhymed Chronicle* of Saint-Claude (*Libellus metricus de fundatione et primis abbatibus monasterii Condatescensis*, in Jean Mabillon, ed., *Annales ordinis S. Benedicti* [Lutetia, 1703]; see Benoit, *Histoire*, 76) states that Saint Injuriosus, the eleventh abbot of Condat and

We could not locate a crypt, and apparently no excavations have revealed any traces of the original abbey church (as they have at Romainmôtier). We were left standing in a vast late-gothic nave, trying to conjure up images of how things might have looked at the time Condadisco was a thriving monastery. Although Saint-Claude grew out of the monastic settlement founded by Romanus and Lupicinus, as often happened in the Middle Ages, little remains in the town that can help us recreate the life and times of the Jura Fathers. Fortunately, however, the outlying areas of Saint-Lupicin, Saint-Romain, and Romainmôtier have more to offer the modern pilgrim.

We backtracked a bit from Saint-Claude on D436 and turned onto D470 to Lavans-lès-Saint-Claude; from there we took D118 a few kilometers to Saint-Lupicin. This village of two thousand in an attractive mountain setting has at its center the graceful romanesque church of Saint-Lupicin, the best preserved in the Jura Region, built on the site where Lupicinus founded his monastery of Lauconnus. As early as the eighth century the name Lauconnus had been replaced by Saint-Lupicin.[145]

---

the predecessor of Saint Claude, had the remains of both Romanus and Lupicinus translated to Condat. It appears that the remains of both Romanus and Lupicinus were divided, some remaining in La Balme and Saint-Lupicin, respectively, and some ending up in Condat. The remains of Romanus in La Balme were hidden in two reliquaries during the French Revolution (Lupicinus' were buried beneath the church at Saint-Lupicin) and later placed in the large reliquary on the altar at Saint-Romain, where they can be seen today; other remains are on view in Saint-Claude. The remains of Eugendus, too, made an eventful journey. Initially they were buried in the monastery cemetery of Condat, then translated by his successor, Saint Antidiolus, to a church built especially for them. Saint Claude was also interred there, the church then assuming the names of both saints. By 1754, when the remains of both were translated to the Cathedral of Saint Peter, the church, subsequently destroyed, had become known only as Saint-Oyend (Eugendus) because of the saint's thaumaturgical workings. A stained glass scene in Saint Peter's depicts the dying Eugendus imparting to monks his final instructions (see Benoit, *Histoire*, 157–60).

[145] Benoit, *Histoire*, 106.

Figure 3

Apse of the church at Saint-Lupicin.

The exterior of the structure is especially attractive when viewed from the east, where three absidoles are crowned by a belfry with lombard arcades, all offering an extremely harmonious picture. Inside, the rib-vaulted nave (a replacement of the original wooden barrel vault) is flanked by slightly lower

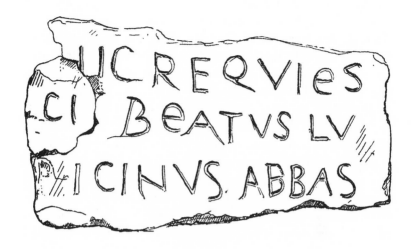

Figure 4

Facsimile of the inscription on the tomb of Lupicinus.

side aisles. Parts of the porch go back to the sixth century and parts of the superstructure to the ninth; the greater portion of the church, however, dates from the eleventh and twelfth centuries. In the left absidole, on an altar, rests the baroque reliquary of Saint Lupicinus, of gold-leafed wood with three small oval windows for viewing the remains. Three cherubim prance atop the reliquary in typical baroque fashion. In 1989 the church celebrated the third centenary of the discovery of the remains of Lupicinus, which came to light on 6 July 1689 when the altar was moved. A stone sarcophagus was discovered containing a skull and bones with a lead tablet bearing the inscription *Hic requiescit beatus Lupicinus abbas* ('Here rests the blessed abbot Lupicinus'). The tablet has been dated to the seventh century. Also in the left absidole stands a reliquary statue of Romanus as monk. In the right absidial chapel is a reliquary chest of Romanus. Tasteful modern stained glass windows depict Romanus and Lupicinus in monastic garb with Moses-like visages. Another scene shows a young Romanus (looking much like Saint Francis) giving the monastic veil to Yole, his sister. In the background is the convent of La Balme (Balma), looking anachronistically like the twelfth/thirteenth-century chapel of Saint-Romain.

Slightly to the west of Saint-Lupicin, near Lac d'Antre, recent excavations have unearthed a gallo-roman temple. This, coupled with new excavations at Saint-Claude that have revealed traces of a gallo-roman settlement, has led some scholars to conjecture that Romanus may have followed a roman road north from Izernore to a pagan village he wished to christianize. Even though the *Life of the Jura Fathers* makes no mention of early missionary work, the possibility should not be ruled out. The presence of an ancient road certainly makes more sense of the author's declaration that hordes of people were coming to Condadisco soon after its founding to seek counsel and healing from the monks (¶¶ 14–15). By having Romanus leave civilization to enter the 'desert', the author of the *Life* follows a topos, placing Romanus in the honored line of Antony and the desert fathers. The *Life* indicates that Lupicinus set out to found a new monastery because of the growth of Condadisco and the need to find a more fertile area to feed the growing number of brothers (¶¶ 22–4). Although we found no speculation regarding Lupicinus and the founding of his monastery, it is possible that he too moved into an area where a roman temple stood in order to convert the local inhabitants. There may be truth in both scenarios.

From the gallo-roman excavations near Villards-d'Héria, we took D470 back toward Lavans-lès-Saint-Claude, turning south onto D300, which leads to Saint-Romain (or Saint-Romain-la-Roche) named after Saint Romanus. Outside the quaint little village we left the car, as only residents are allowed to drive further. The size of the parking lot led us to believe that the Chapelle de Saint-Romain, to which we were heading, must be a popular pilgrimage site. (The *Michelin Guide* states

Figure 5

Chapel of Saint-Romain.

that the first Monday after Pentecost Sunday is an especially important date, but does not say why).

We strolled through the ancient village, which boasts a number of lovely cottages, to the point where the path to the chapel begins. On the way we saw numerous stunning views of the forested hills as they ease down towards the Bienne river valley. After about ten minutes we sighted the chapel and came to a sign explaining the history of the romanesque structure. It has been dated to the late twelfth-early thirteenth century and was constructed near the site of the women's monastery of La Balme (Balma) which was founded by Romanus for his sister and which by the twelfth century had probably ceased to function. We could, however, find no traces of any other buildings in the vicinity. Still, it is nice to think that Romanus came to this lovely site overlooking the Bienne which must have meant a great deal to him: when Romanus was near death, 'he sought

out his sister in order to say good-bye to her' (¶ 60).[146] The *Life*
also says that he was buried here (¶ 25).[147]

The lines of the little chapel are graceful; the thin belfry and
small buttresses that support the interior barrel vault blend in
well with the landscape. The interior consists of a nave and choir
of nearly equal size with some seventeenth-century additions.
Modern stained glass in the central window depicts an ascetic-
looking Romanus giving the monastic veil to Yole.

One last venture remained for us as we followed in the
footsteps of the Jura Fathers: the monastery church of Romainmôtier, in the Vaud region of present-day Switzerland.
Romainmôtier lies outside of the Jura, and we cannot say for
certain that the monastery, despite its name ('Monastery of
Romanus', or perhaps 'Roman Monastery') has any connection with the Jura Fathers. The most convincing arguments
in favor are the name Romainmôtier and the recent discovery
of a fifth-century structure beneath the present abbey church.
Most scholarly literature names Romanus as the founder or at
least the inspiration for the original monastic settlement, but
contemporary sources are vague or silent about its origins.[148]
This may be due in part to later invasions and the destruction
of buildings and dispersal of the brothers.

In any case, it is possible that Romanus ventured northeast
through the Jura past the long and narrow Lac des Rousses and
Lac de Joux and the jagged Dent de Vaulion to the charming
valley where now lies the village named after him. Since he
seems to have made the difficult pilgrimage along Lake Geneva
to Saint-Maurice d'Agaune (ancient Acaunus) as the *Life* reports

---

[146] Present-day Saint-Romain does not, however, lie in a valley.

[147] Another scene from the choir stalls of Saint Peter's Cathedral in Saint-
Claude depicts a visit of Romanus and Lupicinus to the women's monastery
(Benoit, *Histoire*, 62).

[148] Paragraph 16 of the *Life* states that the monks from Condat 'spread so
far that not only the more remote parts of the province of Sequania, but also
many regions far and wide in different regions of the earth, were filled with
monasteries and churches by means of the grace spread abroad by that godly
group of people'.

Figures 6 and 7

- Romainmôtier.
- Dent de Vaulion.

(¶ 44) there is no reason he could not have made his way to Romainmôtier.[149] The modern-day traveler will be well rewarded in following him to the north. Not only is the village of Romainmôtier picturesque, but the church, one of the oldest in Switzerland, is stunning, both inside and out. Extensive restoration of the exterior is nearly complete, and work will soon begin on the interior. There one can view an exceptional video presentation (in English, French, or German) on the abbey and monasticism in general. When all is completed, Romainmôtier will be a sparkling jewel in the romanesque crown.

By its portrayal of fifth-century monastic life, its vivid account of the three abbots, and its depiction of the region, the *Life of the Jura Fathers* stands out among early medieval *Lives*. The names and deeds of the Jura Fathers are still among us, still to be found on maps and in place names, and still to be seen in person, in an area of breathtaking beauty. During our stay in the Jura region, we talked on several occasions with residents about our project. To our surprise, all were well informed about the lives of the Jura Fathers, several loaned us books pertaining to the abbots, and all were very interested that some Americans had come to their region to see the sites related to the Jura Fathers and were translating into English the history of their founders. It would be going too far to say that we felt in these people the spirit of the Jura Fathers—those ascetics who had withdrawn into the 'desert'—and yet both town and country in the Juras are alive with reminders of these ancients, even to crowded Sunday worship services in Saint-Claude and Saint-Lupicin.

In visiting other important sites of fifth-century monasticism in Gaul, such as Lérins, Arles, Marseilles, and Tours, one hears but a faint echo of those who founded religious establishments there and the spirit of their times, emanating from ruins, museums, street signs and historical markers that

---

[149] Unfortunately, limited visiting hours and unlucky timing prevented us from visiting the former abbey.

signal where religious structures once stood. Had Romanus not set out northward from Izernore one day, Christianity would have eventually come to the jura region. Yet, nowhere in former Gaul does one find, as around Saint-Claude, an area so marked by what began as one man's hermitage. Churches, monasteries, villages, towns, creeks, and forests attest to the influence of the Jura Fathers. The most lasting testimony of these early monks, perhaps, although not as tangible, and perhaps the most compelling, is that the Jura Fathers live on in the people, fifteen hundred years after the beginnings in a valley where two rivers come together.

The feast day of Romanus (Saint Romain) and Lupicinus (Saint Lupicin) in the Roman Catholic Church is February 28 and of Eugendus (Saint Oyend) January 1.

the life and rule of the holy fathers romanus, lupicinus, and eugendus, abbots of the monasteries in the jura mountains[1]

---

[1] For our translation, we have used the latin text edited by François Martine, *Vie des Pères du Jura* (Sources chrétiennes 142; Paris: Cerf, 1968). Paragraph numbering follows that of Martine; section headings are those of the translators.

preface

HAT HOLY AND MYSTERIOUS FRIEND, as reported in the Gospels, while teaching mystically[2] that his mercy would not be denied to mortals, adds that the loaves of the Trinity are not refused to a person who insistently knocks on the door in the dead of night.[3] Once the chains of obstinacy have been broken, this great and secret mystery allows itself to be opened up through an entryway of mercy. Although the divine and ineffable mystery[4] I have mentioned is of surpassing value, nevertheless it is profitable,[5] in a limited way, even if one looks at matters simply and literally.

This is why, John and Armentarius, my dear devout brothers, you with twin affections knock so insistently at the door of your friend. If I delay in opening the bolted doors of my mouth and heart, you censure my flagrant and obstinate greediness and declare, in accordance with the Apostle's teaching, that you are no longer able to eat with me.[6]

2. Breaking, therefore, the modesty appropriate to an unlettered heart, I shall put myself forward for your benefit as the trinal narrator of the life of the three abbots of the Jura Mountains, that is, the holy fathers Romanus, Lupicinus, and

---

[2] Latin *mystice*. For another example of 'mystical' interpretation of Scripture, see Eucherius, *In Praise of the Desert* 15 (Appendix III).

[3] See Lk 11:5–8; the insistent friend in Jesus' parable asks for three loaves of bread.

[4] Latin *sacramento*. The word translated 'mystery' earlier in the paragraph is *arcanum*.

[5] Reading *in murca re munerationis* with François Masai, instead of *in murca remunerationis*. See François Masai, '[Review of *Vie des Pères du Jura*]', *Revue d'histoire ecclésiastique* 65 (1970) 520–24, esp. 522–3, and Martine, 237 n. 3 and 439–40.

[6] See 1 Cor 5:11.

Eugendus, and I shall present it in the form of the loaves of bread mentioned above. Your life and conduct is, to be sure, one of spiritual contemplation:[7] you, John, following the Apostle John of old, recline upon the sarcophagus of Saint Maurice, head of the legion of theban martyrs,[8] just as the famous apostle and companion[9] of Christ reclined upon the breast of the author of our salvation;[10] you, Armentarius, like the dove from the seafaring ark,[11] are content to remain enclosed there in the monastery in your private cell and laugh at the swirling commotion of the world. Neither of you, however, is able, without spiritual nourishment, to devote himself fully to these exercises without harm.

3. Your 'Acaunus', in the ancient gallic expression,[12] is recognized to be a rock, as much primordially from nature as now also because of the Church, through the truthful prefiguration of Peter. Nevertheless, may your Charity acknowledge among the forests of pine and fir of the Jura Mountains that same rock allegorically 'discovered' long ago by the psalmist 'in the fields of the forest'.[13] There the holy brothers who have followed, firm in their monastic stability, now tread upon this rock, whose hidden meaning is now made clear.

And although poverty of style cannot detract from the greatness of excellence, I nonetheless ask prayers of your Charity.

---

[7] Latin *theoretica illa conversatio vitaque vestra*.

[8] Martine suggests, 238 n. 3, that John was overseer of Saint Maurice's shrine, but perhaps he lived at the shrine and literally slept upon the saint's tomb; see n. 3, p. 287. See Appendix II for *The Passion of the Martyrs of Agaune* by Saint Eucherius, Bishop of Lyon.

[9] Latin *symmystes*, borrowed from Greek. Honorius Augustodunensis (12th c.), in his *Gemma animae sive de divinis officiis* 1.176 (PL 172), defines the word thus: *id est secretarius vel secreti conscius, qui mysteria Christi explicat* ('that is, a confidant or intimate friend who unfolds the mysteries of Christ').

[10] See Jn 13:23; 21:20.

[11] See Gen 8:8–12.

[12] Modern Agaune *Acaunus* is the latinized form of the celtic word *ac-auno* which, as our author suggests, means 'rock'. The Abbey of Saint Maurice was there (present-day Saint-Maurice d'Agaune); see the map. For a contemporary description of Acaunus, see Bishop Eucherius' account in Appendix II.

[13] See Ps 131:6 (Vulgate).

Then, if the praise and worthy life of the venerable abbots cannot, as we know, be opened up by an ignorant person, enough may nevertheless shine of itself so that it cannot be disfigured by my chattering mouth.

the life of the holy aBBot romanus

ROMANUS' ORIGINS

4. I shall now therefore endeavor to reproduce faithfully in the name of Christ—according to what I saw there[14] with my own eyes or received from the tradition of the elders—the deeds, the way of life, and the Rule[15] of the esteemed fathers of the Jura Mountains, of whom I have spoken above. First I present blessed Romanus as a true standard-bearer for the Lord in battle, a model for holy emulation by your monastic order and by the entire host of monks.[16] This Romanus, it is known, was the first of the three to be named abbot, at the very beginning. He came from a not insignificant family[17] (as those descended from his parents bear witness) from Gallia Sequanorum.[18]

---

[14] That is, at Condadisco (Condat, modern Saint-Claude), where the author was a monk.

[15] Latin *actus vitamque ac regulam*. *Regula* can mean the 'Rule' of a monastery, and can also suggest unwritten traditional observances, lessons, and examples of the ascetic life handed down orally. See Introduction, pp. 74–78.

[16] Latin *professioni vestrae monachorumque exercitui*.

[17] Latin *non adeo exiguae familiae*. Saint Antony, according to Evagrius' latin *Life of Antony*, came from a 'noble' family, *nobilibus religiosisque parentibus* (PL 73.427A). On the gallic nobility, see Jacques Fontaine, 'L'aristocratie occidentale devant le monachisme aux IVème et Vème siècles', *Rivista d'Istoria e Letteratura di Storia Religiosa* 15 (1979) 28–53.

[18] That is, what is termed Maxima Sequanorum. Gallia Sequanorum was apparently not a formal administrative title, but referred to the part of Gallia Belgica occupied (originally) by the Sequani, that is, the region of the Jura. By the fourth century, the administrative region was called Germania Superior; it had been broken off from Gallia Belgica. According to the *Life* (¶ 120), Eugendus was born 'not far from' Isarnodurum, modern Izernore, some nineteen miles (thirty kilometers) southwest of Condat. 'By province of birth'

5. Before Romanus, not a single monk had dedicated himself to the religious life in this province, either to solitude or to communal observance.[19] Although he was not especially well-educated, he was nevertheless gifted with sincerity and distinguished by the virtue of charity (which is more excellent), so that he never fettered himself as a child with childish foolishness,[20] or as a young man with human desires or with the bonds of marriage.[21] He was almost thirty-five years of age when, attracted by the solitudes of the desert,[22] he left his mother, sister, and brother and entered the forests of the Jura near his estate.[23]

ROMANUS FOUNDS A HERMITAGE AT CONDADISCO

6. Moving about here and there in these forests, so suitable and appropriate to his monastic intention, he at length

---

he was the 'countryman and fellow citizen' of Romanus and Lupicinus; thus, Romanus and Lupicinus were from the same area. Romanus must have been born around 400.

[19] See *Life of Antony* 3.2: 'there were not yet monasteries in Egypt neighboring on one another, and no monk at all knew the remote desert'. Translations from the greek *Life of Antony* are from Tim Vivian and Apostolos N. Athanassakis, trans., *The Life of Antony* (Kalamazoo: Cistercian Publications, forthcoming), based on the new text edited by G. J. M. Bartelink, *Vie D'Antoine* (Sources chrétiennes 400; Paris: Cerf, 1994) 123–377.

[20] See *Life of Antony* 1.2.

[21] See Cassian, *Conferences* 21.9.

[22] As Martine points out, p. 244 n. 3, the phrase 'secretis heremi' connects Romanus with the monks of the egyptian desert (*heremus* is the latinized form of Greek *eremos*). Saint Eucherius had earlier written an *Epistula de laude heremi*, 'In Praise of the Desert'; see Introduction, pp. 32–42 and, for a translation of *De laude eremi*, Appendix III. Saint Martin retreated to a place 'so secluded and remote that it had all the solitude of the desert' (Sulpicius Severus, *Life of Martin* 10 [Noble and Head, 13]). According to the *Rule of Saint Benedict* 1.5 (hereafter RB), anchorites do 'single combat in the desert'. English translations of RB are taken from Timothy Fry, ed., *RB 1980: The Rule of St. Benedict in English* (Collegeville, MN: The Liturgical Press, 1982).

[23] Latin *vicinas villae*. *Villa* carries a wide range of meanings, from a farm or a village to an estate or a royal palace. Romanus was probably the son of a gallo-roman landowner, and made his hermitage not far from his family's estate.

discovered beyond them, among rockbound valleys, an open area that could be cultivated. There, on the other side of three mountainous ridges, the natural steepness lessened and settled into a small plain. Since two streams which by nature ran separately came together there, the people soon gave the place the name 'Condadisco' because the streams had already become one.[24]

7. When the new arrival was seeking an appropriate place to live, he found to the east, at the foot of a rocky mountain,[25] a dense fir tree whose branches, spread out in a circle, were covered with an abundance of leaves. Just as the palm tree once covered Paul, this tree now covered Paul's disciple.[26] Outside the circle of the tree's branches, a flowing spring poured forth an icy cold stream of water; even today its waters, channeled with wooden pipes to the distant monastery, are placed at the disposal of Romanus' heirs as a pledge of the inheritance that was to come.[27]

8. This tree, then, as I have said, provided Romanus with a continuously green roof against the burning heat of summer days and the freezing rains of winter because, owing to the merits of the saint, it enjoyed a truly perpetual spring. There were also a few wild bushes that provided berries—undoubtedly bitter for those seeking pleasure, but sweet for one at peace. When the saint arrived at this place, downstream from where

---

[24] Latin *Ab unitate elementi iam conditi*. Condadisco may take its name from the latin verb *condo* (*conditum* is the passive participle), 'to put together, to build, to found', or it may be Celtic in origin, meaning 'confluent' (see Martine, 245–6). The two rivers are the Bienne and Tacon. Condadisco is the modern Condat.

[25] Mount Bayard.

[26] Not Saint Paul the apostle, but Saint Paul the hermit. See Jerome, *Life of Paul* 5, in Vincent L. Wimbush, ed., *Ascetic Behavior in Late Antiquity: A Sourcebook* (Minneapolis: Fortress Press, 1990), and *Life of Antony* 50, where date palms shelter Paul and Antony.

[27] Once called 'Fontaine de Saint Romain' by locals. Antony had 'very clear water, sweet and very cold' from a spring (*Life of Antony* 49.7). The desert monk Paul also had a spring of water available to him (Jerome, *Life of Paul* 5).

the rivers joined, it was many miles distant from any habitation because of the scarcity of dwelling places; the abundant cultivation in the distant plain had given no reason to cross a succession of forests in order to come live in the vicinity.

9. Moreover, if someone decided, with audacious daring, to cut across this roadless wilderness toward the territory of the Equestres,[28] in addition to the dense forest and the heaps of fallen trees, he found high and lofty mountain ridges and steep valleys dividing the regions. There stags and broad-horned deer live. Even if the traveler were strong and lightly equipped, he would scarcely be able to cross it in a day, even the longest day of the year. Given the distance and the difficulties of its natural inaccessibility, no one could blaze a trail through this mountain range, to right or to left, from the regions of the Rhine and the raging of the north wind all the way to the farthest wooded regions.[29]

10. Therefore, having brought seeds and a hoe with him,[30] the blessed one began, between the times required for frequent prayer and reading, to support a modest way of life there by means of the monastic institution of manual labor.[31] He had a plentiful abundance since he required nothing; he dispersed enough, since he had no poor people there to whom to disperse.[32] He never moved further into the wilderness, nor did

---

[28] The fourth-century *Notitia Galliarum* lists civitas Equestrium within Maxima Sequanorum, with its center at Noviodunum (colonia Iulia Equestres), the present-day Nyon, on the southwest shore of Lake Geneva, some 30 miles (50 kilometers) due east of Condat. See ¶ 13 and the map.

[29] Reading *usque pagi nemoralis extimum* with Masai, instead of *usque pagi Nemausatis extimum*. See Masai, 'Review', 521–2. *Nemausatis* (taken to equal *Nemausensis*, 'of Nîmes') is unattested, and if it were adopted, the distances involved would present considerable difficulties. See the map. For Martine's reasons for adopting *Nemausatis*, see 249, n. 3, and 'Note complémentaire', 442–4. Professor Ralph Mathisen has suggested in correspondence that perhaps Nemausatus (?) is a local name, otherwise unattested.

[30] Antony does the same; see *Life of Antony* 50.5 (Latin: 25; PL 73.449A).

[31] Antony 'was accustomed to working hard' (*Life of Antony* 53.1).

[32] This paragraph presupposes the monastic practices of frequent prayer (the divine office), reading (*lectio*), manual labor, and care of the poor; either these

he retreat towards civilization. As a hermit he prayed without ceasing,[33] and as a true monk he worked in order to provide sustenance for himself.[34]

11. Before he embraced the religious life, Romanus had observed a certain venerable man, Sabinus by name, abbot of the Monastery of the Confluence in Lyon, his strenuous regulations, and the way of life of his monks;[35] like a honeybee[36] that goes from flower to flower, after gathering from each the small flowers of perfection, Romanus returned home.[37] He also took from that same monastery (without revealing anything of his most holy ambitions) the book *The Life of the Holy Fathers*

---

are 'institutions' Romanus brought with him from Lyon (see ¶ 11), or our author is reading back to the time of the origins of the monastery practices established later.

[33] 1 Thes 5:17, one of the most important biblical texts in early monasticism. See Cassian, *Praefatio* to *Conferences* I-X (Pichery 1:75); Conf. IX.3 (SCh 2.42) and X.10 (SCh 2.85–90). See also Lk 18:1 and *Life of Antony* 3 (PL 73.128C).

[34] Antony spent his time working and praying; see *Life of Antony* 3. On the importance of manual labor, see RB 48.8.

[35] As Martine notes, 250–1, n. 3, there is no agreement where this monastery was; no other ancient sources mention an Abbot Sabinus. The monastery could have been in Lyon proper, where monks had resided since at least the fifth century, or in an outlying area (the monasteries of l'Ile-Barbe or of Ainay).

[36] See *Life of Antony* 3.4: 'While there, if he heard about someone who was seriously practicing asceticism somewhere, he would go and search out that person like the wise honeybee, and he would not return again to his own village unless he had seen him'. The metaphor of the honeybee was a popular one in ascetic circles. Thomas of Marga enthused about Mar Cyprian: 'And just as the bee that is skillful in her handicraft formeth and buildeth up the honeycomb in her dwelling from herbs and grasses, so also did this holy man gather together habits of the monastic life from each of the holy men and did perfect them in himself'. E.A. Wallis Budge, trans., *The Book of Governors: The Historia Monastica of Thomas Bishop of Marga, A.D. 840* (London, 1893) I:586–7.

[37] See *Life of Antony* 4.1: 'Thus Antony conducted himself, and he was loved by everyone. He went to those who devoted themselves to ascetic practice and sincerely submitted himself to them and closely observed the excellence of each one's zeal and ascetic practice. . . . He recorded in his mind the devotion to Christ and the love for one another that they all shared'.

and the admirable *Institutes of the Abbots*;[38] completely polite, yet insistent, he was able to obtain the books through entreaty[39] or purchase.

12. In his deserted valley in the Jura, the imitator of the venerable Antony long enjoyed the angelic life. Apart from divine contemplation, he enjoyed the sight of nothing except wild beasts[40] and, rarely, hunters. Meanwhile, his esteemed brother, Lupicinus (the abbot[41] whom I shall presently write about; although a younger brother to Romanus, he was soon to be his equal in holiness), advised at night by his brother in a dream, left his sister and mother for the love of Christ, as blessed Romanus had already done, and ardently sought out his brother's hut and monastic profession. There was no doubt—and future events proved it—that in that humble nest, that wilderness set apart,[42] like 'a pair of turtledoves or two young doves'[43] they would conceive spiritual offspring by the inspiration of the Holy Word, and that these, born of a pure birth, would spread to the monasteries and churches of Christ.

---

[38] See Introduction, pp. 37–38; see also Martine, 252–3 n.1.

[39] Latin *supplicando*, which is nicely ambiguous, suggesting both prayer and entreaty. 'Polite' might also be rendered 'artful'.

[40] Wild beasts figure prominently in egyptian monasticism; see *Life of Antony* 50–51.

[41] Latin *abba*. Abba originally meant 'father', the title give to an esteemed, usually older, monk; later it came to mean 'abbot', as in ¶ 4 above. Both meanings may be suggested here.

[42] Latin *secreto heremi*.

[43] Lk 2:24 (Lv 12:8). Luke says that when Jesus was presented in the temple, he was designated 'as holy to the Lord' with an offering of two birds as prescribed by Torah; thus for our author, Romanus and Lupicinus, like 'a pair of turtledoves or two young doves', offer themselves as sacrifices to the Lord. Romanus and Lupicinus, however, conceive offspring 'of a pure birth', unlike a woman's childbearing which makes her unclean and calls for purification (Lv 12:2–8).

OTHERS JOIN ROMANUS AND LUPICINUS

13. At that time two young men, clerics from the city of Nyon,[44] having heard of the renown and the way of life of the saints, crossed that nearly impassable region (not without great risk, except that their faith was stronger than the peril). They wandered here and there in the wilderness,[45] not knowing where the holy ones lived. The day before the two were to arrive, the holy abbot Romanus is said to have made this prediction to his brother: 'Two young men', he said, 'attracted by the desire to imitate us, will come to us tomorrow. The elder, having lost his wife, lives celibately; the other retains intact the favor of virginity'.[46]

Since that birthplace of the saints (if I may speak this way about it) could now scarcely contain their increased numbers, they took up residence not far from the tree, on a small hill with a gentle slope, where the oratory reserved for private prayer now stands to their memory. Once the wood had been hewn and planed with the utmost care, they constructed small dwellings for themselves and prepared others for those who would come in the future.

14. In the meantime, the renown of the holy ones had spread so far in all directions that the sweet fragrance of their good reputation persuaded throngs of believers to abhor the horror and stench of worldly life and to flee it in order to observe for the Lord the divine gift of renunciation and perfection. Some came there to see the miracles of this institution[47] and to take home with them exemplary and harmonious gifts.

15. Others brought people tormented by demons and by

---

[44] See ¶ 9, n. 28.

[45] Latin *heremo*, which again suggests here, and throughout the *Life*, 'desert', the wilderness of the first desert fathers.

[46] Antony also had the gift of foresight; see for example *Life of Antony* 59–60. Saint Martin also often foresaw events before they happened; see Sulpicius Severus, *Life of Martin* 21 (Noble and Head, 23).

[47] Lat *institutionis. Institutio* conveys a number of meanings: building, foundation, institution, (monastic) order.

other spirits of the Devil, along with the insane and paralyzed, so that through the prayer of the saints and their own faith these might be healed.[48] Most of the sick returned home after being restored to health, but others remained at the monastery observing fasts and vigils with so much compunction of spirit that, by a remarkable turn of events, they now—in less time than it takes to say these words—drove out the Devil, along with his subordinates and followers, from those who were possessed. Those who witnessed this said, 'Truly this change is owing to the right hand of the Most High'.[49]

16. The holy community, with its twin founders, like a very abundant crop—one that is not yet adulterated with noxious weeds—will surely be stored in the Lord's granary.[50] United in faith and love, it grew so much that the monks realized that the buildings could hardly hold those who had already been admitted. The venerable swarms of fathers, impelled by the Holy Spirit, then began to spread out from there as from a beehive filled with bees; they spread so far that not only the more remote parts of the province of Sequania, but also many regions far and wide in different regions of the earth, were filled with monasteries and churches by means of the grace spread abroad by that godly group of people.[51] Nevertheless, it is of course at the source—which these religious institutions,

---

[48] The reader needs to balance this sudden influx of people, enthusiastically described by our author in ¶¶ 14–15, with his earlier description of the remoteness and inaccessibility of the monastery. But see Part V of the Introduction, p. 88, for the possibility that these people, like Romanus, used a roman road. The bringing of the ill and demon-possessed to the holy man is an important theme in the *Life of Antony* (see, for example, ¶¶ 55–58).

[49] Ps 76:11 (Vulgate).

[50] See Mt 13:25.

[51] Sources do not indicate any monasteries or churches founded by the jura fathers aside from the three monasteries mentioned in the *Life* (Condadisco, Lauconnus, and Balma), although we should not preclude foundations made by disciples, such as Romainmôtier. This list is probably an example of exuberant hyperbole.

flowing like small rivers, had as their origin—that the institution of the masters reveals itself: ancient, to be sure, but ever more new and pure.

ROMANUS AND LUPICINUS

17. The two Fathers surpassed each other in the requisite and complementary skills of ruling and governing. Blessed Romanus was very loving towards everyone and perfectly tranquil,[52] while his brother was more severe, both towards others, correcting and ruling them, and especially towards himself. Romanus, even when pardon was not to be expected, was eager to forgive those who had done harm; Lupicinus, on the other hand, afraid that repeated light punishment would have no effect, rebuked people very severely. Romanus, in laying privations on the brothers, would order only those that their will and spirit could bear; Lupicinus, offering himself as an example to everyone, did not allow anyone to refuse what is possible with God's help.

ROMANUS IS ORDAINED BY HILARY OF ARLES[53]

18. When report of their renown reached Saint Hilary, Bishop of Arles, he summoned, through clergy he had sent for this purpose, blessed Romanus to come near where he was,

---

[52] Antony, too, was known for his tranquility of spirit; see *Life of Antony* 14. Martin also evinced this monastic ideal: 'No one ever saw him angered, no one saw him excited, none saw him grieving, none saw him laughing'. Sulpicius Severus, *Life of Martin* 27 (Noble and Head, 28).

[53] For the background to this story, see Mathisen, *Ecclesiastical Factionalism and Religious Controversy in Fifth-Century Gaul*, 147–53; on Hilary, 141–72. Calidonius was bishop of Vesontion (Besançon), the metropolitan see of Gallia Sequanorum. He was deposed by Hilary, apparently for having an uncanonical marriage (he had married a widow) and for having sentenced several people to capital punishment while serving in government. He appealed to Pope Leo I, who ruled in his favor.

at the city of Besançon.[54] Extolling his initiative and way of life by means of a well-deserved proclamation, he conferred on him the honor of the priesthood and allowed him to return to the monastery with honors.[55]

(The aforesaid Hilary, arrogating to himself improper monarchical power over the Gauls with the support and approval of the *patricius* and the praetorian prefect of Gaul,[56] had deposed, for no good reason, the esteemed Calidonius,[57] patriarch of Besançon, from his episcopal seat. 19. Because of this action, Hilary was convicted of improper conduct in an audience with blessed Pope Leo in Rome. Calidonius was restored to his episcopal see, while Hilary was rebuked by the Apostolic Authority, in accordance with the rules of ecclesiastical discipline, for illicit usurpation of power. There also exists a decretal of the above-mentioned and esteemed pope addressed to the bishops of Gaul which, along with the investigation of the facts, is included with the canons; in this document the Pope, striking down the vain pretensions of Hilary, re-established the ancient privileges of the metropolitan bishops in Gaul.)[58]

---

[54] Besançon (Vesontion) was quite a ways from Condadisco, some eighty miles (one hundred-thirty kilometers) north.

[55] Martine, 259, dates this event to 444, when Romanus was around 44 years of age.

[56] Latin *patricio praefectorioque*. The *patricius et magister utriusque militum* was the highest military officer in the western empire, while the praetorian prefect was the highest civil official in Gaul. The patricius would have been Fl. Aetius, while the praetorian prefect was either Eparchius Avitus or Marcellus. We wish to thank Professor Mathisen for this information.

[57] Or, possibly, Chelidonius.

[58] Mathisen concludes, *Ecclesiastical Factionalism*, 154, that our author has adopted 'the very unfavorable depiction of Hilary in Leo's letter to the Gauls', while also including the contradictory 'local tradition' that connects Romanus positively with Hilary: 'Romanus therefore would have been a valuable local ally for Hilary and his party at the time of Chelidonius' deposition, and the alliance may have been pointedly ratified by his ordination as presbyter near Besançon. The ordination also shows that Hilary was exercising episcopal rights in another province, and indicates that here, as in the south, a

ROMANUS' HUMILITY AND THE DANGERS OF CLERICALISM

20. So blessed Romanus, invested with the priesthood, returned to the monastery, as we said above. Mindful of his original profession, with monastic humility he made so little of[59] the rights and authority of ecclesiastical office that when it came time for the solemn service the brothers could only with difficulty compel him to go up higher in order to celebrate the sacrifice. On other days, showing himself to be a monk among monks, he displayed on himself nothing of sacerdotal dignity.

21. But as I report this about that most holy man, others rise up before the eyes of my heart. After making their monastic profession, through mad ambition these attain clerical rank. Without delay, wearing the pretentious fashions[60] of an inflated self-esteem, these perfumed and delicate[61] young fellows are borne aloft, not only above their deserving equals, but also above their elders and seniors.[62] Uninstructed[63] in even the most basic and rudimentary principles, they make every effort to take advantage of their priestly office and to preside from their seats of authority—they who, because of their vanity and youthful lack of seriousness, still need to be disciplined and reined in!

---

metropolitan bishop, either Eucherius of Lyon or Inportunus of Besançon, was yielding precedence to him'.

[59] Latin *calcabat*, literally 'trampled under'. In a further slap at Hilary, our author uses the same verb in the previous paragraph to say that the 'vain pretensions' of the bishop of Arles were 'struck down' (*calcata Hilarii superfluitate*). What was *done* to Hilary, Romanus, in our author's eyes, does of his own accord, because it accords with 'monastic humility'.

[60] Latin *cothurno*, literally 'boot', an image dating back to classical times *Cothurnus* (Gk. *kothornos*) originally designated a hunting boot, then a boot worn by tragic actors on stage; it then came to represent a tragic and elevated style, then affectation.

[61] See also ¶ 39 and n. 98.

[62] Especially their elders in monastic profession, the abbas.

[63] There is an untranslatable word play here. 'Perfumed' translates *delibuti*, literally 'steeped', while 'instructed' renders *inbuti* (*imbuo*), which also suggests steeping or saturating ('imbue'), then comes to mean 'initiate, accustom, instruct'. See ¶ 24, n. 65, below.

UNDER DIFFICULT CONDITIONS THE MONASTERY EXPANDS

22. But that is another matter. As I am hastening to port along a right path, my discourse will avoid this crooked course. And because I have decided to be silent about these things, let me endeavor now to add this: how the site of the community of Condadisco, crowded with an astonishing and unheard of number of monks, could now barely supply enough food—not only for the multitudes that were coming there, but even for the brothers themselves. Suspended as the place was in hills and declivities, between overhanging cliffs and rocky ground, and disturbed by the frequent flooding of the rugged landscape, the cultivation of crops there waned and decreased, not only because of the limited and difficult terrain, but also the mediocre harvests and uncertain yields.

23. The harsh winter not only covers the place with snow but buries it; so too in the spring and summer and fall either the summer heat, warmed by the nearby rocks, burns everything, or the irresistible rains carry away in torrents not only the tilled and cultivated land, but often the uncultivated and stony earth, too—along with grass, trees, and shrubs. When the rocks are laid bare, the very clods of earth that still remain are carried off from the monks and given over to the waters.[64]

24. Wishing therefore to relieve this situation as much as possible, the holy fathers cut down and removed the fir trees in the neighboring forests, which were by no means lacking in level and fertile areas. They leveled the fields with the sickle, and the plains with the plow, so that these places, now fit for cultivation, would alleviate the needs of the monks of Condadisco. Romanus and Lupicinus were abbots of both monasteries. Father Lupicinus, however, of his own free will stayed especially in Lauconnus (for this is the name that the place enjoyed), so much so that after the death of blessed Romanus he left there

---

[64] There is a chiastic play on words here: 'carried off from the monks and handed over to the waters' translates *auferetur monachis, aquis inferetur*.

as many as one hundred and fifty brothers embued[65] with his own monastic discipline.[66]

25. Near that place, on a very high cliff dominated by a prominent and natural stone arch that concealed vast caverns within, Romanus and Lupicinus with parental love installed an abbess[67] for virgins and handed over to her the governance of that religious community; there she ruled one hundred five female monastics.[68] This place, cut off from above by an inaccessible cliff and isolated naturally beneath the wide archway, offered no way out from that side; from the east, after confining and narrow passageways, it suddenly widened to offer a way out on to solid ground and level earth. In that place (that is, in those same remarkably narrow passes) the blessed fathers constructed a church that not only received the remains of the virgins but

---

[65] Latin *inbutos*; see ¶ 21, n. 63 above.

[66] The *Life* associates Lupicinus closely with the monastery of Lauconnus; he was its abbot and was buried there (see ¶ 117). Lauconnus was later named Saint-Lupicin; it lies approximately four miles (six kilometers) due west of Saint-Claude (Condadisco), or seven-eight miles (twelve kilometers) by car. The area around Saint-Lupicin is indeed more favorable for agriculture.

[67] Latin *matrem*.

[68] Latin *monachas*. In ¶ 60, the *Life* says that this abbess is the sister of Romanus and Lupicinus; local tradition gives her the name Yole. Yole (if that was her name; it is French, not Latin) joins the sisters of Antony, Pachomius, and Caesarius of Arles (among others), all of whom were placed in convents by their brothers. Paragraph 60 also identifies the site of Yole's monastery as Balma (La Balme); it was located three miles (five kilometers) southwest of Lauconnus (Saint-Lupicin), in Saint-Romain-de-Roche (yet another place named after the Jura Fathers), where the relics of Romanus are kept in the parish church; see part V of the Introduction. Nothing remains of the convent, where Romanus was interred (see ¶¶ 60–61). The monastery may have been abandoned sometime during the fifth or sixth century; the nearby woods, however, bear the name Bois de la Balme. Another community for women formed later in the Juras, at Neauville-les-Dames, and may have been dependent on Condadisco. See the map.

also, as a sepulchre, had the honor of containing the hero of Christ himself, Romanus.

26. So severe was the strictness observed in that monastery at this time that none of the virgins who had entered it for the purpose of renouncing the world were seen again outside its doors unless they were being carried on their final journey to the cemetery.[69] When a mother by chance had a son, or a sister a brother, in the neighboring monastery of Lauconnus, neither of them knew, either by sight or report, whether the other were still alive; as a result, each of them considered the other already buried, so that the bonds of monastic profession would not be worn down little by little by a kind of softening due to memories of things of the flesh.[70]

But now I must return to blessed Romanus and to the monastery of Condadisco.

AN ENVIOUS MONK: ROMANUS DEFEATS THE DEVIL[71]

27. While these things were being accomplished because of the admirable way of life of the monks, the Devil, the enemy of the very name of Christian, was indignant that[72] the monastic life was increasing for so many by daily renunciations of the

---

[69] See Caesarius of Arles, *Rule for Nuns* 2 and 50; Maria Caritas McCarthy, trans., *The Rule for Nuns of St. Caesarius of Arles* (Washington, D.C.: The Catholic University of America Press, 1960), 171, 188. The nun 'must never, up to the time of her death, go out of the monastery'.

[70] The *Rule for Nuns* 40 of Caesarius of Arles allows nuns to have relatives of both sexes as visitors (McCarthy, 184).

[71] Martine plausibly suggests (270–71, n. 4) that Romanus' speech here reflects opposition to Augustine's late writings on predestination. Such opposition was strong among the monks of southern Gaul, especially the monks of Lérins, and was formally reversed in favor of Augustine by Caesarius of Arles at the Council of Orange in 529. For the monastic opposition in southern Gaul to Augustine, see most recently Rebecca Harden Weaver, *Divine Grace and Human Agency: A Study of the Semi-Pelagian Controversy* (Patristic Monograph Series 15; Macon: Mercer University Press, 1996).

[72] The beginning of this sentence closely follows the latin *Life of Antony* 4 (PL 73:129B).

world. He dared to assault blessed Romanus, under pretense of offering him good counsel, with the ancient weapon[73] of envy. Accosting one of the elders who was enflamed with the fires of jealousy, the Devil persuaded him to speak in this manner: 'For a long time now, holy Abbot, I have been meaning to suggest to your Charity certain beneficial things for the sake of your good health and the administration of the monastery. Since opportunity now affords us reason to meet privately, I beseech you to allow me to disclose to you some helpful words that have for some time lain hidden in my heart'.

28. Seeing that this fellow was an elder (owing not to his way of life or habits, to be sure, but solely to his age, because of which he was puffed up with vain pretensions), the abbot granted him permission to offer him counsel. 'I am grieved, my father', the man said, 'that every day you take delight without reason in the enormous number of converts. You bring into the cenobitic life in droves the old and the young, the honorable and virtuous as well as the dishonorable, instead of carefully discerning and selecting a chosen few who have been found acceptable while eliminating and driving out from our sheepfold all the rest for the worthless and undeserving creatures that they are.[74] Just look! If you examine closely and thoroughly investigate our cells or the oratory or guest house, the jumbled multitude of monks that I have called to your attention hardly offers room now for anyone else to enter'.

29. Then, as the one who promised in the Gospel makes known, 'I will give you a mouth and wisdom that your enemies will not be able to withstand',[75] so swiftly did the holy father take up the shield and sword of the Apostle against the spirit of

---

[73] Literally 'arrow' or 'spear'.

[74] An historical situation undoubtedly lies behind this complaint: Pachomius and his brother John had a disagreement over expanding their monastic ranks that led to a break between them. See *The First Greek Life of Pachomius* 15; Veilleux, 1.307. Large numbers were again a problem immediately prior to and after the death of Pachomius.

[75] Lk 21:15.

the ancient Persecutor[76] that with the swift blade of the word
of salvation he cut off the head of the snake-like enemy.[77] 'You
who love our humility', he said, 'if you possess the ability to
offer pious counsel, then without a doubt beneficial powers
of discernment have also been entrusted to you. Tell me, are
you able to distinguish and divide all those you see around you
in our community by such a method as you suggest, so that
without any doubt your examination of them, man by man, can
distinguish before their death the most approved and the lazy,
those who are going to perish and those who are perfect? Or by
means of that examination—by which the Creator alone sees
humanity's secrets of the past and of the future—are you able to
elect or to condemn, without condemning and imperiling your
own salvation?

30. 'Through his inexhaustible and merciful majesty with regard to human weakness, God, by virtue of his foreknowledge,
raises no one at all before death to the bliss of sitting at his
right hand (if one excepts the assumption of blessed Enoch and
Elijah)[78] or immediately shuts him away because of his faults in
the abyss of Gehenna and its cavernous fold. And you, blinded
by diabolical error, do you now already dare to distinguish and
condemn those who doubtless are your betters in the humility
of their upright consciences? Do you not read that Saul and
Solomon (not to mention others) were chosen by the Lord to
rule over the people of Israel before they fell as a result of their
own sin?[79] That Judas too, and Nicholas, who were called along
with the others to the highest ranks of the sacred ministry, were
lost, the latter to heresies and the former to the end of a noose?[80]

---

[76] See Eph 6:17: 'Take the helmet of salvation, and the sword of the Spirit,
which is the word of God'.
[77] See Gn 3.
[78] See Gn 5:22–24 (Heb 11:5) and 2 Kings 2:11.
[79] See 1 Sm 13:11–14 and 15:9–30; 1 Kings 11:1–11.
[80] See Mt 27:5 and Acts 1:18 for Judas; Nicholas, one of the deacons appointed
by the Apostles (see Acts 6:5–6), was—improbably—connected in the early
Church with the heretical Nicolaitans. See Cassian, Conference 18.16 (SCh
3.33), where Nicholas is grouped with Judas.

31. 'Do you not remember the story of Ananias and Sapphira,[81] part of that earliest and purest apostolic crop? Choked by weeds, they failed miserably.[82] After being chosen for the highest ranks, they were punished with divine severity unheard of before then. And conversely, do you not marvel, with veneration and admiration, that Saul the persecutor became Paul the preacher;[83] that Matthew the tax collector suddenly became a disciple of Christ;[84] that the prodigal son became a generous son;[85] that Zacchaeus, who had become wealthy through fraudulent means, now became a "son of the patriarch";[86] that the thief, condemned for his crime and crucified, was suddenly made wealthy with the Lord in the pleasant reaches of paradise?[87] How many others besides these, if I were to continue, fell from the heights to the depths, while some ascended from the most humble and lowly of places to the most exalted? Finally, for how many monks who have disgraced themselves do we weep? By contrast, of how many prostitutes and executioners who rushed to martyrdom with a sudden inspiration do we read?

32. 'And so as not to talk any longer about the past: have you not seen some monks right here in our own community eagerly take on what, after a while, in an apathetic and lukewarm conclusion,[88] they trample underfoot? Or how many times have monks left the cenobium under varying impulses? Yet how many times have some of these returned from the world two and three times and, notwithstanding, regained their strength and brought the monastic profession they once forsook to the palm

---

[81] See Acts 5:1–11.

[82] See Mt 13:24–30.

[83] See Acts 9.

[84] See Mt 9:9.

[85] See Lk 15:11–32.

[86] That is, a son of Abraham; see Lk 19:2, 8–9.

[87] See Lk 23:39–43.

[88] The irony is thick here. What we have translated as 'conclusion' is Latin *consummatione*, 'end, conclusion'; but *consummatio* also suggests 'perfection, consummation', and recalls Christ's last words (Jn 19:30), 'Consummatum est', 'It is completed'.

of victory?[89] Some return guiltlessly not to their original vices
but to their homes; they observe our way of life with such love
and diligence that with the love and acclamation of the faithful
they preside as the worthiest of priests over monasteries and
churches.

33. 'I will give you one more example, if you do not refuse my
offer, something that happened very recently. Did you not observe Maxentius in our community yesterday? After nakedness
and privations unheard of in Gaul, after vigils and persistent and
unwearying perseverance in reading,[90] he was deceived by evil
pride. Seized by this filthiest of demons, he showed himself to
be far more insane and violent than those sick persons whom he
once treated when he was powerful owing to the meritorious
progress he was making.[91] Tied up with straps and ropes by
those whom he had once healed by virtue of the Lord, he was
freed from this deadly spirit by the anointing of holy oil.[92]

34. 'Acknowledge, therefore, that you are being secretly
battered by this same pride, that the Devil is the instigator,
and that you are no different from this fellow Maxentius. You
have a similar wound that inflames you—envy; as a result you
merit the same deserts'.

---

[89] Latin *palmam victoriae perduxere*. The image of the palm branch of victory
was an old one; our author's metaphor here may have Rv 7:9 ('stantes ante
thronum . . . et palmae in manibus eorum') and, more distantly, 2 Tm 4:7
and 1 Cor 9:24 in the background.

[90] *Lectio* was the private reading, chanting, or praying of holy texts, usually the
Bible, often the psalms, sometimes the fathers, especially the desert fathers
such as Antony or Cassian, or the *Apophthegmata*. For Saint Martin, according
to Sulpicius, not 'an hour, not a moment passed without his either giving
himself to prayer or applying himself to reading. But in truth, even during
his reading or anything else he happened to be doing, he never let his mind
relax from prayer' (Noble and Head, 28). See paragraph 10 and n. 32 there.

[91] See ¶ 15. Our author has earlier said that many insane and possessed people
were brought to the monastery. Perhaps Maxentius had charge of them.

[92] Martine seems correct in saying (276–77, n. 1) that there is censure here
of an overly-severe penance as practiced in the East (see par. 179). Cassian
criticizes such practices, and Benedict institutionalizes moderation. See pars.
71–77 below.

When he heard what Romanus said, that brother was completely shaken and almost fell to the floor. Thanks to the prayer of the blessed man, however, he soon abandoned his presumption, showed deep sorrow for his sin, and mended his ways. Thus those who are possessed and insane, when their demons have been driven out through the servants of Christ, are restored cleaner and purer than before.

OTHER WILES OF THE DEVIL

35. Meanwhile, because his plan had been rendered ineffective by the servant of Christ, the ancient Enemy turned his customary craftiness to easier devices; producing adversity from prosperity, he incited the brothers to rise up, not only against the Rule, but almost against the abbot himself. The original means he used in this plan was the abundance and fruitfulness of the harvest; next, the Devil overwhelmed the monks by means of this very abundance and, as they grew more remiss each day, made them think highly of themselves;[93] after this he made them haughty as they paraded their knowledge around, so to speak, in fancy footwear.[94] I will repeat, therefore, the situation that Romanus' brother Lupicinus, faced with unheard of opposition, resolved with admirable grace.

LUPICINUS CORRECTS SOME GLUTTONOUS BROTHERS

36. One year the monastery of Condadisco was favored, as I have said, with an unusually abundant harvest (unusual in that cultivation had only recently been begun). Made confident by that fertility and fecundity, and with disrespect and contempt for their abbot, certain brothers eagerly strove to stuff into their throats and bellies not what would have sufficed according to

---

[93] See Cassian, Conference 5.6; Pichery 1:93–95.
[94] Latin *cothurnasitate superbos*. See ¶ 21 and note 60. Gregory of Tours, *Life of the Fathers* 1.3, in telling this story, uses *cotornosi atque elati* ('vain and proud') to describe these monks, which suggests that he and our author had a common source.

the Rule or the norm, but what abundance allowed. When, because of this, they were repeatedly rebuked by blessed Romanus, who was the gentlest of souls, they became not only more impudent but, because of their extreme dissoluteness, even more wanton, so much so that Romanus, whose staff was truly gentle and easy, had to seek out the rod of his brother's severity.[95]

37. Having gone to his brother Lupicinus, Romanus declared that these gluttons were at this very moment rising up against his humble person; indeed, given over to pleasure and debauchery, they refused to serve God by living by the Rule. Abbot Lupicinus then ordered his brother to return secretly and declared that he himself would arrive at his monastery, as though unexpectedly, after about six days. Now when this man of great good sense[96] arrived, he saw that gluttony was the cause of all this insolence. He kept silent for the space of two days, until on the third day, acting as though he was stuffed and had an aversion for the food served so abundantly since his arrival, he requested meanwhile some bitter herbs to eat in order to regain his appetite. While the brothers were eating, with a cheerful expression he made this request to Abbot Romanus:

38. 'As nourishment, lord brother, I ask that tomorrow you order prepared for us as a light meal only porridge made of strained barley. And because I enjoy eating it so much, I beseech you, your Kindness, order it to be served without salt or oil'.[97] Since no one dared to grumble about this or oppose it, the next day the fare, changed to what it had been in the beginning, was served both to the gluttons and to the abstinent. Since Lupicinus and his brother had made this preemptive decision without, as the saying goes, asking the belly for its opinion,

[95] See ¶ 17 for a description of the different characters of the brothers.
[96] Latin *vir altioris ingenii*, a favorite expression of Sulpicius Severus for Hilary of Poitiers (*Life of Martin* 5.2) and for Saint Martin himself (*Dialogues* 1.25; Hoare, trans., 98). F. R. Hoare translates the phrase 'deeply understanding man'; Noble and Head, eds., 9.
[97] Eating food without salt or oil was a tradition going back to early desert monasticism.

these gourmands left the table without eating anything at all. In private, abbot Lupicinus ridiculed them:

39. 'My gentle brother, if you want to give me the greatest satisfaction, I beseech you to order that we be fed delicacies like these every day until I leave your monastery for Lauconnus. But I confess to your Charity that I advise you—almost on my knees in my request—to leave this place and come to Lauconnus while I stay here permanently and enjoy such delightful things[98] with my lords and brothers'. When, therefore, the gruel—the gruel that put these monks to the test—was served up a third time, all the hot air, along with its authors, dissipated under the cover of night: not one of these fellows remained at the monastery except those whom gluttony and a voracious desire for food had not corrupted.

40. In the morning, when blessed Lupicinus saw that these thick puffs of smoke[99] had vanished from the monastery he said, 'Come now, my brother Romanus, order regular food prepared as usual[100] since I see that this sort of fellow has disappeared, "not to serve Christ, but his own belly".[101] Now that the chaff has been tossed out and scattered by the wind, keep the wheat; now that the jackdaws and ravens have flown away, peacefully feed the gentle doves of Christ'.[102]

---

[98] Latin *deliciis vescar*. The root meaning of *vescor* is 'to eat', and so we could translate this phrase 'and eat such delicacies' (as above). Either way, the sarcasm is clear.

[99] Latin *turgidos fumos*. *Turgidus* also means 'swollen, puffed up', and is used earlier to describe these monks.

[100] This section clearly suggests that the food at the monastery had changed from the simple fare served 'in the beginning' (¶ 38). After Lupicinus' experiment, the menu is changed back to 'regular food prepared as usual'.

[101] See Rom 16:18.

[102] According to Gregory of Tours (*Life of the Fathers* 3), twelve disgruntled monks left the monastery. Gregory also reports that Lupicinus, in character, contemptuously gives up on the twelve while Romanus, also in character, prays for them. As a result, Gregory reports, the Lord 'touched their hearts and, doing penance for their defection, they each gathered together a community and founded for themselves monasteries which, until today, continue to praise God' (Rose, 169).

MIRACLES OF SAINT ROMANUS

41. With regard to the remarkable miracles related about Romanus, which, protected as he was by divine grace, he worked to repel unclean spirits, I should recount a few of them, as best I can. Much more excellent, however, are those that for the sake of secrecy he strove to perform with only God as witness. Therefore, because the grace enkindled by good works can never be extinguished, let the pious and diligent reader seek these gifts of the Holy Spirit, particularly around the tomb of this holy man. There, according to the faith and good works of those who seek him out, each person gains more belief from what he sees than he does from the things he reads and perhaps doubts.

42. I still remember how my blessed lord Eugendus was accustomed to relating this event: Among those whom he saw there in his childhood, he saw one unfortunate person, one among many who were tormented in a number of ways by the same Power; this one was lying face down, stretched out upon the sarcophagus of blessed Romanus as criminals and malefactors under sentence of judgement lie prostrate, bound hand and foot for flogging. And there, suspended four feet in the air for half an hour, wailing and crying out, the man proclaimed the wicked deeds and crimes[103] of the Power who possessed him.[104]

43. But, as I have said, the blessed father took such pains to conceal the miracles he worked that what happened in the parish of Poncin[105] (while on a trip there he restored to youthful

---

[103] Latin *scelera vel crimina*; immediately above, 'criminals and malefactors' translates *criminosi ac scelera*.

[104] Was he lying prostrate on the tomb, which was four feet in height? Or was he literally 'suspended' (*suspensus*) in the air? Our author accepts the story without comment. In Dialogue 3.6 Severus reports that some of the possessed 'would be lifted up by their feet into the air and hung as if from a cloud' (Hoare, trans., 129).

[105] Pontianum, the modern Poncin, is some thirty-one miles (50 kilometers) southwest of Condadisco, thus about halfway to Lyon. Here and hereafter,

health a certain paralytic long debilitated by disease) would doubtless not have come to our attention if our holy brother Palladius had not accompanied him and made it impossible for him to conceal what had occurred.

ROMANUS HEALS TWO LEPERS

44. And since I have made mention of Palladius, a very holy man, whose faithful support blessed Romanus enjoyed at the monastery as well as on the road and who was his true companion in charity, I shall also relate an incident in which this same brother participated. Once it had been done and published abroad, this one could not be hidden from the city and its people. Enflamed with the ardor of faith, Romanus had decided to seek out in Agaune[106] the basilica of the saints. (I should say, rather, the encampment of the martyrs, as the published report of their martyrdom testifies. I will not say that six thousand, six hundred men could be enclosed in the building, nor could they, I suppose, even be held in the field around it).[107]

45. When he had left for Geneva, no one was notified that the poor man was coming—and certainly he had no wish at all to be noted or known. With evening coming on he happened to enter a cave near the road where two lepers lived, a father with his son. Since these unfortunates (fortunate now that mercy had entered) had gone a short distance away to gather wood for use in the cave, blessed Romanus, having knocked at the doorway to their small home, opened it and entered the cave.

'parish' (Latin *parrochia*) indicates a secular district, and not an ecclesiastical parish in the modern sense.

[106] Acaunus, the modern Saint Maurice, approximately nineteen miles (thirty kilometers) from Montreux at the eastern tip of Lake Geneva. The monastery of Saint Maurice (Saint-Maurice d'Agaune), founded about 515, was where John and Armentarius, the recipients of the *Life*, lived. See ¶¶ 1 and 179, and the Introduction, pp. 51–52.

[107] At the end of the third century, Emperor Maximian supposedly ordered that a contingent of soldiers encamped near Acaunus be massacred because of their christian faith. An important pilgrimage site soon arose, and later the monastery of Saint Maurice. See Appendix II.

46. When Romanus and Palladius had finished praying as required of them by their vows, these laborers entered carrying their wood. Throwing down the heap of wood at the front of the cave, they saw—not without surprise—their newly arrived and unexpected guests. Saint Romanus, conspicuous for his singular goodness, greeted and embraced them in a very friendly way, as Saint Martin used to do,[108] and, with a most holy demonstration of faith and kindness, kissed each. After partaking of prayer and other rites, they all ate together, lay down as one for sleep, and rose at the same time. As dark was turning to light, Romanus, giving thanks to God and their hosts, again took up the journey he had begun.

47. What wonderful faith! As soon as Romanus had left, the similarity of his works to those of Saint Martin (whose constancy had already served him as an example) became clear. These lepers, while talking about and remembering their momentous guests, looked at one another. Each considered the other, and, with voices loud with joy, exulted with one another in their common cure. Running quickly to the town (because they were known to many people there who had given them alms), they proclaimed (through the obvious evidence of their own persons) to the bishop and clergy, to the peoples and nobles, the glorious act of their healing and the joys that the miracle had brought.

48. Then, in wondrous fashion, rushing at each of them in crowds, the people eagerly sought out the one who had done this thing. Their eyes sought everywhere to see if he were anywhere about. When they realized that he had hastily left there when it was barely light, the prefect[109] ordered men

---

108 See Sulpicius Severus, *Life of Martin* 18.3–4, where Martin, 'to everyone's horror', 'kissed the pitiable face of a leper and gave him his blessing' (Noble and Head, 20).

109 Reading with Martine *praefectus* instead of *perfectos*. On the office of prefect, see n. 56 above. If one accepts the emendation, this prefect would have to be, at this time, the praetorian prefect of Gaul. Sidonius Apollinaris' father (perhaps named Alcimus), a native of Lyon, was prefect around 448/449, and was known to have been a Christian. This unnamed prefect could be he. Our thanks to Professor Mathisen for this suggestion.

chosen from the church to run out in a holy search and to guard the narrow and rocky passes of Mount Bret.[110] Then on his return the one who seized the heavenly kingdom, constrained to use that narrow and confined pathway, could perhaps be seized by the Genevans.[111]

49. Then, when they found him, by the most cautious questioning they bound him with the chains of love, as though they were looking for an opportunity to accompany him.[112] Suddenly one of them ran ahead and announced the news to the town; the others so thoroughly tied him up with holy conversation that he had no suspicions until he fell into the hands of the bishop and the people who had come out to meet him outside the walls. Those who had been cleansed of their leprosy were present and, approaching him repeatedly with tears, threw themselves at his feet, prostrating themselves before him. Through the great rejoicing of the lepers, the whole citizenry, weeping together, undoubtedly wiped away through inward faith the sins that had accumulated through deadly contagion, just as the lepers had put off the last vestiges of their dire misfortune.

50. The servant of Christ, then, was first led away—or rather snatched away—by the holy bishop; then he was pressed upon by all the clergy and citizens, by the common people, too, both men and women, an enormous, milling crowd, clamoring for his saving cures. Despite the crush, as a servant of Christ he

---

[110] The pass of Bret is located some thirty-eight miles (sixty kilometers) to the east, following the curve of the southern shore of Lake Geneva; it is near the modern town of Saint Gingolph (see the map). The chronology and geography of this episode are curious. 'With evening coming' (¶ 45) implies the first day of wandering, yet Geneva is some thirty-eight miles (sixty kilometers) from Condadisco, often over tortuous terrain.

[111] R. A. Markus has observed: 'The vocabulary of military life found in so much monastic literature is a permanent reminder of the extent to which the monk's fortitude shown in the battle with the demon, with pride, with lust and with avarice, came to be seen as equivalent to the martyr's courage in rendering faithful witness in his fight with the adversary' (*The End of Ancient Christianity*, 71; see 71 n. 28 for examples).

[112] This event is reminiscent of a scene in the *Life of Martin* 9: townspeople wait for Martin; he is tricked to come out and taken by the people 'practically as a prisoner' (Noble and Head, 12).

gave his blessing to all of them as was most appropriate: he
encouraged those who were taking their first steps in the way
of faith; he warned procrastinators, because of the uncertainty
of life, not to wait too long to mend their ways; those in true
mourning he consoled with fatherly goodness; the infirm he
restored to their former health in accord with their faith.[113]
Then he returned as quickly as possible to the monastery, as was
his custom, afraid that if he were defiled by human conversation
with its seductions of worldly flattery, he might contract, either
through what he heard or saw, some unfortunate impurity.

51. But blessed Romanus did not shine alone at his monastery
through these wondrous abilities of his. The example of his
perfection and charity were such that all the brothers in their
wondrous deeds followed the model that he offered to everyone.
Thus one often saw there the venom of serpents extracted and
hordes of demons driven out of many people. Because of this the
ancient Enemy also laid many traps there for the Lord's flock;
goading the monks with jealous envy, he prowled around[114] the
Lord's sheepfold with such unbridled madness that he forsook
the usual series of temptations and strove to drive the monks
out from the monastery by force, physically attacking them with
hostile and monstrous phantasms. I shall relate, therefore, how
the Enemy attacked one of the brothers there in order to show
more readily, to those who desire to know, the steadfastness of
all the others at that time.[115]

THE DEACON SABINIANUS DEFEATS THE DEVIL

52. At the monastery there, among the other men with strong
abilities whom I have spoken about, was a certain deacon named
Sabinianus. Through sanctity of mind and body he sought

---

[113] See Lk 8:48.

[114] See 1 Pt 5:8.

[115] Our author states for the first time what will become a—perhaps *the*—
dominant theme from here on, which the Devil himself summarizes when
he tells Saint Martin, 'Wherever you go, and whatever you attempt, you will
have the Devil against you' (Sulpicius Severus, *Life of Martin* 6 [Noble and
Head, 10]).

both to be a colleague in purity with the first person to hold
this ministry, Stephen, and also demonstrated to the world
through his spiritual strength that he was Stephen's disciple.[116]
Industrious and active, he was in charge of the mills and weirs
on the nearby river below the monastery of Condadisco, which
served the brothers. From the river valley he would hurriedly
clamber up to the monastic assemblies, not only during the day
but also at night, and arrive at the meeting[117] ahead of almost
all the other monks.

53. The Devil tormented this fellow every night and every
moment with such fury that he did not allow him even a
moment's rest. In addition to repeated blows on the walls, with
stones he cracked so many holes in his roof that the brother
was scarcely able to repair each day the damage done at night.
When the Most Evil One perceived that the wickedness that he
was working outside was in vain, he went inside the brother's
hut one night while the deacon was home. Taking a burning
stick from the fire, he quickly and hurriedly ran about here and
there, trying to set the cell on fire.[118] He would undoubtedly
have succeeded if the holy deacon, on his guard and spurred on
by his love for the Lord, had not been keeping watch.

54. When the deacon had chased him away by invoking the
name of Christ, on the following night the Devil changed from
masculine form and arrived in the guise of two young girls in
order to entrap this most chaste servant of God:[119] while the
latter kept vigil in front of the hearth, the doors were forced
open, and with soft and seducing words the harsh Tempter
entered. The brother was provoked by various giggling noises
here and there in the room, but when he refused to look at

---

[116] For Stephen, the first deacon, see Acts 6–7.

[117] Latin *synaxi*. Synaxis, a word imported to the latin west from the earliest
days of desert monasticism, can designate any kind of meeting or, more
specifically, the Divine Office or the Eucharist.

[118] Antony was frequently assailed in his cell by demons; see *Life of Antony*
40–41, of numerous examples

[119] In *Life of Antony* 5.5, the Devil 'dared to take on the form of a woman at
night and imitated all of a woman's ways, solely for the purpose of deceiving
Antony'.

the monstrous images, the most evil Enemy devised—or rather added—even more detestable things than he had done before.

55. When the two girls had pulled off the misty clothing covering them, wherever this chaste servant of Christ looked, the Devil confronted him with female genitals.[120] Since the Devil could not weaken his soul as a man, he tried craftily to defile at least his most chaste sight and vision with such a shameful sight. When the brother recognized in the twin appearance a single monster, however, he said, 'Whatever you do, Enemy, you will not be able to drive me out from this place, protected as I am by the name of Christ. You will never be able to harm my heart, which is armed with the standard of the Lord's passion,[121] either by corrupting it with pleasure or by weakening it through fear. Why do you assault me so often under so many different guises?[122] You foolish thing! You're turning red with embarrassment, aren't you, because I, with the Lord's help, remain one and alone—and you will never see me any other way than you have already seen me!'

56. Then the Devil, inflamed with fury, having withdrawn the iniquitous apparition of the two girls, threw out his arm and struck the brother so sharply in the face that he caused his jaw not only to swell up from the blow but to became fetid, lacerated, and contorted. And as he is accustomed to do, the Devil turned into vapor, and disappeared into thin air. In the morning, when the astonished community of brothers asked Sabinianus why he was bruised and wounded, he explained what the tireless plotter had done.[123] Immediately he anointed his jaw with holy oil and returned to his cell, and from then on the despised Tempter no longer vainly attempted to throw him down.[124]

---

120 Latin *feminea pudenda*. The verb *pudere* means 'to cause shame'. *Pudenda*, literally 'shameful things', in post-classical Latin came to mean 'private parts'.

121 That is, the cross. See *Life of Antony* 13.5.

122 See *Life of Antony* 23.3.

123 In *Life of Antony* 8.2–3 Antony is beaten half-dead by demons.

124 Latin *non eum temptavit . . . temptator. Temptare*, cognate with *temptator*, means both 'to tempt' and 'attempt', which our author is playing on.

SABINIANUS AGAIN DEFEATS THE DEVIL

57. Afterwards, holy Sabinianus wanted one day with the help of the brothers to carefully raise the channel of the river by which water was brought to the mill to activate the machinery of the wheel; they fixed into place a double row of pilings and, as is the custom, plaited sticks and filled the spaces between with a mixture of straw and rock. While they were vigorously pressing the wattle between the rows, suddenly an enormous snake, driven out from the straw, showed itself and, just as quickly, disappeared. Meanwhile these brothers, fearful of the snake's venom, searched in vain for the snake hidden in the icy waters. Without accomplishing a thing, they used up the daylight hours available for work.

58. Then the holy deacon said to the brothers, 'Why are we fearful and apprehensive, afraid of our ancient Waylayer in snake's clothing? Come', he said to one of the brothers, 'arm my hands and feet with the sign of the Lord's cross'. When his companion, after saying a prayer, carried out this order, the deacon stepped among the rows of wattle in the canal and said, 'Hey you, our Waylayer, harm me now! And, if you're stronger than me, strike the person who is trampling you underfoot!' Standing there, the brothers were then saying to one another, 'Truly our deacon is one of those to whom the Savior promised in the Gospel: "See, I have given you authority to trample on snakes and scorpions, and over all the power of the enemy; and nothing will harm you"!'[125]

CONCLUSION

59. So, then, although I have said very little about things so significant and important, it is nevertheless time to bring the narration of this book to a close so that the reader's effort is brought to a conclusion in a spirit of desiring more rather than in the torpor of prolixity. Therefore I admonish and beseech

---

[125] Lk 10:19, also quoted in *Life of Antony* 30.3.

you, my brothers, whom I named in my preface,[126] regard my faith more than my writing. May my garrulousness not offend you, just as the rustic nature of our holy fathers was not found offensive by the Lord. Nevertheless, I must advise you of this one thing: since I promised that I would at the same time set down the Rule of these same fathers, know that I am reserving that for the third book. To produce this in the *Life* of blessed Eugendus who, inspired by the Lord, more artfully arranged these same regulations, is more proper.

60. Now then, with this first little work completed, the second discourse will be devoted to our holy father Lupicinus.

THE DEATH OF ROMANUS

When, therefore, with death approaching him at a protracted age, bodily infirmity beset the hero of Christ and he sought out his sister in order to say good-bye to her, since he was now assured by a revelation from the Lord of his coming departure.[127] (They had appointed her head of the monastery for women in that area of the stone arch or 'Balma'—I believe this is what they call it in the gallic language.)[128] Stricken there by a violent illness, Romanus summoned the brothers to him, and he passed on to them as a great legacy the peace of Christ that he had always preserved through a pure and clement devotion, imparting it to each one with a kiss.

61. Having given his valedictory blessing, and kissing his brother Lupicinus last, he earnestly commended to him the entire community of brothers to be ruled with pastoral love. Pure of any offense as well as free from any accusation, and contemplating death with joy, he expired. His poor body was borne to the basilica, and there, at the top of the hill (as I related in the previous narrative), his dear sons from both monasteries

---

[126] See ¶ 1.
[127] Antony knew of his approaching death; *Life of Antony* 89.2–3. Our author's knowledge of the geography of Balma seems poor. However, the most explicit monastic 'rules' that he cites concern the female monastery (see ¶¶ 25–26).
[128] See ¶¶ 25–26 and n. 68.

buried him. This venerable place, witness to the merits of this man, blooms with a succession of signs and powerful acts. It is adorned more and more abundantly each day, at every moment, to the glory of Romanus' children.[129]

---

[129] In ¶ 2, the narrator says that Eugendus as a child saw 'one unfortunate person . . . lying face down stretched out upon the sarcophagus of blessed Romanus'. The *Life* suggests, then, that Romanus was not buried in the earth but was placed in a tomb in the 'basilica'.

the life of the holy abbot lupicinus

INTRODUCTION

62. Now that a third of my obligation and promise has been paid, with the help of the Lord, it remains for me, dear brothers, with the support of your sanctity, to pay off the promissory note of my Introduction, at least as far as my poor purse will permit. Until I recognize that I owe these secured debts, without a doubt (and my conscience summons me to do so) I am rightly detained by those to whom I am indebted. Although I remember having said a few things in my earlier book about the way of life[1] and the practices of blessed Abbot Lupicinus (even if not done as splendidly as he deserves, at least it was done from a desire to be faithful and straight-forward), let me now with the aid of memory undertake to speak about those things that he did after the death of his holy predecessor; let me reveal right from the start how mean his clothing was, with what frugality he was accustomed to eat and, finally, his extraordinary and inimitable seriousness in the religious life.

LUPICINUS' PRACTICES AND WAY OF LIFE

63. Therefore, to protect himself against the frosts of that extremely cold land and to wear down the wantonness of the body, he always used a tunic made out of hide and fur, which for the sake of humility was patched or sewn together from various animal hides; not only was it shaggy and hideous, it was also soiled and made in a kind of variegated ugliness.[2] His cowl,

---

[1] Latin *conversatione: conversatio.*

[2] For Antony's clothing, see *Life of Antony* 91.8; Lupicinus' dress, as described by our author, is far more wretched than Antony's.

equally ugly, protected him only from the rain, and was of little use in warding off the bitter cold of that place, of which I have spoken. As for his shoes, he wore them only when he happened to leave the monastery to go to the court in order to intercede on behalf of this or that person.[3]

64. At the monastery, even if he went some distance to work in the fields, he would take with him only wooden clogs, which they commonly call *socci* in the monasteries of Gaul.[4] It is reported that he never used bedding or a bed.[5] In mild weather, once the evening meeting[6] was over and the others went to their beds to sleep, he went into the oratory in order rather to meditate than to rest; there he took only as much sleep as nature managed to steal from him when, getting up off the ground after his prayer, he would doze a little on a bench.

65. If harsh and powerful cold assailed him, he had a bag shaped like a cradle. It was measured to fit his size, made from bark stripped from an oak and closed off at each end by pieces sewn from the same bark. After he had privately and lengthily warmed up the part of the bag that was open toward the coals, he either rested in it, enjoying the warmth for a bit, or he immediately carried the bag under his arm, while it was still warm, into the oratory in order to sleep there. In fasting and keeping vigils he was so mighty that gallic nature defeated even the excellence[7] of the monks of Egypt and the east.

66. Although no one, especially at the monastery of Condadisco, dares even today in the name of Christ to taste anything taken from animals except milk, or anything taken from poultry

---

[3] Martin is described by Sulpicius in similar terms: 'his insignificant appearance, his sordid garments and his disgraceful hair', and his "poverty-stricken clothing" (*Life of Martin* 9 and 10 [Noble and Head, 12 and 13]).

[4] In medieval Latin, *soccus* designated a 'wooden sole, sandal, slipper', and, later, a 'sock' or 'stocking', from which, via french *socque*, English gets its 'sock'.

[5] *Life of Antony* 7.7: 'A mat would suffice for him to sleep on, but usually he would just sleep on the ground'.

[6] Latin *vespertina synaxi*; see p. 127, n. 117 above.

[7] Latin *virtutem*.

except eggs (and then only the weak when they are ill), most often Lupicinus would not permit even a drop of oil or milk to be put in his gruel. As far as wine is concerned, from the time of his monastic profession he could never be compelled to taste it, not even a drop; he abstained even from tasting water for about eight years before his passing.[8]

67. During the summer, when the time for dinner had arrived, if thirst violently assailed his stomach and parched his body, he would break up his bread into little pieces in a small dish, moisten it with cold water, and eat it with a spoon. That was the extent of his dinner. I would recount greater feats of abstinence that he did if I did not know that the Gauls are incapable of imitating the deeds that tradition says he performed. I would be afraid that someone, unsuitably following his example, might perhaps eagerly desire to imitate those things that, by the dispensation of grace, divine beneficence allots not to everyone but only to some.

LUPICINUS' MIRACLES

68. Let me now speak a while of his miracles. Once, because of imminent scarcity and the danger of famine, the enormous community of monks and the multitude of lay people who had come to the monastery seeking food were troubling the steward of the monastery; these people had absolutely nothing more than a fifteen-day supply of food for the three months that remained until the new harvest promised relief. The steward, with five elders accompanying him, tearfully went to meet holy father Lupicinus and swore that soon everyone, including himself, was going to die of hunger. Lupicinus, however, fearlessly trusting in the Lord, lifted up his soul and the eyes of his heart to the living bread that came down from heaven.[9] 'Come, my dear children', he said, 'let us go into our granary here, where only a few handfuls of grain remain, and let us pray; we too,

---

[8] See ¶ 116.
[9] See Jn 6:41.

who have left our towns, follow the Savior into the desert in order to listen to him'.[10]

69. When the father had entered, lying prostrate he prayed long and hard. Later, he got up on his knees a bit and, with his hands extended, raised supplicating eyes to heaven; finishing his prayer in a kind of ecstasy, he said, 'Almighty God, through your servant Elijah you allegorically[11] promised the widow that neither the jug of flour nor the jar of oil would diminish until the rains came.[12] This church, having left behind the need for symbols, is defended by Jesus Christ your Son, the eternal bridegroom. Just as it is filled with the Word, in the same way revive it by filling it up with bread; until we obtain rains for a new harvest, do not allow our granary here to lack an abundance of wheat'.

70. When the brothers had responded 'Amen!' Lupicinus turned to the steward and said, 'Thresh out now that which the Lord has blessed; in response to these petitions of faith the Divinity speaks thus: "They shall eat, and have some left" '.[13] Abba Eugendus, then a young boy of happy disposition,[14] was present, and he (along with all the elders who with him remembered what was done and who were saved by that blessing) used to testify that they would never have been able to manage all that wheat and get it threshed unless, by the same blessing, once the cycle of seasons came around with a new crop to add to what had already been accumulated, Lupicinus had not mixed the new with the old. Thus the man of God, trusting in faith, delivered both the community of brothers and the multitude of lay people from the danger of famine.

---

[10] See Mt 14:13–14: 'Now when Jesus heard this, he withdrew from these in a boat to a deserted place by himself. But when the crowd heard it, they followed him on foot from the towns'.

[11] Reading *mystice*, which one manuscript has, instead of *mysticae* (*viduae mysticae*). See p. 97, n. 2.

[12] See 1 Kings 17:14 and 16.

[13] 2 Kings 4:43. See also Lk 9:17, the conclusion of the feeding of the five thousand.

[14] See 1 Kings 11:28, 1 Chr 12:28, and Ws 8:19.

LUPICINUS HEALS A SEVERE ASCETIC

71. At that time a certain monk there had, by the severity of intense abstinence, caused his poor body to be shriveled up with a kind of mange and with extreme emaciation. Half alive and knotted up like a paralytic, he could neither straighten his spine, nor control his walking, nor bend or extend his arms in order to use them. Except for the weak breathing that still sustained his body, you could have almost believed that he had departed this life.

72. For about seven years he had been eating nothing except crumbs from the monks' tables: after the brothers had had their meal, he would diligently sweep the crumbs together with a feather whisk and, moistening them with a little water, eat them in the evening. The blessed elder came to his aid with a plan to restore him to health. Lupicinus treated him, it is said, with such discrete ministrations that not only did he not censure the man for his excessive abstinence but he was not even seen to criticize him for anything whatsoever.

73. One day, when the brothers had left for the fields (to do what kind of work I do not know) and the monastery was completely deserted, the abbot said to the brother, 'Come, let me support you in my arms, and let's go to the community garden; for a long time now, held captive by this terrible weakness, you have neither felt the sunshine on your face nor have you touched anything green whatsoever'.

74. Then, after spreading out sheepskins on the ground, he carried the man, whose arms and legs were numb, to an open area in the garden. He himself lay down alongside the brother. Acting cramped, as though he himself were knotted up by a similar affliction, he began to stretch out now his arms one at a time, and now his legs one after the other. Then, lying on his back, he straightened his spine by repeatedly and pleasurably rocking back and forth, first one way and then the other. While doing these things, in order to dissuade the brother from his excessive austerity, the elder added, 'Good God, what relief! I feel as good as new! Come on, brother, I'm going to roll

you back and forth as I did myself in order to bring back your health'.

75. Then Lupicinus, like a masseur, stretched the man's limbs and massaged each part of his body, one by one. He applied his healing touch to that poor twisted and debilitated body, and the brother, though still half-dead, began to stretch out his limbs, now made straight and fit for human use. Running then to the steward, the father entered the storeroom; mixing together small pieces of bread soaked in wine, he carried this into the garden, along with the rest of the meal, which he had liberally sprinkled with oil, and said, 'Come, dearest brother, lay aside your willful severity, and if it happens that my injunction is onerous, at least to follow my example will not break you. What you see me do, without a doubt you will do, obediently and without argument, under the stipulations of the Rule'.

76. When he had prayed, Lupicinus sat down at his brother's side and revived the limbs weakened by cruel excess. Supporting him, he revived his brother's 'ass',[15] which was collapsing in the road from the weight of the load, and got him on his feet. After singing a hymn,[16] he carried him, restored, back to his cell. The next day he took him back to the garden with his usual kindness and expended the same efforts that he had the day before. At last, on the third day, when the brother was out walking, supported now not by others but solely by his own efforts, the elder provided him with a bent piece of wood like a light-weight hoe and showed him how to weed the vegetables, sometimes standing, sometimes lying down, either with a rake or with his fingers.

77. What more is there to say? In this fashion, within about a week—once the brother had set aside what nourished his foolish vanity—Lupicinus gave this man's life back to him when he ought to have died;[17] as a result, the brother lived many years

---

15 Latin *fraternum asellum*. As Martine notes, p. 322, n. 1, this is a traditional image of the human body.

16 See Mt 26:30; Mk 14:26.

17 The Latin *sepeliendum* is much more graphic. *Sepelire* means 'to bury', so the english 'one foot in the grave', though a cliché, gives the idea.

afterwards, and his testimony was a compelling witness to the old man's charity and power. Thus by means of a clear and divine example, Lupicinus clearly taught that no one, once he has embraced the monastic precepts, ought to walk along the heights to the right nor along the slopes to the left, but ought to undertake the middle course of monastic discipline that is 'the royal path'.[18]

78. Divine largesse, which works together with the grace of good works, was so fully bestowed upon this brother[19] that if someone placed a sick person on his bed, the illness was driven completely away and the person was immediately fully restored to his former good health. I myself, still a young child at this time, saw many of the brothers corroborate this, both from having seen it happen to others and from repeated experiences of their own. Let each person conclude, therefore, that none of the good works of that man will remain silent, since whatever words cannot spell out, deeds proclaim.

LUPICINUS SAVES TWO BROTHERS

79. Let me now speak about the night watches of the blessed father. Once, when no one in the place was assured of rest, he had a watch kept everywhere throughout the night. Two brothers, united in their intention to carry through their common plan to leave, agreed to enter the oratory as though they were going to pray and, as it were, bid farewell to the place of prayer. After praying they admonished each other in whispers: 'You', the one said, 'take from here my hoe and my ax, and I

---

[18] For references regarding this 'traditional' image, see Martine, 324 n. 1. The phrase may be found in monastic literature as early as the *Apophthegmata Patrum*; see Apophthegmata Poemen 31 (Ward, trans., 171) where Poemen says with regard to fasting that 'the royal way' of moderation is to eat a little each day rather than to fast three or four days at a time, which he did when he was younger. Lupicinus' regimen, however, does not seem all that different from this monk's; see ¶ 66–67. RB 39, as is well known, is much more moderate.

[19] It is not clear whether 'this brother' is Lupicinus or the brother cured by Lupicinus in ¶ 77.

will carefully remove your cloak and your cowl from your bed. When both of us have separately got everything removed and packed up, let's again meet together in one place or another'.

80. Although the darkness was a hindrance, the divine presence shone nevertheless, thanks to the servant of Christ. The father sensed (since all things are foreordained) that a step was being taken outside the bounds of Paradise, and so he, the abbot, spoke from the corner: 'Since, my dear children, you offered a prayer for me as you were about to leave, you ought not, before you depart, withhold from me the kiss of peace'. Those wretches fell down right on the spot as though they were preparing to come before a judge; pouring forth great sighs from the bottom of their hearts and deep groans and incessant sobbing, they testified that their innermost parts were being lashed.

81. But Lupicinus called each of them by name and, slowly putting forth his hand, took each of them by the chin; gently caressing each one, he warmly kissed them. With no further discussion, he knelt down and, with fatherly love, took up the weapons of prayer. Then, with divine help, the good-for-nothing Abettor of evil was driven from their souls. The brothers, praying and invoking the name of Christ, repeatedly crossed themselves on their breasts and on their eyes; then, fearful and trembling, they returned to their cells. They were so shaken by fear and shame that neither one dared to speak or breathe a word of what had happened to them. Their only hope for forgiveness lay in the fatherly love and compassion that sensed that they were being lashed in such fashion by their own confusion.

LUPICINUS ADDRESSES THE COMMUNITY

82. I call upon Jesus Christ as my witness—may he not allow us who have been redeemed by his passion to perish through the repeated blandishments of the Enemy—that the father, because of the compunction they showed as a result of their correction, so thoroughly covered over this matter with silence that it was almost twenty years later (one of the two had already journeyed

to be with Christ) that the father related as a cautionary example to the whole community, with the survivor present as a witness, what had happened.

Mixing sorrow with joy, he preached to the assembled brothers: 'You see, my dear sons, by what subtle and secretive methods our ancient Enemy tries to destroy the servants of Christ.

83. See how the Redeemer, bestowing his mercy, allowed his servants to be tempted for a while as they followed their own nature and understanding. But extending his right hand in mercy, the Lord did not allow them, although they wavered, to be devoured by the Seducer. See how one of them', he continued, 'has laid down his fleshly burden and possesses the rewards of Paradise prepared for him; the other, as you can see, rejoices with us, exulting in Christ's mercy. You clearly see then that the disposition to something is not of itself considered a sin; rather it is the doing of a thing that is a sin. Nor are all evil inclinations blameworthy; let those that are evilly carried out be reproached as crimes.[20]

84. 'Therefore, let each of you who is standing always be afraid of falling, as the Apostle has expressed it,[21] and conversely, if through the fault of weakness someone has fallen, let him get up again,[22] in accord with the prophet's word.[23] What gain, what advantage, would I have accrued if with severe strictness I had made their plans public and punished them with inappropriate harshness when they were ashamed and trembling? In truth, only this: I would have forced them, after a few days perhaps, to entangle themselves, compelled by shame, even more tightly

---

[20] This understanding of sin may be found in very similar form in the *Sayings of the Fathers*. See Tim Vivian, 'Words to Live By: A Conversation that the Elders Had with One Another Concerning Thoughts', *St Vladimir's Theological Quarterly* 39.2 (1995) 127–41: 'Waves will never injure rock; in the same way an unsuccessful assault will never harm a person, for it is written that any sin not brought to completion is not a sin' (p. 137; see also 137 n. 35).

[21] 1 Cor 10:12: 'So if you think you are standing, watch out that you do not fall'.

[22] Latin *consurgat*; see n. 23 below.

[23] See, perhaps, Is 52:1–2 (Vulgate): 'Consurge, consurge' ('Arise, arise').

in something that now, through the Lord's mercy, they have dispelled by their ashamed apology.

85. 'Just as the contumacious and proud, therefore, ought to be rebuked more severely, those who feel remorse through humility of conscience should be treated with mild medicine. Who among you does not know that in the administration of this community that has been entrusted to me I must preserve a treatment in accord with the art, just as medicine is administered by skilled doctors to each patient in accordance with the nature of his wounds or the cause of his infirmity?

86. 'I must not put a patient under the surgeon's knife or cauterize him with burning instruments; often he should be treated with poultices and warmed with plasters lest, through hasty treatment or treatment inconsistent with fevers, the doctors not bring healing to the person but instead, through untimely and inopportune practice, weaken him'.

This speech of the blessed father occasioned in the brothers great caution in ascertaining the exact nature of the facts and discerning the particularities of each case.

THE DEVIL ATTACKS THE MONK DATIVUS

87. After some months had passed, our ancient Enemy (who with such great craftiness ties up and captures men's souls) sought to ensnare one of the most respected and outstanding of the brothers in the same way. Once this brother was stripped of the armaments of discernment and the power of prayer, the Enemy then bound him captive with invisible restraints. This brother was a person of the greatest humility and gentleness and, in addition to the virtue of obedience, by divine help he was also adorned with great qualities and gifts for every kind of work.

88. Into this brother, little by little, and slowly, the Devil put a spark of pride regarding his own self-worth. Immediately, when he saw it kindled, the Devil enflamed some of the brothers against the man by inciting an argument. Some of the monks daily blew upon him, who was already overheated with pride,

with the winds of offenses, while others, using ropes made out of gossip and the alluring bonds of the world, pulled him out of the monastery, encouraging him not to put up with such people as live there but to leave everything. Thus, gathering up and tying together his tools and utensils,[24] he deserted in secret, lest someone detain him, and quickly hastened without stopping to the city of Tours.[25]

89. When he entered the courtyard of the basilica of blessed Martin and reverently went into the church itself in order to pray, one of the possessed people suddenly ran up to him and joyfully cried out, 'Here is a monk who by all rights belongs with us!' Calling him by name, he said, 'Dativus! How are you, comrade?' When Dativus, terrified and groaning aloud at being taunted by the Devil, sighed deeply, the possessed man added, 'All right! You are my horse, and by rough treatment I have tamed you. So let us live together!' The monk quickly prayed and went home; prostrate, he begged to be received again into the monastery. From then on, soberly and diligently, and with the divine help that is always necessary, he more wisely now kept the Devourer from having access to him.

LUPICINUS' PRAYERS AID DATIVUS

90. Two years later, however, his old rider returned. Just as before, the Devil had him make a bundle of his tools and a blanket so he could depart.[26] When the holy abbot learned that that same poor sheep was not going to leave and return as before, he wept and deeply lamented that he would be lost. Dativus, standing before the brothers, had placed his load on his shoulders in order to depart. He stood, however, for half an hour, stupefied, in the courtyard; through the prayer of the

---

[24] It is interesting that here and in ¶ 79 the monk has tools 'to pack up', since supposedly all things were held in common (see ¶¶ 112, 173). See also ¶ 90.
[25] Tours is over 400 kilometers (250 miles) northwest of Condadisco.
[26] With regard to the question of private ownership (see ¶ 88 and n. 24), the Latin here does lack 'his', but the sense seems to require it (Martine, 335, translates 'son matèriel'). Perhaps he is stealing the tools.

servant of God he blew out[27] the one who was inciting him to
wander, and having thrown down onto the vestibule floor the
pack he was carrying around his neck, he said,

91. 'Come on, you who encourage and advise me, *you* carry
my load! Walk in front of me to where you are pushing me to
go. As for me, I will follow you if I see you carrying it'. The
diabolical delusion fled his soul on the spot, and the monk,
jumping for joy, turned and embraced and kissed the entire
community of brothers. Nor, from that time did the ridiculed
and despised Vassal dare to bind Christ's poor sheep with his
usual seductively persuasive rope.

LUPICINUS DEFENDS THE POOR—AND HIMSELF—AT COURT[28]

92. Moreover, this blessed father spoke with an authority[29]
that was absolutely admirable, accompanied as it was by sincerity of conscience. He did not burst with vainglorious pride at the
flattery of state officials, nor was he ever moved or shaken from
his devotion to justice by fear of princes. Indeed, one time he
was moved by the plight of some poor persons whom a certain
man, puffed up by the prestige of being at court, had through
unlawful coercion violently subjected to the yoke of servitude.
The servant of God, through the holiest of testimony, sought to
defend them before the illustrious Chilperic, formerly *patricius*
of Gaul.[30] (Public power had at that time gone over to a royal

---

[27] Latin *exsufflans*, a word commonly used in describing exorcisms. Normally
the exorcist 'blew on' the demon. In *Dialogues* 3.8 (Hoare, 130), Martin blows
on (*exsufflans*) a demon 'of astonishing size'. Sulpicius says that 'exsufflans'
is 'hardly Latin'.

[28] For the version of Gregory of Tours, see *Life of the Fathers* 5 (James, trans.,
8–10).

[29] There may be an echo here of Lk 4:32, where the people are astounded
at Jesus 'because he spoke with authority', although the Vulgate has *potestate*
whereas the *Life* uses *auctoritate*.

[30] Chilperic I, king of the Burgundians, *Galliae patricius*, ruled in the 460s and
470s; he was the father of Clotilde, who married Clovis. Clotilde, then, was
the mother of the sons who conquered the Burgundian kingdom. As James
notes, *Gregory of Tours*, 9 n. 10, 'It is significant that Gregory, unlike [the

government.) The execrable oppressor, inflamed by a furious anger and filled with rage, frothed at the mouth and spewed forth these words designed to blemish the reputation of that most holy man:[31]

93. 'Are you not that impostor who has been in our midst a long time, the one who about ten years ago arrogantly denigrated the honor of being a Roman citizen when you proclaimed to this region and to our fathers that ruin was imminent?[32] Why, then, I ask you, have these terrible predictions that you made publicly not been confirmed by any unfortunate event? Explain that to us, false prophet!'

Then Lupicinus, his hand held out to Chilperic, whom we mentioned above, a man of singular intelligence and remarkable goodness,[33] said boldly,

94. 'Look here, you faithless and lost soul, await the wrath I predicted for you and those like you! Do you not see, you ignoble and miserable person, that law and justice have been thrown into confusion on account of your sins and those of your followers—I mean your exactions against the innocent— and that the authority of the purple-banded fasces has been handed over to a judge clothed in skins? Finally, take a look at yourself just a little and see whether a new enemy, through unexpected disdain for the law, does not lay claim to your lands and acreage and make them his own!

95. 'Yet just as I have every reason to believe that you know these things, or can sense them, I also believe that you have

---

Life of the Jura Fathers], simply bestows on [Chilperic] the title of king, the constitutional niceties of the fifth century being long forgotten'.

[31] On this incident and the context of 'informers', see Mathisen, *Roman Aristocrats in Barbarian Gaul*, 74–6.

[32] Mathisen, *Roman Aristocrats in Barbarian Gaul*, 123, dates this episode to 457/458, 'in the troubled times immediately after the fall of Avitus, when the Burgundians were extending their control into the area of Lupicinus' own monastery. Presumably, Lupicinus had been speaking out on the failure of Roman policies, and his predictions of gloom and doom may have involved a catastrophe which he felt was sure to follow the Burgundian takeover'. See Martine, 337, n. 3.

[33] The Burgundians, although Arian, were tolerant of Catholic Christianity.

sought to diminish my humble person with a two-pronged
hook—either I will be afraid of the king or frightened by what
has happened—in order to besmirch my name by branding me
with this accusation'.[34]

To be brief, the aforementioned *patricius* was so delighted by
Lupicinus' truthful audacity that, with numerous examples and
lengthy argumentation, and with members of the court present,
he confirmed that this had happened through divine judgement.
Then, with a decision promulgated with royal authority, he
restored the freedom of the free men and, presenting gifts for
the needs of the brothers and the monastery, gave permission
for the servant of God to return to the monastery with honor.[35]

LUPICINUS' PRAYERS AID COUNT AGRIPPINUS[36]

96. Once Lupicinus (and I have no doubt that those who are
old will perchance remember this), praying at the monastery,
brought about the great and wonderful release of a friend
being held in a prison in Rome whom he had promised to
aid. At that time the illustrious Agrippinus, a man endowed
with rare sagacity, had been appointed Count of Gaul by the
emperor on account of his reputation in the secular service. He
had been defamed before the emperor in an underhanded and

---

[34] Martine (p. 341, n. 2) suggests that the 'hook' (*uncus*) may refer to the
instrument the Romans used to lead prisoners to the Tiber to be drowned.
'Two-pronged', he suggests, refers to Lupicinus' fear of Chilperic and his
unfulfilled prophecy, although Lupicinus suggests that the two 'prongs' are
fear of the king and being hauled to the court.

[35] For other examples of intervention on behalf of the poor or captives, see
Mathisen, *Roman Aristocrats in Barbarian Gaul*, 101–2; it is interesting to note
that the noblewoman Syagria of Lyon, who makes an appearance in the *Life
of the Jura Fathers* (¶ 145), on one occasion contributed to the release of
captives (Mathisen, 101).

[36] Mathisen, *Roman Aristocrats in Barbarian Gaul*, 218, dates these events to
around 458. 'Although the details of this story might be questioned', he
adds (p. 200), 'it appears as if the ecclesiastical *topos* of appeals to Rome
by disaffected clerics has here been applied by a hagiographer to a secular
incident'.

malicious manner by Ægidius, who at that time was head of the army, because, he said, Agrippinus, envious of the Roman fasces and doubtless favoring the barbarians, was trying through surreptitious and underhanded means to remove the provinces from the control of the state. Ægidius had defamed Agrippinus with the fetid stench of accusation, as I have said, before the latter was able to overturn this false accusation in person with a true account of his innocence.[37]

97. Soon, enflamed imperial orders commanded the head of the army, who had accused him, to send 'the enemy of the state' to Rome to be severely punished by the emperor. In the meantime, the aforementioned Agrippinus, having heard the barest whisper of a rumor regarding these matters while stationed with his troops, was forced to hurry to court under guard. While still stationed at his post, he perceived, through the whisperings of certain persons, that the mind of the emperor had been prejudiced against him, as I have said, by a jealous rival; he began to resist and to protest loudly that under no circumstances would he return to Rome unless the person who had secretly accused him came forward and publicly proved the charges in his presence.

98. But Ægidius did not undertake to argue with him. Fearing the reproach of his conscience and secretly alarmed, with frequent oaths on the sacraments he began, not to loosen the

---

[37] See Martine, p. 445. Ægidius († around 465) was *patricius* and *magister utriusque militiae*, and friend of Emperor Majorian († 461); he rebelled against the *patricius* Ricimer, who claimed power after Majorian's assassination, and the puppet emperor Severus. Agrippinus was *magister militum Galliarum*. Before the death of Majorian, Ægidius had accused Agrippinus of dealings with the Visigoths. After Majorian's death, the Visigoths sided with Ricimer, who favored rapprochement with the 'barbarians' (Ægidius accuses Agrippinus of 'favoring the barbarians'), and a small civil war ensued, pitting Romans against Romans. When Ægidius besieged Narbonne, the Goths heeded the call of a roman general and entered the city. Ægidius accused Agrippinus of delivering the city to Theodoric, king of the Visigoths. D.P. Benoit, *Histoire de l'abbaye de de la Terre de Saint-Claude* (Montreuil-sur-Mer: Imprimerie de la Chartreuse de Notre-Dame des Prés, 1890) 92, adds that one tradition had Lupicinus and Agrippinus being schoolmates.

net around the innocence of Agrippinus, but to pull it tightly around him: 'Why' he said, 'Agrippinus has nothing to fear! No guiltless person that I know about has been branded as guilty before the emperor merely because of the suggestion of wrongdoing. It seems clear to me, at least, that Agrippinus, if he has been accused by someone, would make suspicions grow by refusing to appear. And if he does appear, why, he'll clear himself of the suspicion of treachery!'

99. 'If indeed, my lord and superior Ægidius', Agrippinus replied, 'I have nothing to fear there, even though I have been accused, I beg that, for my sake, the holy servant of God, Lupicinus, who is present here, act from this time forward as a guarantor of Your Nobility'. 'So be it', said Ægidius. Immediately taking the right hand of the servant of God and kissing it, he placed it in the hand of the accused as a pledge of the agreement they had made.

100. Agrippinus undertook and completed his journey and arrived at the Great City; he immediately presented himself, in accordance with the previous summons, to the *patricius* [Ricimer] in the presence of the senate. Now the emperor [Severus], who had followed the case, was asked what punishment was appropriate for someone who had falsely pretended to act on behalf of the state, someone in conspiracy with the enemy. The result was that he ordered Agrippinus to submit soon to a sentence of capital punishment, without being heard or having his case discussed. But God doubtless commanded (or, rather, deferring to the prayer of his servant, agreed) that an innocent person who has not been justly sentenced should not be immediately put to death with the ax by the state.

101. For the time being, an order was given for Agrippinus to be thrown into prison, and everywhere the murmuring crowd rejoiced and insulted[38] him: 'The man who was seen to curry the favor of the barbarians and kindled their desire for insurrection has at last, with divine help, been reined in, and barbarous temerity will no longer possess its former audacity'. But Saint

---

[38] Latin *exsultante insultanteque*.

Lupicinus knew right away all about the villainy because the above-mentioned Agrippinus was by constant petition through the Spirit asking for his pledge and surety.[39]

102. The servant of Christ therefore laid upon himself, with unceasing prayer, unwearying acts of penance. Except for food such as raw cabbage hearts and uncooked turnips, crude and straight from the field, he made use of absolutely nothing more for his daily fare until he could see that Agrippinus had been released. With untiring determination the friend of Christ knocked on the ear of the Lord's kindness with petitions that lasted through the night. One night he came in a vision to his friend in prison, to whom he had pledged his support. He urged him not to be upset and, pointing to one of the corners of the prison, said, 'Push there very gently and, by crawling slowly and quietly, quickly make your escape before dawn comes'.

103. Thus shaken from sleep, and as though he had been shut up in Herod's prison and had spoken with the angel who once visited the Apostle,[40] Agrippinus immediately took down his prisoner's sack that was hanging from a peg. Gathering together his chains, and cautiously shaking and tossing aside the rock in the corner, he uncovered a way out similar to a tunnel. Then, as though he had become a very small child again, he stretched out flat and placed his hands on the ground; crawling at times, he extricated himself, but he did not know how to find the basilica of Saint Peter[41] where he could find refuge.

104. Nevertheless, coming upon a square, he hurriedly hastened his steps in order to get as far away as possible, and avoid recognition once he had mixed in with and joined the passersby. With his head covered by a cowl, he had no idea where he was going. Meanwhile, looking to the right, he saw a certain venerable and God-fearing monk; pretending to be a pilgrim, he asked how he could get to Saint Peter's[42] by the

---

[39] Agrippinus, then, is a Christian, not typical for a roman commander.
[40] See Acts 12:6–9, where an angel helps Peter flee prison.
[41] Latin *apostolica limina*.
[42] Literally 'the basilica of the Head of the Apostle'.

shortest route possible. The monk responded, 'By way of the Vatican', that most famous place, where on one side of the public porticos small shelters have now been pieced together for the sick. Giving him instructions, he told him about all the squares and intersections he would have to cross; since Agrippinus was ignorant of these places, the monk left no detail of the correct route uncertain.

105. When he had entered the basilica of Saint Peter he prostrated himself, wailing with tears, and letting out from deep within his chest all his hardships. In whispers the wounded man begged pardon for all his sins and asked to be freed by the Physician from the snares surrounding him in his present circumstances. Night then followed, and once again Lupicinus, Agrippinus' guarantor, appeared in the basilica in a vision to comfort his protégé with words of encouragement. During the familiar exchange of words Agrippinus rejoiced that he had been led from the darkness of the prison into the light, but now, discomforted by the needs of nature, he confessed that he was very hungry. In fact, from the time he had escaped from custody, as he fled repeatedly from this place to that place, he had asked no one at all for food. 'Be calm', the servant of God told him, 'just a little longer. At dawn I will send you plenty to eat'.

106. When dawn began to break the following day, a certain senator's wife turned away from the tomb of the Apostle after praying. As she was about to leave she observed Agrippinus in the corner, and said to her slave, 'This fellow here is a pilgrim and, judging from his obvious natural superiority, not a person of low estate.[43] For the time being, offer him these two *solidi* [44] left over from our almsgiving; when I return home I shall give him (I want you to remind me) a larger amount'.

107. Immediately taking possession of the coins, he bought food at the nearby market and returned much happier to the

---

[43] This motif runs through much of Middle High German literature.
[44] In the fifth century a *solidus* was a gold coin about the size of a U.S. five-cent piece or a U.K. five pence coin. It is impossible to say what its purchasing power was at the time.

outer court. And now he heard some sad and anxious men from the palace talking among themselves: 'This Agrippinus, who has escaped from prison, compelled by the grave injustice done to him, is without a doubt going to incite the barbarians to invade the state'. When he heard this, and because he had gone unrecognized by them, he joined them and nonchalantly spoke with them for a little while. Acting as though he were a native of the place, he carefully questioned them. Skillfully directing the course of the conversation, he mixed in with the discussion shrewd advice:

108. 'How much better the emperor would have done if he had made a person like this indebted to the good offices of his mercy (even if the fellow had been guilty as charged) rather than push him, without a hearing or a trial, and perhaps goading him, by the injustice done to him, to commit the very thing he had falsely been accused of'. They responded, 'What you are saying is exactly what the emperor and the *patricius* and the whole senate is asking; they are bewailing together the fact that it was not done'. Agrippinus said, 'And how, if he were discovered, would he escape?' They replied, 'If he could be tracked down and discovered, not only would he be unharmed, but he would also be raised to the highest honors; he would recover his property and be showered with gifts—provided that he release the state from this fear right now!'

109. 'Know', Agrippinus said, 'that Agrippinus, falsely and iniquitously accused, would indeed have been able to flee to the enemy, but that if he is guilty, he wishes to be convicted and to be condemned, with the truth brought out into the open. Go now, and announce to the emperor and the *patricius* that I, Agrippinus, am here!' Dumbfounded, they embraced Agrippinus on the spot, warmly kissed him, and quickly dispatched a courier to the palace. When the emperor heard the news, he was greatly relieved. All the people rejoiced at this turn of events and, having changed their opinions and their expressions, their joy was all the better.

110. The senate, quickly called into session, concurred in turn. When contempt for Agrippinus had been dissipated, he

was immediately showered with great kindness and numerous
small gifts. Everyone testified in his favor without even being
asked to by a lawyer. He was presented to the emperor without
delay; he was publicly presented with the charges, and cleared
of all suspicion. He returned to Gaul and, when the servant of
Christ came to see him, he prostrated himself before him, gave
thanks, and related before everyone the events I have recounted
here.[45]

111. At that time the sweet scent of the servants of our
Lord Jesus Christ flourished everywhere[46] (or, rather, their
fragrance was met everywhere) because deceitful envy had not
laid hold of anyone, and consuming jealousy was lacerating no
one. Everyone, I say, was one[47] because everyone belonged to
the One.[48] If, therefore, one of the fathers[49] perceived that his

---

[45] As Mathisen notes, *Roman Aristocrats in Barbarian Gaul*, 84, Agrippinus
returned "'loaded with honors" to Gaul, where he later served as a partisan of
Ricimer: in 462, he was the agent of the Italian administration for the cession
of Narbonne to the Visigoths'.

[46] See 2 Cor 2:14–16.

[47] See Acts 4:32. The beginning of the 'Second Rule of the Fathers' (Griffe,
I.274) echoes Acts: 'Ut omnes unianimes, sicut scribtum est [sic], et unum
sentientes, invicem honorantes' ('So that all might be of one spirit, as it is
written, and thinking the same, honoring one another'), and later directly
refers to Acts: 'sicut scribtum est in Actus Apostolorum'. Both the *Lives*
of Lupicinus and Eugendus uphold 'the archetype of the truly Christian
community' (Markus, *End*, 165) that Acts 4 represents (see ¶ 170 n. 71
below). Cassian traced communal monasticism back to the primitive apostolic
community; see Conference 18.5 (SCh 3.15, and n. 1 there). See also Vogüé,
'Monachisme et église dans la pensée de Cassien', in *Théologie de la vie
monastique*, 213–40 (Lyon, 1961) 214–20 (ET in *Monastic Studies* 3 (1965).

[48] See Jn 17:22.

[49] See Martine, 380–81, ¶ 132 and n. 24 there. He translates 'one of the
two fathers' as Lupicinus and Minausius; Minausius, he notes, is listed in the
'Catalogue of the Abbots of Saint Eugendus' (Saint Eugendus was the later
name of Condat, before it became Saint-Claude). The author had said at the
beginning of his *Life of Lupicinus* (¶ 62) that he would 'speak about those things
that he did after the death of his holy predecessor'. See p. 46 n. 68 above.

brother at the helm[50] (that is, his fellow abbot) possessed and burned with any of the gifts that the Holy Spirit bestows, he raised his eyes and his hands to heaven as though he himself had received it, and promptly poured forth tears of joy to Christ.

THE APOSTOLIC WAY OF LIFE

112. If someone possessed from God the Creator greater eloquence in speech or showed greater facility in holy learning, Lupicinus' awareness[51] of a pure simplicity in the brother brought him more delight than his own diligence and sophisticated speech. As for the more humble brethren,[52] they wished with all respect to be instructed or taught by those whose 'mouth is opened'[53] (according to the Apostle), who are competent in telling more effectively and surely the mysteries of Christ.[54] Absolutely no one, in accordance with what was laid down by the apostles, said that anything was his own.[55] One person differed from another only in the ownership of his name, and not with respect to possessions or reputation.

113. So content with nakedness[56] were they, so fervently of one heart and mind in charity and faith, that if a brother, say, were ordered for some necessary reason to go somewhere out in the cold and if, say, he returned soaked by the winter rains, each monk eagerly, of his own volition, removed his drier and more comfortable clothes and took off his shoes and hastened to warm and comfort his brother's body rather than his own. Up to that time no brother, sent out of the monastery by the abbot for

---

[50] Latin *gubernaculum*, figuratively, his 'fellow governor'; in ¶ 175 our author uses the metaphor of the helmsman (*gubernator*) piloting his ship.

[51] Latin *conscientia*.

[52] Latin *simpliciores*.

[53] There is a play on words here. 'Mouth is opened' translates *adapertio oris*, which is being contrasted with 'sophisticated speech' above, *sophistici oris*.

[54] See Eph 6:19; Col 4:3.

[55] See Acts 4:32.

[56] Latin *nuditate*; perhaps 'privation', but one recalls Saint Jerome's famous exhortation: 'Nudum Christum sequere nudus'. ('Follow, naked, the naked Christ'.)

some reason or other (and it provokes shame to refer to this or speak about it now that the monastic ordinances are everywhere thwarted), had himself, a creature of two legs endowed with reason, conveyed by a horse, a creature with four legs. Rather, each person was satisfied with the support of a walking stick, just as he made do with the coarse and substantial wheat bread of the monastery.

114. And this is why the servants of the Lord, accompanied by grace that gave them their powers, frequently accomplished gifts of healing and other wonders; each monk, however, would leave the scene of the wonders before his face or name could be known by anyone.[57] Thus the monks would teach their admirers that they had to seek out the fountain and source of God's gifts. There they hastened, as soon as possible, once their missions had been completed and fulfilled in love and with burning faith, without receiving any kind of monetary gift in return. They were afraid that if they set up market places for business in the temple of their hearts, both the money-changers and their tables and the merchants selling pigeons would be severely whipped by the Lord.[58]

THE DEATH OF LUPICINUS

115. When the blessed father, having lived long, was struck by the twin forces of old age and illness, he chose first a father for Condadisco, the older monastery. Then, with his death now imminent, he appointed an abbot for the monastery of Lauconnus. Day by day he began to be troubled increasingly by illness until his arms and legs, long since withered, burned with constant and unceasing fever.

116. He was pevailed upon by the monks to take some water (he had abstained from water, as I said, for about eight years)[59] so that he could, as was the custom, rinse his mouth by swirling a

---

[57] See ¶ 43 for the example of Romanus' humility.
[58] See 1 Cor 3:16, and Mt 21:12 and parallels.
[59] See ¶ 66.

bit of water around with his tongue. His venerable sons, bound by chains of love, broke the vow that their father had made: by making a late but minimal change, they secretly mixed in a spoonful of honey in the little cup from which he was going to take a small amount of water. From where he was lying down he sat up with support and tasted what was offered with just the front of his lips; moved by his desire to keep the vow he had made, he immediately said, 'Enemy! Even at the end you try to corrupt my humility with the pleasure of perishable sweetness!' Then, lying down a little, he eagerly and quickly departed to Christ.

117. Drawing inspiration from his natural devotion (which I have spoken of),[60] his dear sons buried their father's corpse at the monastery of Lauconnus. Since his brother already honored the place of prayer at Balma,[61] and Saint Eugendus would one day honor Condadisco,[62] Lupicinus would for the time being furnish the monastery of Lauconnus with his powers, imbue it with his example, adorn it with his patronage, and aid it continuously with his prayers.

---

[60] See ¶ 24.
[61] See ¶¶ 60–61.
[62] See ¶ 178.

the life of the holy abbot eugendus

INTRODUCTION

118. Insofar as I have, with the Lord's help, fulfilled part of my debt in order to satisfy your fervent desires, blessed brothers, my mind is now partly at ease. Before my own conscience and the judgment of others, however, I am anxious about carrying out those things that you have enjoined upon me (undertaken not by ignorant presumption but, as you know, through monastic obedience). Human weakness, while delighting in a chant or in music, and while admiring lovely oratory with its appropriate utilization of vocabulary and verb tenses, is inclined toward judgment; may the Divinity, then, who favors my undertaking, see to it that my simple and unadorned style is not trampled upon by the boasting of arrogant judges with their windy verbiage.

119. Moreover, as I have already said, I have dedicated these little works especially to you, whom I know to be the disciples not of orators but of fishermen.[1] You look for 'the kingdom of God not in philosophic language but in virtue',[2] and prefer to beseech the Lord through a pure and continuous observance rather than through a foolish and perishable eloquence. May this, then, bring to a close the introduction of my report as I narrate the life of this most blessed man.

---

[1] For this phrase, see Sulpicius Severus, *Life of Martin*, Dedication 4: oratoribus . . . piscatoribus (Martine, 367 n. 7); for an english translation, see Noble and Head, 4.

[2] See 1 Cor 4:20 (Vulgate), which, however, lacks 'philosophic' (*philosophia*). See also 1 Cor 2:1–5.

EUGENDUS' ORIGINS

120. The holy servant of Christ, Eugendus, in the ascetic life[3] a disciple of the blessed fathers Romanus and Lupicinus, was also by province of birth their countryman and fellow citizen. Indeed, he was born not far from a village that, on account of the fame and the mighty stockade of its temple (a shrine for the most superstitious of practices),[4] the pagans had long ago named, in the gallic language, 'Isarnodorum', which means 'Iron Gate'.[5] In that place today, where the shrines lie partially in ruins, the roofs of the heavenly kingdom consecrated to the worshipers of Christ[6] shine out.[7] There the father of a most holy son, by an episcopal decision and with the witness of the people,[8] was a priest in the high office of the presbyterate.[9]

---

[3] Latin *in religione*. In ¶ 121 'two monks' translates *duobus religiosis viris*, 'two religious', a term still used for persons under religious vows.

[4] On this temple, see Albert Grenier, 'Le Temple d'Izernore', *Manuel d'archéologie gallo-romaine* 31(Paris: Picard, 1931- 60) 403–6.

[5] The modern town of Izernore, some thirty kilometers (nineteen miles) southwest of Saint-Claude, forty-five kilometers (twenty-eight miles) by car. See the map. Martine (pp. 367–8) questions our author's etymology of the town's name; rather than being named after the temple, he suggests that Isarnodorum comes from two celtic words, the first a proper name (*Isarnos*), and the second (*duros* or *durum*) signifying 'marketplace' or, perhaps, 'fortress'.

[6] Latin *Christicolis*: either 'Christians' or 'monks'.

[7] Today one can still see the ruins of the temple, which was dedicated to Mercury. See Grenier, 3.1: 403–406, for a description. On pre-christian religion in Gaul, see J. J. Hatt, 'Essai sur l'évolution de la religion gauloise', *Revue des études anciennes* 67 (1965) 80–125. Christianity's defeat of paganism, symbolized concretely by the building of christian sanctuaries over the ruins of pagan shrines, is an important theme in fifth-century christian writing. Saint Martin 'immediately built a church or a monastery in every place where he destroyed a pagan shrine' (Sulpicius Severus, *Life of Martin* 13 [Noble and Head, 16]). Paganism, however, strong in the countryside, persisted 'until the late eighth and early ninth centuries', 'when the Carolingian Church made a serious attempt to bring Christianity to the rural population' (James, *The Origins of France*, 98). See James, 93–101, and Wallace-Hadrill, *The Frankish Church*, 17–36. Wallace-Hadrill, 27, terms the conversion of pagans to Christianity 'a lengthy business'.

[8] Martine notes (p. 369, n. 2) that this *testimonium* of the people was a gallic rite.

[9] Priests at this time could be married.

EUGENDUS' VISION

121. The blessed child grew, impelled almost from the cradle by a prosperous happiness and light, as divine power, I believe, foretold. One night, so that the venerable father and his holy offspring might not remain uncertain about the child's disposition and progress toward future blessedness, in a vision the holy child was carried away by two monks. He was made to stand on the far side of the porch of his father's house so that he could, by gazing intently, see the eastern region of the sky and the stars there, as once the patriarch Abraham gazed upon his numerous progeny. He too was already told, figuratively, 'So shall your descendants be'.[10]

122. A little later first one[11] appeared on this side, then another from that side, and another from this side, until the growing multitude became innumerable; they surrounded the blessed child and the holy fathers (doubtless Romanus and Lupicinus, who had led him away in the Spirit from the mire of his father's house) just as an enormous swarm of bees crowds together, like a bunch of grapes, to make honey.

123. And suddenly, from the direction where he was gazing, Eugendus saw something like a vast doorway thrown open in the heavenly heights. On a gentle slope leading down to him from the summit of heaven, in the form of an inclining stairway of sloping crystal and accompanied by light, he saw angelic choirs, effulgent and snowy white, dancing and praising Christ, coming toward him and his companions. In spite of the ever-growing congregation in that place, not one of them, thoroughly terrified with awe of the Divinity, uttered a word or moved a muscle. Slowly and carefully the angelic multitude mixed in with the mortals; the angels, singing harmoniously together, gathered and joined the earthly beings to themselves

---

[10] See Gn 15:5: God brought Abram 'outside and said, "Look toward heaven and count the stars, if you are able to count them." Then he said to him, "So shall your descendants be." '

[11] Latin *unus*; the author, with admirable style, by not immediately identifying who these beings are, creates suspense in his readers.

and then ascended as they had come, returning to the holy places of heaven.[12]

124. The holy child understood only this one thing amidst the singing of the songs. He learned it about a year later, after he had entered the monastery, when it was recited from the Gospels; this, then, sung antiphonally (I remember it well because he himself deigned to repeat it for me), the angelic multitude sang together, their voices alternating: 'I am the way, the life, and the truth'.[13] The huge multitude then withdrew; the starry spaces, after Eugendus contemplated them a long time, closed up too; and the child, seeing himself alone in that place, arose with a start from his sleep. Struck with fear by what he had seen, he immediately told his father what had happened. The holy priest knew right away to what, above all, his most holy offspring ought to be consecrated.

EUGENDUS IS GIVEN TO ROMANUS AND LUPICINUS

125. Soon, therefore, his father instructed him in the basics of reading and writing and, after a year, he was offered by his father to Saint Romanus, just as Samuel had once been—not to keep watch in a figurative temple, but rather to become a temple of Christ.[14] In him a twofold abundance of graces belonging to the blessed abbots who had spiritually led him away from his earthly dwelling flowed together; the next generation wavered in its judgement, uncertain whether in Eugendus they saw Lupicinus or Romanus.

EUGENDUS' WAY OF LIFE

126. While Romanus and Lupicinus often left the monastery, going here and there on acts of mercy, Eugendus, after he

---

[12] See Gn 28:12, the story of Jacob's ladder, though the description here is much fuller, reminiscent of details from Revelation.

[13] Latin: *Ego sum Via et Vita et Veritas* (Jn 14:6: 'I am the way, the truth, and the life'). Martine notes (p. 373, n. 2) that the author, by reversing the order of *Veritas* and *Vita*, embellishes both the rhythm and the alliteratation—an interesting liberty taken by our author.

[14] See 1 Sm 3:3. RB 59 allows the offering of children to the monastery.

entered the monastery, never took a step outside, from the time he was seven years old to the day he died, when he was over sixty. After completing and fulfilling all the things enjoined upon him by the prior[15] or the abbot, he gave himself so fully to *lectio*, spending all his time at it day and night, that in addition to being learned in Latin works, he was also fluent in Greek.[16]

127. With regard to clothing, he never used two tunics;[17] moreover, he never changed, for any reason, the one he had until it was worn out with many years' use. The same conditions applied to his cowl also. He had a bed made of straw; the straw, rarely shaken, was compressed by a rough ticking. He slept on this, with an animal skin as a covering.[18] During the summer months he used a *caracalla*[19] and an old scapular made of goats' hair which a man conspicuous for his sanctity, Abbot Leunianus of Vienne, had given him as pledge of his love.[20]

A DIGRESSION ABOUT ABBOT LEUNIANUS

128. This holy man had once, when the barbarians poured over Gaul, been abducted from Pannonia and taken away captive in chains.[21] He lived enclosed in his own cell for a long

---

[15] Either 'prior' as in RB or 'dean' as in the Rule of the Master.

[16] See Introduction, p. 51, n. 82.

[17] See Lk 9:3, where Jesus commands his disciples: 'Take nothing for your journey, no staff, nor bag, nor bread, nor money—not even an extra tunic'. This literal understanding with regard to clothing goes back to early desert monasticism.

[18] Saint Martin was more abstemious: 'it was his habit to lie on the bare earth with nothing but a piece of sackcloth over him' (Sulpicius Severus, Epistle 1; Hoare, 50).

[19] Martine, 376, n. 1, says that a *caracalla* was 'a kind of shirt in use among the Gauls', while Lewis and Short, *A Latin Dictionary* (Oxford: Clarendon, 1879), 290B, defines the celtic word as 'a long tunic or great-coat, with a hood, worn by the Gauls, and made of different materials'. From this tunic the emperor Antoninus Caracalla (211–17) took his nickname.

[20] Martine observes that the *Life of the Jura Fathers* is one of the few sources with information about Abbot Leunianus, who resided in Autun and Vienne. In the church museum of Saint Peter in Vienne one can still see Leunianus' sarcophagus, whose epitaph is drawn from the *Life of Eugendus*.

[21] Perhaps a reference to the invasion and occupation of Pannonia by the Huns. Pannonia was a former Roman province between the Danube and

time, not only in Vienne but also in Autun, shut in so long—
for more than forty years—in one city or the other that no
one, after his first sequestration, recognized him by his face or
body, only by the way he talked. He directed a small number
of monks next to his cell; far away in the city he directed and
nourished with admirable guidance more than sixty cloistered
female monastics; the greatest of them he sent on to heaven
ahead of him, but he did not spiritually abandon the great
women who survived him. But I must return to my subject.

EUGENDUS' WAY OF LIFE (CONTINUED)

129. Blessed Eugendus wore sturdy country shoes in the
manner of the ancient fathers; his legs were wrapped with
leggings and his feet with *fasciola*. For the offices of nocturnes
and matins,[22] he never put anything on his bare feet, either
during freezing cold or when there was a great deal of snow,
except wooden clogs worn in the gallic manner; with great
frequency he walked in the snow a long way in these shoes, in
the early morning hours, to the cemetery where the brothers
were buried, in order to pray.

130. No one ever saw him leave either the daytime or night-
time gathering[23] before it was finished. Just as he entered the
oratory at night a long time before the others in order to
pray privately and at length, so after everyone had left he was
spiritually nourished no less by a long prayer of set words that
he recited lying down on a bench. He would leave there at
whatever hour it was and approach the brothers with a glad and
joyful face, just as other men, once their ambitions have been
satisfied, are accustomed to showing faces awash with laughter
and good cheer.

131. At all times he took refreshment only once a day. During
the summer it was at noon with the other monks when he

Sava rivers, encompassing modern western Hungary and Croatia. It was also
the homeland of Saint Martin.

[22] Latin *nocturnis matutinisque*.

[23] Latin *synaxi*. See p. 127, n. 117 and p. 134, n. 6.

was tired, while at other times he restricted himself to eating with those who were having a second meal in the evening; however, he never tasted anything at the table except what was set before all the brothers. But let us return to the beginning of his administration of the monastery.

EUGENDUS ASSUMES AUTHORITY AT CONDADISCO

132. When, therefore, that father[24] whom blessed Romanus and Lupicinus had appointed as their successor at the monastery of Condadisco was beaten down, not only by his labors and concerns at the monastery, but also by troubling physical infirmities, he summoned the brothers to him and divided his office and cares with Saint Eugendus in such a way that he in no way reduced or diminished his superior paternal authority.

That same abbot attempted to tie down the above-mentioned and holy Eugendus more tightly with the dignity of the priesthood along with the burdens of administration.

EUGENDUS REFUSES ORDINATION; HE SPEAKS ABOUT HUMILITY

133. Not only did Eugendus very frequently and very piously oppose the will of the abbot in this matter,[25] but he also, when approaching the holy high priests[26] who had come together there to pray, circumspectly and deliberately fled away in deference to the honor of their office. Moreover, he often told me in private that it is much more beneficial for an abbot, because of the ambition of the young, to preside over the brothers free

---

[24] Martine, 381 n. 4, says that the Catalogue of the abbots of Saint-Oyend gives the name of this person as Minausius; see also Martine, 33. See ¶¶ 111 and 135, and above, p. 152, n. 49.

[25] Refusal of ordination by monks is a common theme in early desert monasticism: Pachomius fled ordination. For Pachomius and other examples, see Tim Vivian, *Histories of the Monks of Upper Egypt and the Life of Onnophrius* (Kalamazoo: Cistercian, 1993) 111 n. 53. Closer to Eugendus' time, Martin refused ordination as a deacon; see Sulpicius Severus, *Life of Martin* 5. RB 60 and 62 assume that priests will be part of the monastery.

[26] Latin *sacrosanctos pontifices*.

of the office of the priesthood, and not to be tied down by that dignity for which it is scarcely fitting for those who have renounced the world and who live in seclusion to strive.

134. 'We have known', he used to insist, in addition to the reason we have just adduced, 'many fathers who, having exercised to perfection their profession of humility, have grown deeply and secretly proud in their office and have placed themselves above the brothers whom it would have been more fitting to go before as an example of humility'. Therefore, the saint of God took on (as Father Lupicinus had done) the labor imposed on him of being a replacement and partner without the title of priest. With great peace of mind he trusted in the fact that the foresight and care of his father were guaranteed.

But soon he was shaken by a very clear revelation, so that he did not hesitate to take complete control, and had no lack of clarity with regard to anything.

EUGENDUS' VISION OF DARKNESS AND LIGHT

135. The following night he was suddenly seized by a vision: both blessed abbots, Romanus and Lupicinus, were present, as had happened in the beginning. Now, however, the vision took place in a sacristy of the oratory, to the right of the church. He also saw brothers among them, old men who had survived Romanus and Lupicinus, carrying candles and lighted lamps. After he was blessed and given the kiss of peace by the holy fathers, he immediately saw that blessed abbot who was to be his predecessor[27] brought in, and he saw a white pallium set with purple bands fall the length of his back and over his shoulders.

136. Blessed Romanus loosened the cincture of that holy man and immediately fastened it around the loins of Eugendus. Then, pulling off the pallium which, as I have said, he was wearing over his other clothing, and in like manner placing it over the shoulders of Eugendus, he said, 'Know that these things are being consigned to you immediately, for a time'.

---

[27] See n. 24 above.

Holding tightly with his fingers the dalmatic of the above-mentioned predecessor, he said, 'Know also that this dalmatic is to be assigned to you because you have made good use of what you have already received'. Soon, while the brothers were standing there with their candles, they all, after one had begun to do so, immediately dashed the bright and comforting lights against the wall, snuffing and extinguishing them.

137. The astonished saint, imprisoned by the confining darkness, waited to see what would happen next. Then a voice was heard: 'Eugendus', it said, 'do not sadden yourself because of these deceptive lights, material and present only for the moment. Turn your gaze to the east of this room and there you will see, without human assistance, a light that will be given to you by God'. And Eugendus, immediately turning to look there, saw, as the dawn slowly increased its light, a ray of daylight come streaming toward him. Coming to himself, he jumped from his bed, overjoyed. That vision came true without delay.

EUGENDUS BECOMES ABBOT; HIS ENEMIES

138. His predecessor very soon journeyed on to Christ; Eugendus, whether he wanted it or not, was unable to evade the administration of the monastery that had been pledged to him.[28] However those who in the vision had taken away the solace and comfort of the light that they had offered him, suffering from some sort of human evil and enflamed with jealous envy, swelled up with burning hatred for the blessed man. At one time despising him in their hearts, at another time even deserting the monastery and their monastic vocation, they allowed monks and lay persons to subject the holy abbot Eugendus to contempt as a novice and an ignoramus.[29]

---

[28] Latin *administratione . . subarratam. Subarr(b)are* can mean 'to pledge or offer as a pledge', 'to pledge oneself'. It can also mean 'to espouse', or 'take to wife'; so Eugendus is, in effect, pledged or betrothed to the monastery, and it to him.

[29] Our author is vague here. It seems that there was a rebellion over the abbatial succession. Martine suggests, 387, n. 2, that the complaints against

DIVINE COMPASSION WATCHES OVER EUGENDUS

139. But Divine Compassion,[30] watching over its servant, did not allow Eugendus to be tormented by prolonged difficulties. Immediately it extended to him, with an overflowing abundance of signs, the power and strength of its right hand, giving and demonstrating through its servant so many miracles and gifts of healing that the greatest and most powerful people of the time frequently asked to be protected and blessed by his letters. They did not believe that they could make atonement and receive divine clemency unless they had first obtained, either in person or through a letter, the special favor or intercessions of the friend of Christ.

140. The bishops, too, and the very reverend priests showed themselves quite pleased if they managed to see him in the flesh or had a friendly letter addressed to them. Even those false brothers who, elegantly clothed in their haughty pride, had left him the day before were viewed by the laity as unfortunate and reprobate unless, putting aside their jealous poison, they returned as quickly as possible to the holy servant of Christ.

EUGENDUS HEALS A WOMAN AND DEFEATS THE DEVIL

141. While the reports of these sweet and fragrant events were being carried about, a certain young woman (not among the lowest of people according to worldly standards),[31] who lived on the outskirts of the parish of Secundiacum,[32] was seized

---

Eugendus may have been two-fold: (1) he was too young, perhaps less than forty years old at this time; (2) Minausius himself designated his successor (¶ 132) rather than having him chosen by the entire community.

[30] Latin *divinae pietatis*. *Pietas* has a wide range of meanings, and is much richer than 'piety': goodness, kindness, pity, mercy, and compassion are some of the meanings here.

[31] This parenthetical phrase about the girl's origins is very similar to one in the *Life of Martin* 2.1; Fontaine, ed., 1.254. There the description refers to Martin's family.

[32] An unidentified site; see Martine, 390 n. 2. 'Parish', as noted before (¶ 43, n. 105), designates a civil administrative territory, not an ecclesiastical precinct.

by a horrible demon; not only was she locked away, but she was even restrained by iron chains. As is the custom, a number of people tied written formulas of exorcism around her neck, as she lay all tied up, in order to heal her.[33] She, however, through the unclean spirit, calumniated (which is something to be mourned) the persons—unknown to her—who had written the formulas of exorcism by giving their names and their vices; moreover, she claimed to have long possessed, through this or that sin, those who had written, even if indications of sin had been hidden from human sight. Then one of those present asked the demonic force[34] itself:

142. 'You unclean thing, why do you try to frighten us with the vices of others—or, more accurately, with your own vices? Truly, in the name of Christ, if I am able I will bind around your neck the written exorcisms not only of those whom you derogate, but of all the saints. You will be overwhelmed by a multitude of masters if you refuse to listen, but instead despise these saints who are here, even though they are few'.

'You', said the Devil, 'if you so please, may lay on me a cartload of inscribed alexandrian papyri; you will, however, never be able to drive me out of this vessel I have gained possession of until you bring to me the order of one person: Eugendus, the monk from the Jura mountains'.

143. Those nearby immediately seized what was said and ran with absolute faith to the blessed man. Throwing themselves at

---

[33] These amulets may well have been holdovers from paganism; see Markus, 'From Caesarius to Boniface', 157. For an example of the persistence of pagan practices and their 'relocation' into Christian rites in late antique Europe (in this case, animal sacrifice), see Dennis Trout, 'Christianizing the Nolan Countryside: Animal Sacrifice at the Tomb of Saint Felix', *Journal of Early Christian Studies* 3:3 (Fall 1995) 281–98. More generally, see Claire E. Stancliffe, 'From Town to Country: The Christianisation of the Touraine 370–600', in D. Baker, ed., *The Church in Town and Countryside* (Oxford: Basil Blackwell, 1979).

[34] Latin *inergima*, which transliterates Greek *enérgêma*, an 'action, activity, or operation', sometimes demonic or of the Devil; see G. W. H. Lampe, *A Patristic Greek Lexicon* (Oxford: Clarendon, 1961) 473B.

his feet, they narrated what had happened and testified that they would not go back unless he, once entreated, granted Christ's mercy to the oppressed girl. Won over by either their argument or their prayers, the father wrote a brief letter accompanied by lengthy prayer, as Gregory the Great once did with regard to Apollo;[35] writing the letter and sealing it, the father sent the following to the filthy creature:

144. 'I, Eugendus, servant of Christ Jesus, in the name of our Lord Jesus Christ, of the Father, and of the Spirit of our God,[36] admonish you with this writing:[37] Spirit of gluttony and wrath and fornication and carnal love, demon of the moon and madness,[38] demon of Diana, of midday, of the day and the night, spirit unclean in everything, depart from the human being who has this writing on her person. Through him, the true Son of the living God, I abjure you: Depart quickly, and see that you do not enter into her again! Amen. Alleluia'. Praying and folding the letter, he gave it to the suppliants to deliver. What more is there to say? They had not yet gone half way on their journey when— look!—that gallows-bird, grinding his teeth and moaning, left the possessed girl before those returning had even stepped across the threshold of the house.

A WOMAN IS HEALED THROUGH EUGENDUS

145. From almost that very moment, the name and reputation of the blessed man shone far and wide, with the result that he who was already considered a saint by the local inhabitants also came to be honored by the inhabitants of far-off lands for his power and his truly apostolic character.[39]

---

[35] In one of his additions to his translation of Eusebius' *Ecclesiastical History*, Rufinus tells the story of Gregory Thaumaturgus (not Gregory the Great) spending the night in a temple of Apollo and writing a letter to the god; see Martine, 393 n. 2.

[36] See 1 Cor 6:11.

[37] Latin: *scripturam*.

[38] Latin: *lunatice*.

[39] This sentence is taken almost verbatim from the *Life of Martin* 7.7 (Noble and Head, 11; Fontaine, 1:268): 'The immense renown of this man of bless-

Syagria, formerly mother of a family, and now through her almsgiving mother of churches and monasteries, was beset with a serious illness, and the doctors considered her prognosis desperate.[40] By chance she had received from the blessed man a letter which had been delivered to her; she ordered it to be taken from her cupboard so that she could touch it and kiss it as though it were the right hand of the blessed man.

146. Taking the letter, she held it to her eyes with a prayer, soaking it with a great many fallen tears; then she put the letter in her mouth for a while, gripping it with her teeth while praying; soon she recovered her health and stood up.[41] With what joy and wonder, with what wonderful exultation, what relief did they rejoice, not only she and her household, but even the great city of Lyon!

AS A RESULT OF EUGENDUS' FAME,
THE SICK FLOCK TO THE MONASTERY

147. As the renown and the life of the man grew thanks to the spreading fame of his powers, such a large crowd of unfortunate people began to flock to the monastery in groups that the multitude of secular persons (or, rather, those afflicted) seemed almost more numerous than the companies of monks. In the meantime, while some received the prayed-for blessings at the monastery right away, others did so after two or three days, while for a certain number it took months: the holy man of God, laying his hands on them in a timely manner in order to heal them, removed their weariness and miseries.

148. To those who came as suppliants and who were healthy, he would give, along with a quantity of the holy oil mentioned above, written injunctions against spirits and maladies for them to take with them and bind on those afflicted; they would bear

---

ings dates from this time. He was already regarded by everybody as a saint; now he was looked upon as a man of power and in very truth an apostle'.

[40] Syagria was a philanthropist who lived in Lyon at the end of the fifth century.

[41] See *Life of Martin* 19 for another example of a healing letter.

these notes (which worked in cooperation with faith) to far-flung provinces so that people there might obtain the same remedy of healing as those who had presented themselves to him in person at the monastery. Nor was the blessed father the only one in the community who had the possession of the charismatic gifts of good works, but priests too, and many brothers there; so that jealous desires might cease, the man of God would delegate to them this ministry of healing rather than keep it for himself.

149. Eugendus saw to it in every way possible that each person in the monastery would do the functions or tasks for which he saw he was best suited by the gift of the Holy Spirit. Thus he would assign to a quiet and gentle brother a duty or position where the goodness of his gentle and patient nature would in no way be stained by another's agitation. On the other hand, he would not allow those who perhaps were blemished with the mark of haughtiness or vanity to live by themselves for fear that they would, inflated by their opinionated and rank self-importance, sink even lower and, despite being frequently and publicly rebuked, not recognize their faults and vices.

150. Meanwhile, if he learned with reason that certain brothers, partaking by nature of human frailty, were being eaten up by a consuming sadness, he would come to them spiritually when they were not expecting him, amiable and joyous on purpose, and he would rekindle their hearts with speech so sweet and holy that, once the contagion of pernicious sadness had been wiped away, the unremitting irritant was healed as though by the anointing of a saving oil. To be sure, though, he always exhibited a harsher and more severe nature towards the slackers and the more dissolute monks.

151. Although the bishops often attempted to force priestly duties on him, out of humility he preferred not to become

entangled with the priesthood. As a result, since priests perform the ministry of the saving sacrifice, Eugendus allowed them to keep their consciences pure by having them always remain apart. Thus if he got perhaps a little too gruff over some offense (as often happened), the priests, because they did not know about the culprit and his fault, could distribute the body of the Lord from the altar without knowledge of, or participating in, the other's offense. Thus they did not punish their consciences by taking part in a sin, nor did they seem, perhaps, by granting sacraments to the offender, to have lessened for him the severity of the father's punishment before he had made amendment.

EUGENDUS, PURE IN SPIRIT, CONVERSES WITH THE SAINTS

152. This man was—or rather is—a most blessed person close to Christ. Out of his mouth, as God is my witness, never came an insult; the deadly contagion that comes from a slanderous mouth never polluted his ears. He hated this vice—one should say rather 'shameful crime'—as much as one hates a deadly serpent: not only does one fear its venom; one also avoids even encountering the snake or catching a glimpse of it. His spirit,[42] freed from vice and sin, was so pure that he was able to see and hold conversations with even the most blessed apostles of Christ, Peter and Paul, with Saint Andrew, and in like manner with that apostolic and illustrious man, Bishop Martin.[43]

153. Once, in fact, before Eugendus became encumbered with the burden of ruling the community, on a summer's day he was outside the monastery, resting beneath his favorite tree beside the road that crosses over the mountains and runs to Geneva. Suddenly three men approached him in his sleep, and presented themselves to him. After praying together and giving one another the kiss of peace, Eugendus, having contemplated with astonishment their strange appearance and dress, asked

---

[42] Latin *mens*.

[43] Martin himself 'actually saw angels very often, even to the extent of engaging in continuous conversation with them' (Sulpicius Severus, *Life of Martin* 21 [Noble and Head, 22]).

who these venerable men were from whom he had merited a visit as a blessing.

154. Then one of them said, 'I am Peter; as for this person, he is my brother Andrew, and that is our brother[44] Paul'. Eugendus, immediately prostrating himself in spirit at their feet, says, 'How is it, my lords, that I see you in these rural woodlands— you whose bodies, we read, are buried in the great cities of Rome and Patras after your holy martyrdoms?' 'It is true', they reply, 'we are indeed in those places, as you assert, but we have come now to dwell here also'. With these words his vision came to an end, along with his sleep.

155. After rubbing his eyes and driving the heaviness of sleep from his face, Eugendus spied in the distance two brothers who had left the monastery about two years ago. They were approaching him by the same road on which he had seen the holy apostles approach in the vision. He leaped up immediately to meet them, and, after greeting them in the customary way,[45] asked from where these dear brothers were returning to the monastery after such a long absence. They replied, 'Among other things, we went as far as the city of Rome; having obtained the protection of the saints, we are returning under the intercession of three martyrs—late, it is true, but reliably. We are returning to the fold, our ancient home, with relics that will enrich us: the remains of our lords the apostles Peter and Paul and Andrew'.[46]

156. While the two men remained there, as is the custom, Saint Eugendus ran to the monastery; he himself, who just a little earlier had been the one to behold them in a vision, became for the father [Minausius] and the brothers the news bearer of the saints' coming. The monks immediately rushed

---

[44] *Frater*, rather than *germanus*, like Andrew.

[45] That is, after prayer and the kiss of peace; see ¶ 153. RB 53.4–5 assumes this custom: the superior and guest are 'first of all . . . to pray together and thus be united in peace, but prayer must always precede the kiss of peace because of the delusions of the devil'.

[46] The present-day church in Saint-Claude is named Saint Peter's.

to meet them and, once they had greeted the two brothers and fervently kissed the reliquaries, the relics were displayed with joyful celebration and rejoicing and singing of psalms. The relics were then placed under the altar where now they, whose praises and good works can not be restricted to any one place, grant the protection of their unwearying power to those who pray.[47]

SAINT MARTIN VISITS EUGENDUS IN A VISION

157. Let me not shrink from continuing our account a little longer in order to speak of the holy and blessed Martin, whose face and appearance Eugendus was accustomed to describe for me in private along with the saints of whom I have spoken above. Once the monks feared the terrible incursions of the Alemanni[48] in their very neighborhood. (These men were accustomed to attacking unsuspecting travelers not in a frontal assault but by springing on them like wild animals. The monks wished to avoid death, and even the apprehension of death, for repeated onslaughts of fear kill a person as many times as he is afraid.) Therefore they decided to look for salt for cooking as far away as the shores of the Mediterranean rather than locally in the vicinity of the Herians.[49]

---

[47] Relics, and the cultus surrounding them, became very important in Gaul in the fifth century; see Wallace-Hadrill, *The Frankish Church*, 9, and Brown, 236. However, the main ingredients of the cultus—local saints, martyrs, and how relics were controlled by bishops—are missing from the *Life*; see Wallace-Hadrill, 11–12, and Brown, 240.

[48] In the 480s the Alemanni (or Alamanni) were pushed out of *Sequania* by the Burgundians; this episode would have taken place then at the beginning of Eugendus' abbacy. See Martine, 407 n. 3.

[49] Salt was difficult to obtain before modern times, and often had to be sought far afield. Our author seems to have his details right: Aeriensium ('the vicinity of the Herians') was located some 60 kilometers (37 miles) north of Saint-Claude, in the region now known as 'Salins', an ancient source of salt. The present town is called Salins-les-Bains. Nearby is the town of Pont-d'Hiry, whose name derives from latin *Aeriensium*. Salt was an important commodity in southern Gaul; see Klingshirn, *Caesarius of Arles*, 35.

158. The entire enterprise was undertaken with the advice and encouragement of the blessed man. After two months had passed, when the brothers who had been sent for salt showed no sign of returning, the brothers at the monastery put the blame on the holy one because others had already returned safe and sound from the nearby region of the Herians which they had feared. They said, 'This is not exile that the father, through his encouragement, has inflicted on the brothers who were sent; it is more like being sent to die in a strange country'. Eugendus, because he had removed these men from any possibility of danger, was uncertain whether he was at fault; nevertheless, afraid of unjustified reproach, he prayed every day and every night for Christ's mercy to keep them safe.

159. When, worn out from weeping, he had fallen asleep on his bed, he was suddenly surrounded on his pallet by so much brightness that he saw himself bathed in light brighter than if he were being shone upon by the rays of the clearest sun.[50] Right there, next to his bed, stood blessed Martin who greeted him and asked him if he was well. Eugendus answered, 'I would be doing well if I were not uncertain about the well-being of the brothers I am accused of sending into exile'.

160. And Martin replied, 'Do you not remember that when they left, you commended them in prayer particularly to me, that is, to your beloved Martin? Look! In the name of Christ I am returning to you safe and sound those whom you commended healthy to me in prayer. This very night, indeed, they are spending the night in the parish of Poncin;[51] tomorrow, one of them will come right here to stay and will drive away everyone's apprehensions'. The man of Christ[52] arose and, as though he could see the aforesaid brothers and point them out to the whole community, predicted the day and hour of

---

[50] See ¶ 137.
[51] The town of Poncin is some fifty kilometers (thirty-one miles) southwest of Saint-Claude, seventy kilometers (forty-three miles) by road. For the meaning of 'parish', see n. 32 above.
[52] Latin *Christi homo.*

their arrival.[53] Just as the holy one of God had announced, they returned at once.

A MIRACLE IN THE FLAMES

161. What I will now relate, as I continue, no one will doubt ought to be joined to the miracles of blessed Martin; moreover, I do not know who would be ignorant or stupid enough not to understand that miraculous gifts are especially evident in those places where the gifts of the virtues more readily occur because people are united in their faith. For example, one night the Lord permitted even the aforementioned Saint Martin to be put to the test by fire in the sacristy, but Martin was proved worthy.[54] The same thing also happened at Condadisco where the monastery once went up in flames, but the holy oil of Martin was touched not at all by the devouring flames of fire.

162. Blessed Eugendus bore even this calamity with such patience and calmness of spirit that divine providence soon gave back to him twice as much as he had lost,[55] and not just in food and clothing; the tabernacles[56] themselves were restored, now much more useful and more in harmony with the way they were originally used.

So then, one day toward evening, the whole monastery, as I have said, went up in flames. The monastery had been constructed long ago of wood, with cells joined together by

---

[53] For Antony's similar abilities, see *Life of Antony* 6.21–2.

[54] See Sulpicius Severus, Epistle 1 (Hoare, 50–1). Sulpicius emphasizes in his story the efficacy of prayer and the Devil's attempts to stop it. Martin comes to understand that 'safety lay, not in flight, but in the Lord'.

[55] See Job 42:10: 'and the Lord gave Job twice as much as he had before'.

[56] Latin *tabernacula*, which can mean 'tent' or 'hut'; but the word retains its biblical sense in both Latin and English; see 1 Kings 2:28 and Acts 7:44 ('Tabernaculum testimonii fuit cum patris nostris in deserto': 'Our ancestors had the tent of testimony in the wilderness'). Rufinus of Aquileia, in his additions to the latin translation of the *Historia Monachorum*, says that the monks of Nitria, some three thousand of them, lived in about fifty *tabernacula* or dwellings. See Joseph Patrich, *Sabas, Leader of Palestinian Monasticism* (Washington, D.C.: Dumbarton Oaks, 1995) 13.

wooden framework, and it was also nicely doubled in size with second–story rooms; as a result, it was suddenly reduced to ashes so that in the morning nothing of the structure remained, and the fire itself, quickened by its dry provender, was also almost entirely extinguished.

163. While the brothers, each one having a hoe or an ax (iron implements that were the only things the fire was unable to consume), sifted the ashes looking for their things, the holy priest Antidiolus[57] saw in front of him a little bottle with the oil of blessed Martin. This used to hang at the head of his bed to ensure health and well-being.[58] The cap was on and the bottle was full, just as it had been. After the devastating fire and after the second-floor rooms came crashing down in flaming ruins, it had remained thus, whole and in place, among the glowing ashes and smoking remains of the fire, just as we read that the three youths, refreshed by dew, covered themselves in glory in the persian furnace.[59]

164. That little bottle, with the same oil, is preserved right up to this day in that very monastery as a testimony to its miraculous powers. Thus the fiery misfortune, I believe, was not allowed more power over holy Eugendus than, as I have said, when it retreated from blessed Martin. Consequently, we recall, the monks of Condadisco escaped thanks to the oil and power of Martin.[60]

---

[57] Martine points out (414–15, n. 1) that a certain Antidiolus succeeded Eugendus as abbot; according to the twelfth-century 'Chronique de Saint-Claude', he governed the monastery of Condadisco for thirteen years. Thus, Antidiolus was abbot when the *Life of the Jura Fathers* was written. Whether it is the same person is uncertain.

[58] Latin *salutis gratia*. *Salus*, in addition to 'health and well-being', also suggests 'salvation' and '(divine) deliverance', all of which meanings are apposite here.

[59] See Dn 3:49–50.

[60] The use of oil for healing has a rich tradition. In the *Life of Martin* 16 (Noble and Head, 18–19), Martin heals a sick girl by pouring oil in her mouth; Sulpicius tells essentially the same story in *Dialogues* 3.2 (Hoare, trans., 124). In *Historia Monachorum* 1.12, John of Lycopolis 'did not perform cures publicly. More often he gave oil to the afflicted and healed them in that way'. (Russell, trans., 53). In chap. 21.17 Macarius heals a young girl by rubbing

EUGENDUS PREDICTS THE DEATH OF A BROTHER

165. In addition to these few things that I have touched upon as testimony to his virtues and miraculous powers,[61] there exist such outstanding examples where his spirit, through a pure and divine illumination, foresaw things so clearly that, although he was in the body, it was thought that he already shone to a certain degree with supernal powers.[62] This was true to such an extent that one day he warned the venerable Valentinus, a deacon in that same monastery, saying to him privately, 'Without a doubt, dear brother, within about twenty days you will depart from this world for the rewards that have been prepared for you. Therefore, however much you have laid aside the bonds of sin, however prepared you are to go to the Lord, I nevertheless have this advice for you: Since you are near the conclusion of your life, enrich yourself, while there is still time, by making further progress in perfection so that you may be taken up from the altar of Christ, as I have seen, as a worthy and even more acceptable sacrifice.

166. 'I saw you this night, dressed in snow-white linen, as psalms were being sung, positioned by the holy fathers at the altar of this oratory. Therefore, although you are well aware of your merits and know the manner in which you will be taken up, I recommend nevertheless that in the meantime you add what you can possess there in perpetual happiness'. They ended their conversation with tears of joy and with prayer. About ten days later the deacon, seized by a light fever and afflicted little by little with an illness, completed the course of this present life.

EUGENDUS, LIKE SAINT ANTONY, POSSESSES DIVINE GIFTS

167. Moreover, whenever someone arrived at the monastery, Eugendus discerned (depending on whether the person gave

---

'her all over with oil' (Russell, 110). In the New Testament, see Mk 6:13 and Js 5:14. See also ¶ 148 above.

[61] Latin *meritorum virtutumque.*

[62] For Antony's similar powers, see *Life of Antony* 86.

off a fragrant smell or a fetid exhalation), the signs of that person's merits to such a degree that he could foresee right there on the spot which virtue or vice that person was subject to.[63] Also, he often predicted the arrival of brothers or of secular visitors seeking faith before the guest was in any way apparent to the brothers.[64] Although he was so abounding in great and extraordinary gifts, nevertheless he never judged himself to be better or more eminent than another, not even a little; rather, full of piety, he would weigh carefully not what he was for the moment, but how far he still was from being perfect, as though he were lower and more abject than everyone.

168. Illuminated undoubtedly by the One who dwells within, Eugendus possessed great joy, which showed in his face; just as no one ever saw him sad, in the same way no one observed him laughing. The deeds of blessed Antony and Martin and their way of life never slipped away from his spirit. 'Never', as is reported of Antony, 'did sudden anger snap his patience, nor did he receive glory from being humble'.[65] Never was he puffed up by praise or because he was considered blessed; never did blame break his spirit or cause him to be sad.

---

[63] Discernment of smells is an old monastic charism. In *Life of Antony* 63, Antony alone perceived 'a terrible and very acrid stench' on a boat. Others on the boat said that the stink came from the cargo of dried fish, but Antony 'said that the stench was coming from something else. Even while he was speaking, a young man possessed by a demon . . . suddenly cried out. Antony rebuked the demon in the name of our Lord Jesus Christ and it left the young man. The young man became well and everyone knew that the stench had come from the demon'. Pachomius, according to tradition, 'perceived a strong stench' among some monks who turned out to hold the 'heretical' views of Origen (Armand Veilleux has pointed out that this is a later addition). See Veilleux, ed. and trans., *Pachomian Koinonia*, volume 2, *Pachomian Chronicles and Rules* (Kalamazoo: Cistercian Publications, 1981) 28. For Veilleux's assessment, see 'Monasticism and Gnosis in Egypt', in Birger A. Pearson and James E. Goehring, eds., *The Roots of Egyptian Christianity* (Philadephia: Fortress, 1986) 288–9. In the *Apophthegmata*, a woman's alluring 'stench' is linked with the Devil. See Vivian, 'Words to Live By', Saying 24, p. 139.
[64] See *Life of Antony* 59–62, and ¶ 168 for explicit references to Antony.
[65] See *Life of Antony* 39.1.

EUGENDUS MODIFIES THE EXAMPLE OF THE ANCIENTS

169. Reading so refreshed him that, while being read to during meals, he was often overcome by thoughts of the future as though he had fallen into ecstasy, and he forgot about what had been set before him.[66] Struck by joy and despising the pilgrim nature of the present life, he longed for that city in the heavens that was prepared for him. He it was at Condadisco who, following the ancient fathers, properly introduced the practice of reading [in the refectory].[67]

170. It was also Eugendus who, refusing to follow the eastern archimandrites, more usefully brought everyone together in the communal life. After the separate cells were destroyed, he had everyone sleep with him in a common *xenodochium*[68] so that a common building, with only the beds being private, might also encompass those whom a common room enclosed for the common meal. In this dormitory was an oil lamp, just as there was in the oratory, that provided light without fail the whole night.[69] This holy abbot, I might add, neither sat at his own

---

[66] See *Life of Antony* 22 (PL 73146D; in the greek *Life*, ¶ 45.2–3), which this sentence is modelled on. Antony, however, is distracted not by reading but by his remembrance of 'spritual food'.

[67] The context seems to require our addition, but the author could also mean private reading. Martine notes (421, n. 3) that Cassian talks about the introduction of reading at table by the Cappadocians (Inst. 4.17), and that it is in one of the short rules in Basil's *Asceticon* (180). The *Rule of Saint Benedict* shows how important reading was in benedictine monasteries (RB 48.4–5, 15–16, and 22); see *RB 1980* 32 and n. 91.

[68] In a monastery a *xenodochium* (the word is borrowed from Greek) was usually a guest-house for visitors, pilgrims, the poor, and the sick, but the word seems to suggest 'dormitory' here. See ¶ 178, n. 86. RB 22.3 advises that 'if possible, all are to sleep in one place'.

[69] RB 22.4 states that a 'lamp must be kept burning in the room until morning'. A passage from Thomas Merton's famous 'Fire Watch' strikingly shows that some aspects of monasticism were very similar 1500 years later: 'Perhaps the dormitory of the choir monks is the longest room in Kentucky. Long lines of cubicles, with thin partitions a little over six feet high, shirts and robes and scapulars hang over the partitions trying to dry in the night air. Extra cells have been jammed along the walls between the windows. In each

private table (as I have recently heard that some do) nor ate any food different from what the brothers ate.[70] Everything belonged to everyone in every way.[71]

EUGENDUS LEADS BY EXAMPLE

171. Eugendus never taught anything about authority that he did not first accomplish by his own example or with his own work. With regard to the sick or the very old, he always had the monks pay the gentlest attention to them, ordering in addition that those of the brothers whom the sick especially preferred be the ones to serve them. And not only did he have the brothers serve meals to the sick that were suitable to their condition, but also, on account of their fatigue due to their infirmities, he provided that until they recovered their health they could eat and remain by themselves.

172. In addition, with regard to those who lived in the world,[72] he made himself available without showing personal preference: he embraced the poor in the same way that he did the rich, and he entertained and sat with both. In obedience to the Rule of the fathers, he made sure that no monk present himself to lay visitors, not even to close relatives, without

---

one lies a monk on a straw mattress. One pale bulb burns in the middle of the room. The ends are shrouded in shadows. I make my way softly past cell after cell. I know which cells have snorers in them'. The 'Fire Watch' also reveals that the danger of fire (see ¶¶ 161–2 above) was still very much present for the monks of Merton's day: 'I have seen the fuse box. I have looked in the corners where I think there is some wiring. I am satisfied that there is no fire in this tower which would flare like a great torch and take the whole abbey up with it in twenty minutes'. Thomas Merton, *The Sign of Jonas* (Garden City, NY: Doubleday, 1956) 348, 349.

[70] The *Rule for Nuns* 41 of Caesarius of Arles commands that the 'abbess shall never eat outside the congregation unless some unusual occurrence or illness or business demands it' (McCarthy, 184). RB 56 assumes that the abbot had a private table; however, it 'must always be with guests and travelers'. See ¶ 172.

[71] *Omnium omnino omnia erant.* See Acts 4:32. The *Rule for Nuns* 52 of Caesarius of Arles, also requiring the common possession of property, cites different passages of scripture (McCarthy, 188).

[72] Latin *saeculi hominibus*, that is, 'seculars', those who were not monks.

his orders.[73] If someone happened to receive a gift from his relatives, he immediately took it to the abbot or the steward of the monastery and did nothing with it without the father's orders.[74]

173. No one at the monastery ever, in any way, had a private cell, closet, or box;[75] no one was given the smallest opportunity to work for his own personal needs.[76] Down to the simplest needle, even to woolen thread for sewing and mending, all things were held in common by the community.[77] This custom effectively removed from the monks the smallest occasion for deviating [from the Rule]. Among all the occupations, the only ones that allowed for personal profit for anyone were reading and prayer. All the brothers know what I am saying: in the

---

[73] RB 53.23 commands that 'no one is to speak or associate with guests unless he is bidden'.

[74] RB 54.2 instructs that the monk 'must not presume to accept gifts sent him even by his parents without previously telling the abbot'. For earlier parallels, see the *Rule of the Four Fathers* 2, 37–40, Augustine *Praeceptum (Rule)* 5.3 (George Lawless, *Augustine of Hippo and His Monastic Rule* [Oxford: Clarendon, 1987] 94–95), and *Regula Orientalis* 26 (Sources chrétiennes 298, 437–38). We wish to thank Adalbert de Vogüé for these references. The *Rule for Nuns* 43 of Caesarius of Arles allows nothing to 'be received into the monastery without the knowledge and approval of the abbess' (McCarthy, 185).

[75] The *Rule for Nuns* 9 of Caesarius of Arles is very similar: 'No one may be permitted to choose a separate room, nor to have a cell or a chest, or anything of this nature, which can be locked for private use, but all shall be placed in one room, and shall remain there' (McCarthy, 174).

[76] The *Rule for Nuns* 57 of Caesarius of Arles is to the point: 'All works shall be done in common' (McCarthy, 189); see also *Rule for Nuns* 29 (McCarthy, 180).

[77] Sulpicius Severus reports the same communion of goods for Martin and his disciples: 'No one possessed anything of his own; everything was put into the common stock. The buying and selling that is customary with most hermits was forbidden them' (*Life of Martin* 10 [Noble and Head, 13–14]). RB 55.18 instructs the abbot 'to provide all things necessary' so that 'this vice of private ownership may be completely uprooted'. See also RB 33.2–6. See ¶¶ 79 and 90 for examples of monks who seem to possess tools, although their surreptitious activities may suggest that they are stealing them. In ¶ 163, the monks sift through the fire, 'looking for their things'.

cenobium the most powerful opportunities for backsliding and
falling into sin are never lacking unless even the slightest of
them are eliminated.

THE MONASTIC INSTITUTIONS OF BLESSED EUGENDUS

174. My discourse has caused me to touch upon some of
the institutions of the fathers as they were imitated by blessed
Eugendus. According to the promise that I made above, that I
would reserve this for the third section of my work (as Christ
inspires my memory), I am making known as of first importance
the initial steps of those who renounce the world.[78] In no way am
I belittling, by a disdainful presumptuousness, the institutions
of the holy and eminent Basil, bishop of the episcopal see of
Cappadocia, or those of the holy fathers of Lérins[79] and of Saint
Pachomius, the ancient abbot of the Syrians,[80] or those that
the venerable Cassian formulated more recently.[81] But while
we read these daily, we strive to follow those of Condadisco:
they are more conformable with our local conditions and with
the demands that our work entails than are those of the East.[82]
Without a doubt the Gallic nature—or weakness—follows the
former more easily and efficaciously.

---

[78] The insistence that the way of life at the Jura monasteries is only a
beginning on the spiritual path is very similar to RB 73.1, which speaks of
the rule as 'the beginnings of monastic life'. It is striking that RB 73.5 then
goes on to mention Cassian and Basil, just as our author does here. Martine
(p. 427, n. 2) believes that there is an 'important lacuna' here.

[79] Latin *ea quae sancti Lirinensium patres*. For a different interpretation of this
passage, see Masai, 'Review', 523–4.

[80] Pachomius (d. 346) was the leader of a group of monasteries in Middle
Egypt. This reference to him betrays a woeful knowledge of the pachomian
tradition.

[81] RB 73.5 commends, in addition to holy Scripture, 'besides the Conferences
of the Fathers, their Institutes and their Lives, there is also the rule of our
holy father Basil'.

[82] RB 73.6–7 expresses a different view: 'For observant and obedient monks,
all these [the institutions and rules of the Eastern fathers] are nothing less
than tools for the cultivation of virtues; but as for us, they make us blush for
shame at being so slothful, so unobservant, so negligent'.

THE DEATH OF EUGENDUS

175. Now that this, my modest discourse, having looked upon the oceans of such a great institution like a trembling helmsman, and directed its gaze in every direction, rejoices at reaching the port of silence, I shall briefly report the deeds of the blessed man at the time of his passing.[83] While, therefore, the father about whom I have spoken above, more than sixty years of age now, was suffering during about six months from some bodily illness, he never missed the canonical offices, not even once, nor could he be forced to bestow anything more than once a day upon his poor, worn-out body. Calling to himself one of the brothers upon whom he had enjoined the special privilege of anointing the sick with oil,[84] in secret he asked that he too be anointed, as is the custom, upon the chest.

176. When night had ended, and when we inquired of him at dawn if he had passed the night peacefully, he burst into tears and sobs and said, 'May almighty God spare you for hindering me, sick as I am, from being freed of my bodily chains!' Trembling, and with abundant tears, convulsed also by the sobbing of our hearts, we fell silent. 'My lords, the abbots Romanus and Lupicinus', he continued, 'brought before this bed, on their own shoulders, a litter; after they kissed me and arranged my body, they lifted me and placed me on this bier in order to carry me away.

177. 'When they carried me into the oratory on their shoulders, you all ran into the doorway, violently forced me out, and carried me back on this bed. Because of this, I beg you, if you have any regard for an old man, if you have any respect for the fatherly love I have shown towards you, do not keep me here

---

[83] As Martine notes, 429, n. 2, the conclusion here echoes Cassian, Preface to *Conferences* 1–101 (Pichery, 1:75), especially in the oceanic metaphor and the image of reaching 'the port of silence'. See also Conference 12.16 (Pichery, 2:36) and 24.26 (Pichery, 3:135 and 206).

[84] Martine, 429, n. 4, and 50–1, suggests that this person is our author. The scene here is reminiscent of Jn 19:26–7, where Jesus entrusts his mother to the beloved disciple.

with you any longer but allow me at last to cross over to the fathers. I beg all of you, my dear sons, I implore you, carry on with the institutions and traditions of the fathers that you have received; these are on every point unassailable. In this way you will bring joy to me, to all the saints, and to yourselves, until you claim the palm branch of victory'.[85]

178. He finished speaking amid our cries of lamentation. About five days later he lay down, without assistance, on this same bed, that is, in the dormitory.[86] Suddenly he seemed to fall asleep and gave up his spirit.[87] His holy and blessed remains were buried with great honors and in the name of Christ amid the ranks of sons and brothers at Condadisco, where his offspring continue to serve him.[88]

CONCLUSION

179. Refresh yourselves, holy brothers, and quench for a while your faithful and fervent thirst, with your desires for the moment satisfied. If my rustic garrulousness has not brought peace to your souls, which have for a long time now despised and rejected philosophy,[89] then the institutes regarding the rules and regulations of your monastery (that is, the community of Agaune),[90] which holy Father Marinus, abbot of the island of Lérins, has requested, will, with Christ's assistance, as much because of the distinguished character of that institution as out of respect for the authority of the one who asked for it, magnificently fulfill all your desires.

---

[85] See, perhaps, Rv 7:9.
[86] Latin *mansorio*. A *mansorium* usually indicated a 'rural dwelling', but that is clearly not the meaning here. See ¶ 170, n. 68 above.
[87] Latin *animam exhalavit*, literally 'exhaled his spirit'.
[88] See the introduction, pp. 53–54.
[89] See ¶ 119 The rejection of philosophy for Christ is an important theme in the *Life of Antony*. See *Life of Antony* 72–80.
[90] The monastery of Saint-Maurice d'Agaune; see ¶ 3 n. 12 above.

APPENDIX I

ΛVITUS, BISHOP OF VIENNE
LETTER TWENTY-EIGHT, TO VIVENTIOLUS[1]

INTRODUCTION

THIS LETTER, written shortly after Eugendus' death around 514,[2] is important for several reasons: It is one of the few contemporary references to the Jura monasteries that we have outside of the *Life*; it shows the continuing relationship between the monasteries and Lyon (Viventiolus, a priest at Condadisco, leaves the monastery to become bishop of Lyon), which began with Romanus' visit to a monastery in Lyon before his withdrawal to the Juras; it demonstrates that even a monastery as remote as Condadisco (both geographically and ecclesiastically) could be a nursery for priests and bishops.

LETTER XVIIII, TO VIVENTIOLUS

Bishop Avitus to Viventiolus, priest.[3]

What you have done is doubly dutiful, for when coming to Lyon and sending letters here [to Vienne], you showed great care about two brothers, inquiring about one who was ill and visiting the other, who was distressed. What you related will not be overlooked, for you brought to your brother monk more

---

[1] Avitus (Alcimius Ecdicius Avitus) lived from about 450 to 526. This letter is translated from the latin text edited by Rudolf Pieper, ed., *Alcimi Ecdicii Aviti Viennensis Episcopi Opera Quae Supersunt* (Monumenta Germaniae Historica, Auctores antiquissimi, vol. 6; Berlin: Weidmann, 1883) 50–53. Letter XVIIII is numbered XVII in the edition of Ulysse Chevalier, *Oeuvres complètes de Saint Avit évêque de Vienne* (Lyon: Vitte, 1890) 154–155.

[2] Pieper, 50, dates it to 516–17.

[3] Viventiolus was a priest at Condadisco; despite the urgings of Bishop Avitus, and undoubtedly others, he became bishop of Lyon around 515 (after the death of Eugendus) until his death about 524.

than what is due in love or in honor of his spiritual office, even though the monastery, weakened as it was, had not requested you to do it. Indeed the youth of the priest, your brother by ordination, seemed to call for an exhortation even if his distress had not required consolation. Therefore, utterly cease excusing the labor that you have undertaken, lest you seem to have sinned thus far by being insecure about beginning it and finishing it. Now, in giving you thanks appropriate to the gift that you sent, I feel prayers to be more effective than letters. So that you may say that such things may be made known about the solitude [of your monastery],[4] you attract by an elegance [of style] the desire of people to visit the place where you lived cenobitically. Thus through your care, instruction, and teaching, what in fact was a desert[5] should become a heavenly garden.

Since you have earnestly sought a bishop's chair[6] in place of the seat[7] [as monk] that you have left, I ask that you cherish and protect with your spiritual comfort and priestly leadership the wavering community of Eugendus, dear to both of us, especially because it has got to its present state owing to its being bereaved of its abbot. And do not let this pull you away from the charity that is due, because I believe that [the brothers] entreat the care of your administration more in simplicity than in an unworthy spirit of blame. We wish that, with God's help, you may impart this understanding to the greatest number of the faithful in order to provide greater guidance and, by summoning up your strength, to double the five and then the two talents you have been given.[8] Then, having been proved in a lower position [as a monk], you may by your fraternal withdrawal in other ways create holy ground,[9] and your paternal love may be zealous to hold the monastery together.

---

[4] Latin *eremus*.
[5] Latin *eremus*.
[6] Latin *cathedrae*.
[7] Latin *sella*.
[8] Mt 25:15–17.
[9] Latin *eremum*. Avitus is hoping that Viventiolus will create a new 'desert' (*eremum*) in his bishopric, just as he had cared for the monastic desert at Condadisco. Avitus clearly wishes that Viventiolus would stay at the monastery.

APPENDIX II

eucheRius, Bishop of Lyon the passion of the maRtyRs of agaune, saint mauRice and his companions[1]

INTRODUCTION

*t*HE PASSION OF the Martyrs of Agaune purports to be an account of the martyrdom of 'six thousand, six hundred men' in arms of the theban legion under Maximian at Acaunus (Agaune) late in the third century; Eucherius of Lyon sent the account in a letter to Bishop Salvius around the year 450.

After some scholarly fisticuffs, the consensus is that the *Passion* is 'a complete fiction';[2] even the author of the *Life of the Jura Fathers* seems a bit puzzled by the improbable number of martyrs:

---

[1] The translation is based on the edition by Karl Wotke, *Passio Agaunensium Martyrum* (CSEL 31; Prague: F Tempsky, 1894) 165–173.

[2] David Woods, 'The Origin of the Legend of Maurice and the Theban Legion', *Journal of Ecclesiastical History* 45:3 (1994) 385–95, 395. For the most recent summaries of research and bibliographies, see Woods, and W. H. C. Frend, 'Review of *Les passions de S. Maurice d'Agaune* by Louis Dupraz', *Journal of Ecclesiastical History* 14 (1963) 85–86. See further Salvatore Pricoco, *L'isola dei santi: Il cenobio di Lerino e le origini del monachesimo gallico* (Rome: Edizioni dell'Ateneo & Bizzarri, 1978) 204–244. 'Theban' refers to the Thebaid (whose chief city was Thebes) in middle Egypt. For a fascinating look at the continuing importance of the relics of the theban martyrs in both the Roman Catholic and Coptic Orthodox Churches, see Otto F.A. Meinardus, 'About the Translation of the Relics of the Theban Martyrs Saints Cassius and Florentius from Bonn to Cairo', *Coptic Church Review* 13.2 (Summer 1992) 49–53.

Enflamed with the ardor of faith, Romanus had decided to seek out in Agaune the basilica of the saints. (I should say, rather, the encampment of the martyrs, as the published report of their martyrdom testifies. I will not say that six thousand, six hundred men could be enclosed in the building, nor could they, I suppose, even be held in the field around it) (¶ 44).

The author of the *Life*, however, was not concerned with scholarly consensus. We include a translation of the *Passion* here for four reasons: (1) Romanus, as the quotation above shows, thought enough of the theban martyrs to make the difficult trek to their shrine at Agaune;[3] (2) one of the recipients of the *Life of the Jura Fathers* was somehow connected with the shrine: 'you, John, following the Apostle John of old, recline upon the sarcophagus of Saint Maurice, head of the legion of theban martyrs just as the famous apostle and companion of Christ reclined upon the breast of the author of our salvation' (¶ 2); (3) as the quotation above also shows, our author knew the *Passion* as a 'published report'; (4) evidence, ambiguous and sketchy as it is, connects the jura monasteries with the monastery of Saint Maurice at Acaunus (Saint-Maurice d'Agaune) 'the greatest of Burgundian monasteries'.[4] The monastery was founded in 515 at the site of the shrine.[5]

THE PASSION OF THE MARTYRS OF AGAUNE

Eucherius to the holy and most blessed lord in Christ, Bishop Salvius.

I have sent to your blessedness the Passion of our martyrs. I am afraid that through neglect time will obliterate from human

---

[3] Legend had it in the early Middle Ages that Saint Martin visited Acaunus. Whether this was believed at Condadisco is uncertain; however, if it was believed, Martin's veneration at Condadisco (see the Introduction, pp. 38–39 above) might have given further impetus for Romanus to visit Acaunus.
[4] Wood, 4; for a discussion of the possible connection between the jura monasteries and the Monastery of Saint Maurice, see Wood, 16–17.
[5] See Dupraz, 296, and Riché, 106.

memory the deeds of so glorious a martyrdom. Long ago I sought out the truth of the matter from the appropriate sources, those affirmed by Saint Isaac, bishop of Geneva. He acknowledged the account of the passion that I presented to him; it was he, I believe, who had previously received these things from the blessed bishop Theodore, a man of an earlier period.

Therefore, although others in diverse places and provinces offer gold and silver in honor and duty to the saints, and gifts of many kinds, I worthily offer these writings of mine to you, our benefactor, entreating your intercession on their behalf for all their faults and, from my patrons, continuous aid and protection hereafter. In addition, holy lord and deservedly most blessed brother, remember me in the sight of the Lord, as I adhere always to the service of the saints.

1. I here set forth in writing, in a style commensurate with their honorable deeds, and with exactly that faith by which the celebration of their martyrdom[6] has come down to us, the passion of the holy martyrs who honor Agaune with their glorious blood. Through the narrative that follows, the memory of what took place has not yet been lost in oblivion. Although the individual places and cities that possess them are distinguished on account of individual martyrs—and not undeservedly, since the saints pour out their precious souls on behalf of the highest God—with what great reverence ought this sacred place of Acaunus to be honored, where for Christ's sake it is reported that so many thousands of martyrs were killed with the sword? But now let us address the subject of the most blessed passion itself.

2. Under Maximian, who held the *imperium* of the roman republic jointly with Diocletian,[7] people were tortured[8] throughout almost all of the different provinces or were put to death as martyrs. This same Maximian was raving mad with avarice, lust, and cruelty, and was besieged by other vices. Thus, given up to

---

[6] Latin *martyrii ordo*.
[7] Diocletian first made Maximian Caesar, then on 1 April 286, joint-Augustus.
[8] Literally, 'mangled', *laniati*.

the abominable religious practices of the pagans and profaning
the God of heaven by his deeds, he had armed his impiety for
the purpose of obliterating the name of Christianity. If people
at that time dared to profess the worship of the true God—
with troops of soldiers stationed everywhere—they were seized,
either to be punished or to be put to death. Moreover, because
Maximian had been given a respite by the barbarian peoples,
he directed the military against the faith.

There was at that time in the army a legion of soldiers called
the Thebans. (A legion in those days was defined as having six
thousand, six hundred men in arms.) The Thebans had come
from the East, summoned to be auxiliary troops for Maximian.
Men prompt in warfare, noble in ability, more noble still in their
faith, they fought for the emperor with strength and bravery,
while for Christ they fought with devotion. Even under arms
they were not forgetful of the Gospel precept: they rendered
to God the things that were God's, and returned to Caesar the
things that were Caesar's.[9] Therefore, when the Thebans, along
with other soldiers, were chosen to forcibly seize a number
of Christians, they alone dared to refuse such cruel service;[10]
moreover, they refused to comply with such orders in the future. Maximian was not far away, for he had made a wearying
march near Octodurus.[11] There, when it was reported to him
by messengers that this legion had, by going against imperial
orders, fomented rebellion and caused difficulties in Acaunus,
Maximian became furious with indignation. But before I recount the rest of the story, I believe I ought to introduce a
report about the geography of the region.

3. Agaune is almost sixty miles from the city of Geneva,
and fourteen miles distant from the head of Lake Geneva, into

---

[9] See Mk 12:17.
[10] Latin *ministerium*.
[11] A town of the Varagi, in Gallia Narbonensis; modern Martigny, in Switzerland. Martigny lies approximately eight miles (thirteen kilometers) southeast
of Saint-Maurice, following the Rhône.

which flows the Rhône.[12] The place itself is situated in a valley between alpine ridges; a rough and narrow road offers difficult travel to those going there because the Rhône, a dangerous river, deposits heaps of rock on the roadway that make it almost impassable for travelers. Once the narrow defiles have been passed, however, a large plain immediately comes into view between the mountainous cliffs; here the holy legion had taken up position.

Therefore, as I said above, when Maximian learned of the response of the theban legion to his command, he seethed with a rash and dangerous anger because his orders had been ignored. He ordered a tenth of this legion to be killed with the sword so that others, terrified with fear, would more readily obey imperial commands. Once his orders had been renewed, he decreed that the remaining soldiers be forced to participate in the persecution of Christians. When this second pronouncement came to the Thebans and they understood that impious actions were again being enjoined on them, shouting and tumult arose far and wide in the camps from those declaring that none of them would ever participate in such a sacrilegious service,[13] that they had always abominated the profane places of idols, that they were imbued with Christian teachings and instructed by their veneration of sacred and divine religion to worship the one God of eternity! Better for them to undergo the worst things possible than to go against the christian faith!

When Maximian found out about these things, he became an even more cruel monster and his savage nature asserted itself once more: he ordered another tenth of the theban legion to be handed over to death; the others, moreover, were forced

---

[12] About fifty-five and thirteen modern miles, respectively. It is approximately fifty-seven miles (ninety-two kilometers) by car around the lake to Saint-Maurice; from the tip of the lake to Saint-Maurice is about fifteen miles (twenty-four kilometers). The French name for Lake Geneva, Lac Léman, preserves its Latin name of Lemannus. The Rhône flows by Saint-Maurice.

[13] Latin *ministeria*; see n. 10 above.

to do what they had previously refused. As these orders were being carried out once again in the camp, the ten percent who had been chosen by lot were separated from the others and cut down. A great number of the remaining crowd of soldiers were exhorting and encouraging one another to stand firm in such a glorious deed.

4. The greatest example and model of the faith in those days was Saint Maurice; at that time, tradition has it, he was *primicerius* of his legion. Maurice was outraged, as was Exsuperius, who was *campi doctor* (as it is termed in the military) and Candidus, who was *senator militum*.[14] By exhorting and counseling the soldiers one by one, and presenting to them the example of their faithful fellow soldiers as well as the martyrs, he was persuading them to die for their allegiance[15] to Christ and for all the divine laws, if necessary, and to follow their comrades and messmates who had already preceded them into heaven. The glorious flame of martyrdom was now set blazing in those blessed men. Animated by their leaders and teachers, they now sent dictates to Maximian, who was still raging in his frenzy. These, as loyal as they were brave, are reported to have been in this manner:

'Emperor, we are your soldiers, but nevertheless we are— and this we freely confess—servants of God. To you we owe military service, to God innocence; from you we receive pay for our labor, from him we obtain the beginning of life. Under no circumstances, our emperor, can we follow you in this if it means denying our true leader, God, who is most certainly our creator. God is also, whether you accept it or not, your

14 All three of these men were non-commissioned officers, the *primicerius* being the highest ranking, perhaps a chief warrant officer, with the *senator* ranking immediately below him. The *campi doctor* was the 'regimental drill instructor'. See A. H. M. Jones, *The Later Roman Empire 284–602* (Baltimore: Johns Hopkins, 1986) 634, 674.
15 Latin *sacramentum*, in its military sense of an oath or allegiance sworn. See n. 18 below.

own creator and leader.[16] If we are not forced to do such dire things that we give offense to him—as we have done up to this point—we will still obey you. Otherwise, we will obey God rather than you.

'We offer our hands against whatever enemy you please, but it is an abomination for us to stain our hands with the blood of innocent people. These right hands of ours are capable of fighting against the holy and the hostile; they are incapable of torturing[17] the faithful and our fellow citizens. We recall that we took up arms on behalf of our fellow citizens rather than against them. We have always fought for justice, for godliness, and for the well-being of innocent people: up to this point these were well worth the dangers.

'We have fought on behalf of the faith; how shall we keep our agreement with you if we do not keep faith with our God? We have first sworn an oath to God; then we have sworn an oath[18] to the emperor: you need to know that the second means nothing to us if we break the first. You order us to seek out Christians for punishment. Others no longer need to be sought for by you: here you have us confessing that God our Father is the creator of all things, and we believe his Son Jesus Christ to be God. We have seen our comrades, those who shared in our toils and dangers, with whose blood we have also been spattered, cut to pieces with the sword, and yet we have not wept over the deaths of our most holy fellows and our brothers' funerals. We have not grieved; instead we have praised them, and with joy we have followed them, because they have been deemed worthy to suffer for their Lord God.

'And now the ultimate necessity of this life has not driven us to rebel; nor has even desperation itself—which is mightiest

---

[16] In this sentence, *imperator*, 'emperor, ruler', is being contrasted with *auctor*, which means both 'originator' and 'creator'. The religious use of *auctor* here may remind one of the phrase from the anglican *Book of Common Prayer*: 'the author of our salvation'.

[17] Literally, 'mangling'; see n. 8 above.

[18] Latin *sacramentum* for both.

when there is danger—armed us against you, Emperor. See! We have arms and we do not resist, because we prefer to die rather than to kill, and we prefer even more to die innocent than to live guilty. If you decide something further for us, if you command or dictate anything, we are prepared to submit to fire, torture, or the sword. We confess that we are Christians; we are unable to persecute Christians'.

5. When Maximian heard these amazing words and saw how firm the men's souls were in their faith for Christ, despairing that their once-glorious uniformity could be restored, he sentenced all of them to be killed. Once the troop of soldiers had been surrounded, he ordered the sentence carried out. When those who had been sent to attack the blessed legion arrived, they unsheathed their ungodly swords against the saints, who did not allow their love of life to prevent them from dying. They were, therefore, everywhere cut down by swords, not even crying out or offering resistance. Instead, when they had laid down their weapons, they offered their necks to their pursuers, and presented their throats and uncovered bodies to their slayers.

They were not exalted by their large numbers or their armaments so as to attempt to assert the righteousness of their cause with the sword. They called to mind only this one thing: to confess the One who did not cry out when he was led to the slaughter. And as the Lamb did not open his mouth,[19] they too, as a flock of the Lord's sheep, allowed themselves to be mangled by ravening wolves.

The earth covered over the bodies of the saints laid low in death, and streams of their precious blood poured forth. What madness, except in battle, ever produced such a heap of human bodies? What savageness, relying only on its own judgment, ever ordered so many accused to perish at the same time? (Lest the just be punished because a multitude sinned, many of the soldiers, although accustomed to going unpunished, did not continue in these acts.) Through the cruelty of this monstrous tyrant, then was murdered that population of saints,

---

[19] See Is 53:7, Jer 11:19, Rom 8:36.

who showed contempt for the present in return for the hope of future things. Thus that whole angelic legion was murdered, which now, we believe, joins with legions of angels in heaven in always praising together the Lord God Sabaoth.

6. The martyr Victor, however, was not a soldier in this legion, nor a soldier. He was a veteran already retired from the army. While traveling, suddenly he came upon those who were joyfully and heedlessly carousing over the spoils taken from the martyrs. Invited to eat with them, he understood very clearly the cause of their merry-making. As he abhorred both the revelers and their revels, he refused to join them. When they asked him if he too were perhaps a Christian, he responded, 'I am a Christian, and I will always be a Christian'. Immediately they fell on him and killed him, and he was joined with the other martyrs there, as in death, so too in honor.

Of all that number of martyrs, these are the only names that are known to us: blessed Maurice, Exsuperius, Candidus, and Victor; the others are unknown to us, but they are written in the book of life.[20] From this same legion, it is said, were also the martyrs Ursus and Victor, whom tradition confirms as having suffered at Salodorum. (Salodorum is a fort above the Arula River, not far from the Rhine.)

7. To indicate what end then followed for the savage tyrant Maximian is also of value for this work. When Maximian, laying plots, planned to kill his son-in-law Constantine, who at that time was in power, his deception was discovered and he was taken captive near Marseilles; not long after, he was strangled, a most disgraceful punishment, and ended his wicked death-deserving life.[21] The bodies of the blessed martyrs of Agaune, however, many years after their passion, were revealed to Saint Theodore, bishop of Agaune. In their honor a basilica was constructed which stands next to a great rocky slope; indeed, it is built right against its side.

---

[20] See Rev 13:8, 20:12, and 21:27, *passim*.
[21] Maximian was defeated, and apparently killed, in 310.

I have not intended to pass over in silence the miracle that occurred then.

It happened that, among the craftsmen still remaining of those who had been summoned to work on the basilica, a certain worker was present who up to that time had been a pagan. On the Lord's day, when the others had left work in expectation of that festal day, he remained in the workshop. Alone there, this worker was suddenly caught up in a bright light, as saints made themselves present to him, and he fell prostrate, either for punishment or in supplication. Seeing a crowd of martyrs becoming visible, he was rebuked and lashed, either because he alone was absent from church on the Lord's day, or because he, a pagan, had dared to undertake the holy work as a craftsman there. What the saints did was done mercifully, in order that the workman, confused and terrified, would beg to obtain the name of Christian for himself, and he immediately became a Christian.

8. Nor among the miracle of the saints shall I omit that other one which is also famous and known by all. When the *materfamilias* of the Quincii, who were outstanding and distinguished men, was so crippled by paralysis that even the use of her feet was denied to her, her husband begged her to make the long trip to Agaune. After she had entered the basilica of the holy martyrs in the arms of her servants, she had returned to her lodgings by foot, with her prematurely dead members now restored to health. Now she herself spread the news of her miracle.

I thought that these two miracles alone ought to be inserted into the Passion of the saints. Suffice it to say that through his saints the power of the Lord daily works miracles there, either in the exorcising of demons or in various kinds of cures.

APPENDIX III

eucherius of lyon

in praise of the desert[1]

a letter to bishop hilary of lérins

E UCHERIUS, LATER BISHOP of Lyon, wrote the following letter possibly between 412 and 420 while living on the monastic island of Lérins (Lirinum) or as late as 427, just prior to becoming bishop. There can be little doubt that Romanus learned about the desert tradition first-hand while living in Lyon, just prior to his withdrawal to the Juras around 435.

IN PRAISE OF THE DESERT

Eucherius to the most reverend Hilary, praiseworthy and highly to be honored in Christ.

1. It was with great generosity that you once left your country and your relatives to penetrate the recesses of the desert as far as the Great Sea, but it is with greater virtue that you seek the desert a second time.[2] For when you first entered the desert as an inexperienced young man, you had a leader and guide for your journey who became your instructor in the heavenly army.

---

[1] Translated by Charles Cummings, ocso; revised by Jeffrey Burton Russell. Father Cummings' translation was originally published in *Cistercian Studies* 11 (1976) 60–72, based on the edition by Karl Wotke, *Sancti Evcherii Lvgdvnensis Epistula de laude heremi* (CSEL 31; Prague: F. Tempsky, 1894) 178–194. A later edition was prepared by Salvator Pricoco, *Eucherius De laude eremi* (Catania: Centro di Studi Sull'Antico Cristianesimo, 1965). Professor Russell's revision draws on Pricoco's edition. Passages are noted where the use of Pricoco's text (Pr) over Wotke's (Wo) required a change in translation. Paragraph numbering is taken from Pricoco.

[2] See Gn 12:1; Acts 7:3.

197

By following him, you followed a father, although you had left your parents behind. Now, however, after having thought you should follow him when he was called to the heights of episcopal office, you feel yourself drawn back again by love of the desert, and now your example is even nobler and greater. When you went into the desert the first time, people saw you following your kinsman;[3] now when you seek the desert again you leave even him behind. And remember what kind of man he was, and how great. Always caring for you with reverence and love, he was bound to you by special affection. To such a love you could prefer nothing, except perhaps your love of the desert. And when you honestly compare your love of the desert with your love for him, you will find that you do not love him any less but the desert more. You show how strong in you is the love of solitary places, since the strongest human love must yield to it. What shall I call that love of the desert if not the love of God in you? Thus you have kept the law of charity revealed by the Gospel, loving your God first and then your neighbor.[4]

2. Still, it seems to me that if he were alive,[5] he would not be against your proposed move. He might have counseled you to go away, even though that is not customary among friends, and the separation would have been as painful for him as for you. He loved you very much, but in that love he always looked to your welfare, and though his love for you was rich and deep and intense, he directed it to what would be profitable for you.

3. You have given me many reasons to esteem you: rich in Christ, you have been giving generously of all your possessions to the poor of Christ; youthful in years, you have displayed the wisdom of maturity; furthermore, you are brilliant in reasoning and in speaking. But from now on I shall esteem and love nothing about you more than this longing you have for a home in solitude. And so, since you have often asked me to write at greater length in response to your long and eloquent letters,

---

[3] Cummings supplies 'your kinsman Honoratus'.
[4] Dt 6:5; Mt 22:37.
[5] Cummings again supplies 'Honoratus'.

you will now have to bear with my foolishness a little while, you who are wise yourself. I propose to pass in review the many graces shown by the Lord to this beloved desert of yours.

I would say that the desert deserves to be called a temple of our God without walls. Since it is clear that God dwells in silence, we must believe that he loves the solitary expanses of the desert. Very often he has let himself be seen there by his saints; he willingly meets with people in favorable places such as the desert. In the desert Moses gazed upon God until his face shone with glory.[6] In the desert Elijah covered his face for fear of seeing God.[7] Although God is present everywhere, and regards the whole world as his domain, we may believe that his preferred place is the solitudes of heaven and of the desert.

4. The story is told that someone once asked a wise man where he could be sure to find God. The wise man told his questioner to come along where he would lead him, and together they went into the solitude of the open desert. 'Behold', he said, 'where God is'. God is more promptly believed to be there, since he is more easily found there.

5. At the beginning of creation when God created all things according to his wisdom and differentiated individual things in such a way that each would be suited to its future use,[8] he did not leave the desert places of the world without honor; still, their worth was not immediately evident. I am convinced that God, in foreknowledge of the future, prepared the desert for the saints to come. I believe he wanted some parts of the world to be rich in the fruits of agriculture and other parts, with drier climate, to abound with holy men. In this way the desert would bear fruit. When he 'watered the hills from the heights above', the valleys were filled with plentiful crops.[9] And he planned to endow the sterile deserts with inhabitants, lest any land go to waste.

---

[6] Ex 35: 29–30.
[7] 1 Kgs 19:13.
[8] Si 16:26.
[9] Ps 104:13.

6. He who possessed Paradise and transgressed God's law lived in a land of delights, but he could not keep the law given him by God.[10] The more pleasant and delightful that place was, the easier it was for him to fall. In punishment God subjected him to the law of death and then extended that sting of death to all his descendants.[11] That is why one who desires to live will dwell in a desert, while the inhabitant of a pleasanter place may not escape a bitter death. But now let us come to further examples showing how the desert has always been pleasing to God.

7. Moses was tending his flock in the depths of the desert when in the distance he saw God resplendent in a shining fire that burned without consuming.[12] Not only did he see God; he heard him speaking.[13] The Lord commanded Moses to take off his sandals and then called the desert holy, saying, 'The place where you stand is holy ground'.[14] The merit and dignity of the desert had been hidden until that public pronouncement. Then God confirmed the sanctity of the place by making a holy covenant there.[15] In my opinion, the lesson implicit here is that those who approach the desert should first unblock the path of their lives from the obligations of their previous concerns.[16] They should proceed to the desert only when they have taken off the sandals that impeded them, so that they will not profane the sacred place.

It was there in the desert that Moses first conversed with God. He received God's words and spoke to him in reply. He asked questions and was instructed about what to do and say. He conferred with the Lord of Heaven in ordinary speech. It was there that Moses acquired a staff powerful in miraculous

---

[10] Gn 2–3.
[11] 1 Cor 15:56.
[12] Ex 3:1–3.
[13] Ex 19:9.
[14] Ex 3:5.
[15] Ex 3.
[16] Pr *vitae gressus* for Wo *vitae se.*

effects.[17] With that staff he had gone into the desert as a shepherd of sheep; he returned as a shepherd of people.

8. In order to be liberated from Egypt and set free from sinful conduct, the people of God sought out the pathless wilderness.[18] They fled into the solitary places and prepared to meet the God who had freed them from slavery. With Moses as their leader, they marched off into the desert with its endless vastness.[19] 'How great is your abundant goodness, O Lord!'[20] Moses had seen God when he first entered the desert, and now he returned to look for him again. The Lord visibly led his people on their march through the desert, showing them the way and night with a burning column of flame or a shining cloud. This was a sign from Heaven given to those worthy to see it. He went on ahead of the people, a white column flashing with fire at night. With the light directing them,[21] Israel followed the brightly glowing beacon wherever it led. The Lord in his goodness provided a light to guide them on their way into the solitary depths of the desert.[22]

9. The doors of the pathless sea that lay in the road of this people on their way to the desert were thrown open wide for them.[23] When the multitude reached the shore of the Red Sea, their feet dusty from the hurried journey, they looked up as from a deep valley and saw threatening mountains of hanging waters looming over them. But the Guardian of the people let them through the shallows beneath.

10. Nor did the divine power end there. God permitted the water to resume its natural course, and the inrushing sea covered the bare ground again, wiping out all footprints both of Israel and of their enemies. I believe that God put the sea back in its channel so that Israel could not turn back from the

---

[17] Ex 4:17.
[18] Ex 13–14.
[19] Dt 1:19.
[20] Ps 30:20.
[21] Pr *intento Israhel* for Wo *intuito Israhel*.
[22] Ex 13:21–22; Dt 1:33; Neh 9:19; Ps 78:14.
[23] Ex 14:21–22.

desert. He had opened a pathway between the waters but then covered it again with inpouring waves; thus he allowed them to enter the desert while closing off all hope of return.

11. This people were favored with great graces from the very beginning of their journey into solitude, and once they had entered it, they merited graces even greater. There in the desert the Lord refreshed them in their thirst with an unexpected miracle, drawing living water from a sundered rock.[24] He brought a stream out of the impermeable stone as from a natural spring, tapping with his invisible hand a hidden vein. Then, after infusing the heart of the dry rock with gushing water, he transformed a flow of bitter water by adding a delicious sweetness to the undrinkable liquid. The first waters he drew out of a rock; the second he purified. Bringing water out of a rock was not a greater miracle than changing bitter water into sweet. The whole people were amazed. They recognized the power of heavenly assistance no less in the transformation of the bitter water than in the water newly created from the rock.

12. In the desert the people collected the bread sent down from heaven.[25] The Lord who dwells in the clouds cast down bread like dry rain. Dropping from the snowy air, the manna fell upon the tents and everywhere in the camp. 'People ate the bread of angels.'[26] Since 'sufficient for the day are the troubles thereof',[27] God in his bounty sent food every day. Thus he taught them already in the old dispensation not to worry about the morrow. In those days heaven itself took care of the people living in the desert, since they could not provide their own food from the land.

13. Besides all this, the Hebrews in the desert received the law and the commandments from heaven. Drawing as close as they dared, they were deemed worthy to see the letters written

---

[24] Ex 17:6; Nm 20:11; Neh 9:15; Ps 78: 16, 20; Ps 105:41.

[25] Ex 16:4–30; Ps 78:24–25.

[26] Ps 78:25.

[27] Mt 6:34.

on stone tablets by the finger of God.[28] They went out of the camp to meet the Lord, took their stand at the foot of the mountain, and waited.[29] They remained there in great fear of the visible glory of God.[30] Terrified, they looked at the peak of Sinai. Thunderstruck, they watched as the mountain began to be covered with whirling smoke and fire. Gradually a great cloud covered and hid the whole mountain in densest blackness. The people were exceedingly terrified by the lightning, flashes of brilliant fire, and frequent crashes of thunder mingled with the echoing peals of trumpets.[31] Thus the children of Israel were deemed worthy to see the throne of God and to hear his voice when they lived in the desert.

14. In the desert that nation was sustained and favored by miracles. They lived on strange food, unexpected water, and clothing that never wore out.[32] The very garments that clothed their bodies were miraculously preserved. Anything necessary that the nature of the land could not provide was supplied by the visible beneficence of God. Scarcely any of the saints have attained such gifts of heavenly grace. It is rightly said of this people, 'The Lord has not dealt thus with any other nation'.[33] The Lord gave them special favors and granted them unheard of things when he nourished his people with his divine gifts in the desert.

15. All these events are recorded as a sign of what happens to us, for the outward appearance of things shines with hidden mysteries. They were all baptized in Moses, in the cloud and in the sea, and they all ate the spiritual food and drank the spiritual drink.[34] Nevertheless, these symbolic events remain true realities in themselves. So the desert still deserves to be

[28] Dt 9:10.
[29] Ex 19:7; Dt 4:11.
[30] Ex 20:18.
[31] Ex 19:16–19; 20:18; Dt 4:11.
[32] Dt 8:2–4; 29:5; Neh 9: 20–21.
[33] Ps 147:20.
[34] 1 Cor 10: 2–4.

praised even if the things done there must be understood as referring to deep mysteries. Grace is not slighted in the least even when we interpret that condition of body and incorruptibility of clothing as the ideal of eternal life. It was by the sheer gift of grace that the kind of happiness the blessed enjoy in the age to come was already possessed in the desert by those people in the present age.

16. Could the children of Israel not have come to the promised land without first living in the desert? In order for that people to take possession of the land 'flowing with milk and honey',[35] they first had to possess this parched and sterile wilderness. From the dwelling places in the desert, the road lies always open to our true homeland. Let those who desire 'to see the good things of the Lord in the land of the living'[36] take up their residence in an uninhabitable wasteland. Let those who strive to become citizens of Heaven be guests first of the desert.

17. But, to go on, David himself could not escape the plots of a hostile king without taking refuge in the desert.[37] Dwelling in the Idumenean deserts, he thirsted for the Lord with all his heart. Because he had thirsted in the desert, in that trackless and waterless land,[38] he could at last appear before God in the holy place and thenceforth see the glory and power of God as one of the saints.

18. Elijah, the greatest of those who dwell in solitary places, closed up the heavens so that it might not rain; he called down fire; he ate food brought by a raven; he revoked the immutable law of death; he divided the Jordan and crossed over while the flow was held in check; carried off in a fiery chariot, he ascended into heaven.[39]

19. Elisha was the successor of Elijah both in power and in way of life. He was famous for working divine miracles. His

---

35 Dt 6:3; 26:9; 27:3; Jos 5:6.
36 Ps 27:13; 116:9.
37 1 Sm 23:14.
38 Ps 63:1.
39 1 Kgs 8:35; 17:6; 2 Kgs 2:6–11.

greatness is remembered because of the river divided, the ax made to float, the boy raised to life, and the oil multiplied.[40] These and many other exploits show that Elisha truly possessed his teacher's power. Though Elijah while alive raised a dead man, Elisha raised one even after he himself was dead.

20. The successors of these two prophets chose to heave the cities and dwell where the Jordan River divides in two.[41] There they built tents next to that remote river. The holy band kept watch on the banks of the desert river, scattered among their tents and other suitable dwellings. Thus in their noble nature they preserved the spirit of their forebears the prophets.

21. Did not he also live in the desert who was greater than any man born of woman, he who was a voice crying in the desert?[42] In the desert he instituted baptism, and in the desert he preached repentance. In the desert the Kingdom of Heaven was first heard of. In the desert he first communicated those mysteries to his listeners, because by going into the desert they could sooner merit them. It was highly fitting that this desert dweller, this angel sent before the face of the Lord,[43] should open the way to the heavenly kingdom. He was both a precursor of Christ[44] and a witness worthy to hear the Father speaking from heaven, to touch the Son as he baptized him, and to see the Holy Spirit descending.[45]

22. Our Lord and Savior himself was led into the desert by a spirit immediately after his baptism, as Scripture says.[46] Who was this spirit? Without doubt, it was the Holy Spirit. It was the Holy Spirit who drew him into the desert. It was the Holy Spirit who ordered this, who silently inspired it. The idea of going into the desert was worthy because the Holy Spirit suggested it. Once steeped in the holy river, he knew that he must not

---

[40] 2 Kgs 2:14; 6:5–6; 4:32–35; 4:2–6; 13:21.
[41] 2 Kgs 6:2.
[42] Cummings supplies 'John the Baptist' Is 40:3; Mt 11:11; 3:3.
[43] Mt 11:10.
[44] Pr *Christi et precursor*; Wo *et precursor*.
[45] Mt 3:13–17.
[46] Mt 4:1.

do anything else before hastening off to a solitary place. His baptism sanctified the sanctifying water; it did not wash or cleanse him from sin, because he had never committed or feared sin. He was burning with ardor for the desert and desired to enflame us all with the same ardor through his salutary example, though he himself had no need of repentance. If God himself, who is without sin, freely chooses it, how necessary must the desert be for people enslaved to wrongdoing? If the desert was sought by the innocent, how much more eagerly must it be desired by a sinner?

23. There in the desert, far from the crowds of noisy people, the silent angels offered their service to the Lord and strengthened him. When he reached the desert, he was served by ministering angels as if he had returned to heaven.[47] There he confounded the ancient enemy, who tempted him with the customary tricks of his art. And the new Adam drove off the seducer of the old Adam. What a triumph for the desert that the Devil, who had been victorious in Paradise, should be vanquished in a wasteland.

24. The desert was also the place where our Saviour fed, filled, and satisfied five thousand people with five loaves of bread and two fish.[48] Jesus always feeds his children with bread in the desert. Just as he once served his people manna as a pledge of divine help, now he served them with fragments of bread. In the same miraculous way that food had then fallen from the sky for the hungry people, he now multiplied loaves for the crowd to eat. When the food had been increased by his miraculous gift, the leftovers were more plentiful than what had originally been on hand for the meal. I do not hesitate to say that the cause and occasion of such great wonders was nothing but the desert; if the crowd had gathered in a place of abundant food, there would have been no need for a miracle.

25. After that, the Lord Jesus withdrew to the summit of a high mountain, and in the presence of three chosen disciples hid

---

47 Mt 4:11.
48 Mt 14:18–21.

face was transfigured by a remarkable brilliance.[49] The greatest of the apostles, who would later proclaim the risen Christ publicly, first came to belief because of the glory glimpsed in that solitary place. 'It is good', he said, 'for us to be here'.[50] He was overjoyed at the powerful transformation he had witnessed in that secluded wilderness.

26. Scripture says that the Lord Jesus was accustomed to go into a desert place to pray. The desert may rightly be called a place of prayer, for God himself has approved it and taught by his example that it is appropriate for prayer. The prayer of a humble petitioner[51] will more easily penetrate the clouds if it rises from the desert, because that solitary place gives it increased merit. The Lord Jesus, seeking that place for prayer, showed us where he prefers us to pray.

27. What shall I say now about John and Macarius and so many others whose way of life was like that of heaven while they lived in the desert? They drew as close to God as divine law permits. They were admitted into the counsels of divine providence in the highest degree permitted to those clothed in mortal flesh. Their minds fixed on Heaven, they were introduced into its mysteries. They progressed accompanied by grace in the form of silent revelations or of eloquent signs. In their ideal, solitary environment, they eventually attained the stage of being already in heaven in spirit though their bodies were still on earth.

28. The cell in the desert truly deserves to be called the ark of strength, the seat of faith, the tabernacle of charity, the treasury of piety, the storehouse of justice. For just as in a home precious objects and valuables are kept in a hidden place behind locked doors, so also those magnificent gifts of desert sanctity are put away in a cell in some desert protected by natural inaccessibility, lest they decay[52] because of exposure to worldliness. The desert

---

[49] Mt 17:1–5.
[50] Mt 17:4.
[51] Pr *humiliantis* for Wo *humilians*.
[52] Pr *obsolescat* for Wo *abolescat*.

is an ideal place for the Lord of all to preserve his precious ornament of sanctity, not only to store it there but to bring it out of its hiding place when it is needed.

29. In former times the desert was under the special and privileged care of divine providence, and this is still so even in our time. Today when an unexpected amount of food is generously given to a monk in the desert, what is this but a gift fallen from heaven? So the monks today have their own manna by heaven's bounty. The Lord works secretly through others to provide nourishment for his servants. And when these monks dig down through the rocky ground, and water finally begins to flow from the stones as a divine gift, what is this but water flowing from the rock as if it had been struck by a blow of Moses' staff?[53] Similarly, sufficient clothing is never wanting to those who live today in the desert waste;[54] one habit may wear out and be replaced by another, and there will be yet another, thanks to divine providence. The Lord nourished his people in the desert then, and he continues to nourish them now. He took care of the Israelites for forty years,[55] but he cares for the monks today all their lives.

30. It is right for a holy man aflame with divine passion to leave his own home and choose the desert as his dwelling. It is right for him to sell all his goods and prefer the desert to father and mother and children. It is right to abandon the land of one's birth and seek a provisional homeland in the desert, never to be called back by fear or longing or joy or sadness. Clearly this desert dwelling is worthy of total devotion.

31. Who can number adequately all the benefits of the desert and the advantages for virtue enjoyed by those who live there? Finding themselves placed in this world, they in a way go beyond this world. As the Apostle says, 'They wander through desert places, in mountains and caves and in holes of the earth'.[56]

---

[53] Ex 17:6.
[54] Dt 8:4; 19:5; Neh 9:21.
[55] Dt 8:2; Neh 9:21; Acts 13:18.
[56] Heb 11:38.

Quite correctly the Apostle says that the world is not worthy of such people, for they are alien to the confusion of human society; they are distant, quiet, silent, and free now both from sin and from inclination to sin.

32. In former times it was customary for illustrious men,[57] after wearing themselves out in business affairs, to turn to philosophy as to their proper home. How much more fitting is it for people today to direct themselves to the study of the highest wisdom, and how wonderful for them to withdraw into the leisure of solitude and the solitary places of the desert! This enables them to be free for philosophy alone and to wander in the desert with more pleasure than athletes exercising in the gymnasium.

Where, I ask, would it be possible to celebrate Easter more freely[58] than in a desert cell? Where possible to practice the virtues more easily? I am thinking particularly of the virtue of temperance, which is a sort of desert of the heart. For Moses undertook an unbroken fast in the desert for forty days,[59] and after him Elijah fasted for the same length of time.[60] They both extended their desert fast beyond the limit of human ability. Then our Lord also passed a time of abstinence in the desert.[61] And after that we never read again about his fasting for exactly forty days, so we must conclude that some special strength for fasting is to be found in desert places.

33. Where, I ask, could anyone find a better opportunity to be still and see how sweet the Lord is? Where can a more direct path be found for those on the way to perfection? Where does a broader field lie open for the practice of virtue? Where is there an easier place to guard the mind and free it for contemplation? Where could the heart be more free of concern in order to devote itself to cleaving to God? Nowhere but in

---

57 Latin: *viri*.
58 Pr *liberius* for Wo *salubrius*.
59 Ex 24:18; 34:28; Dt 9:9; 9:18.
60 1 Kgs 19:8.
61 Mt 4:2.

those solitary places in which it is easy to find God and never lose him again.

34. Desert lands are often covered with fine sand, yet there is no better place in which to lay the foundations of the building of which Scripture speaks. Although a person may stand on those desert sands, there is no way one could build a house on such sand.[62] Nowhere more than in the desert must that building be constructed on rock so that it will last with unshaken stability because it is based on a solid foundation. When the fierce storm breaks, the building will not be undermined by raging wind or torrential downpour. This is the sort of building that those who live in the desert construct for themselves, but in the depths of their hearts. They seek the heights by way of the depths; they pursue exalted things by way of humility. They are unmoved by and unmindful of earthly matters because their hope and desire is for heavenly things. They throw away wealth, preferring to go in want; they pursue poverty, longing for true riches. Day and night they struggle, in manual labor and in vigils, to attain the beginning of the life that never comes to an end. The desert holds them as in their mothers' lap while they long for eternity, despising this brief life; indifferent to the present life, they are confident of the life to come. In this way, by hastening toward the world's end, they manage to attain the world without end.

35. There in the desert the principles of progress in the spiritual life and the obligations of eternal life are observed more exactly. Laws against grave crimes and villainy are not needed there, nor are punishments meted out for capital offenses, for the punishments of an unjust law declare every heart but the purest to be guilty. In the desert even the interior attraction of the mind is diligently kept within the bounds of justice, and the very beginning of idle thoughts is deserving of punishment. Among other people it is wrong to have done evil, but among these people it is wrong to have done no good.

---

[62] Mt 7:24–26.

36. But how can I acknowledge with appropriate words of praise the fruit of this desert spirituality? I cannot pass over in silence the virtues that are almost as well known as they are well hidden in those desert dwellings. For when these monks give up human companionship and withdraw to remote places, they desire to be completely hidden, but merit cannot be concealed forever. The more they give themselves to the interior life, the more the glory of God pours out into their exterior life. In my opinion, God's glory directs them, so that his desert dwellers may be hidden from the world but their example not be hidden. They are that light set upon the lampstand of the desert to shine brightly over the whole world.[63] Out of the desert a brilliant light penetrates the darkest parts of the world, They are that city which cannot be hidden because it is built on the desert mountain, an earthly symbol of the heavenly Jerusalem.[64] Let all who are in darkness draw near to this light, and they will see again. Let any who are exposed to danger come to this city, and they will be safe.

37. How pleasant is the solitude of a remote place to those who thirst for God! How attractive for those who seek Christ are those solitary lands stretching in every direction under protecting nature. All things are silent there, and the joyful mind is spurred on by silence in its search for God, finding nourishment in ineffable ecstasies. No sound is heard in the desert save the voice of God. Only that sound that is sweeter than silence, the holy activity of a moderate and holy way of life, breaks into the state of quiet peace, while only the sound of the desert outpost interrupts the silence.[65] Then with sweetly resounding hymns the eager choirs ring in heaven itself, and the choir reaches heaven as much with voices as with prayers.

38. Then our prowling adversary howls in vain, like a wolf[66] in the sheepfold when the sheep are well guarded, as the vast

---

[63] Mt 5:14–15.

[64] Heb 12:22.

[65] Pr *solus ille animo, dum sonitus* for Wo *solus illi animo, dum sonitus suavis.*

[66] Pr *lupus, et tamquam* for Wo *lupus Lupus et tamquam.*

expanse of the desert protects them like a strong wall. Lest they who guard the city watch in vain, the monks are specially protected by Christ as their defender,[67] so that the particular part of the desert that is open to God's adopted children is thereby closed to all their enemies. Instead, the choir of rejoicing angels visit those beautiful places in the desert and, going up and down Jacob's ladder, enhance the desert by their frequent though invisible visitations.[68] The Spouse rests there at midday,[69] and those desert dwellers wounded with love contemplate him, saying, 'We have found him whom our soul loves, and we will hold him and never let him go'.[70]

39. The soil of the desert is not sterile and unfruitful, as is commonly held; its dry, stony ground is not unproductive. A sower has hidden countless tender shoots and hundreds of fruit trees there. In the desert the seeds are unlikely to fall on the roadside to be eaten by birds, or on rocky soil where they wither in the sun's heat for lack of deep roots, or on thorny land where the thorns eventually choke them out.[71] There the farmer reaps the harvest of an abundant crop; such a great crop is produced from these stones that the desert's dry bones are covered with meat.[72] There also is to be found that 'living bread that comes down from heaven';[73] from those stones gush forth refreshing fountains and streams of living water capable not only of satisfying thirst but of saving souls.[74] Here is a delightful meadow for the interior soul. The untilled desert is attractive with a wonderful pleasantness. The material desert becomes a paradise of the spirit.

40. No field however fertile can compare with the desert. Is some country known for its fine grain? In the desert thrives

---

[67] Ps 127:1.
[68] Gn 28:12.
[69] Sg 1:7.
[70] Sg 3:4.
[71] Mt 13:3–9.
[72] Ps 64:13.
[73] Jn 6:51.
[74] Jn 7:38; 4:14.

the wheat that satisfies the hungry with its richness.[75] Is some
country joyful over its heavy grapevines? The desert yields an
abundance of wine that 'rejoices the human heart'.[76] Is some
country famous for its lush pastures? The desert is the place
where those sheep contentedly graze of whom Scripture says,
'Feed my sheep'.[77] Is some country painted with beautiful flowers? In the desert blooms that true 'flower of the field and lily of
the valley'.[78] Is there a country renowned for its beautiful gems
and tawny gold?[79] In the desert, stones of varied brilliance gleam
with shimmering light. Thus the desert compares favorably
with every other land and surpasses them all in its diverse
advantages.

41. O admirable desert, how right it is for the holy monks to
live or desire to live near you and within you, for you are rich and
fertile in all the good things of him in whom all things are held.
The kind of inhabitant you look for is one who will cultivate
his own ground, not yours. You became fruitful in the virtues
of those who dwell in you and become sterile in their vices.
Whoever strives to become familiar with you shall find God.
Whoever has revered you has found Christ in you. Whoever
inhabits you rejoices to discover that the Lord inhabits you as
well. To possess you is to possess God himself. One who accepts
your hospitality becomes a temple of God.

42. I have great respect for every desert place that is the
illustrious home of a monk, but I honor my own Lérins above
all. Faithful to her reputation, she takes in her faithful arms
those who come to her from being shipwrecked in the stormy
world. For those who come burned from the world's fire she
tenderly provides shade where they can regain their spirits in
the shade of the Lord who refreshes the heart. Its bubbling
fountains, green grass, beautiful flowers, and all the delights of

---

[75] Ps 147:14.
[76] Ps 103:13.
[77] Jn 21:17.
[78] Sg 2:1.
[79] Pr *speciosis exultans metallis* for Wo *pretiosis et speciosis exultans metallis*.

sight and scent show those possessing this paradise what they
shall possess in the heavenly paradise.[80]

Lérins is worthy for having been founded by Honoratus
and endowed with his heavenly teaching; worthy for being
descended from so great a father shining in the strength of
the apostolic spirit;[81] worthy for having taken in Honoratus so
as to send him forth;[82] worthy for nourishing the outstanding
monks and priests it has raised and sent out as missionaries.[83]
Lérins now has as successor of Honoratus the noble Maximus,
who deserves a place of honor after the founder. A famous monk
of Lérins was Lupus, who reminds us of that wolf of the tribe of
Benjamin.[84] Lérins now has his brother Vincent, a jewel shining
with the brilliance of his spiritual life. Still living is the venerable
and respected Capriasius, the equal of the saints of old. And also,
there are those holy elders who brought the egyptian fathers to
Gaul after the destruction of their cells.

43. O good Jesus, what an assembly and community of saints
have I seen there! Precious alabasters with their secret oint-
ments were burning within them: the scent of life was breathing
everywhere.[85] They cared for the appearance of the interior soul
more than for that of the clothing they wore. They were bound
together by love, people tender in piety, strong in hope, meek
in humility, modest in hearing, quick in piety, silent among
themselves, and serene in countenance. By their constant contemplation they resemble a throng of quiet angels. They have
no longings or desires except for God, whom they desire with
great longing. Because they seek a blessed life, they do blessed
things;[86] thus they have already attained it while on earth. They
want to dwell apart from sinners and so they do. They want a

---

80 Pr *exhibet quem possidebunt* for Wo *exhibet.*
81 Pr *vultus* for Wo *vultu.*
82 Pr *emitteret* for Wo *eniteret.*
83 Pr *ambiendos* for Wo *ambiendo.*
84 Gn 49:27. Cummings notes that Saint Paul was a descendant of Benjamin. Ro 11:1; Phil 3:5.
85 Pr *flagrabant* for Wo *fragrabant*; Pr *spirabat* for Wo *consiprabat.*
86 Pr *beatam* for Wo *beata.*

life of purity, and they have it already. They pray to spend all their time praising God, and this is exactly what they do.[87] They want to rejoice with the assembly of the saints, and already they rejoice. They wish to enjoy Christ, and in their spirit they do enjoy him.[88] They desire to live the desert life, and in their heart they do.[89]

Thus it is that many of the very things they wish for the future are given them in the present through Christ's boundless love. Their hopes reach out for things they have in hand. In the labor itself they enjoy much of the labor's reward, because what will be the fruit of the work is already present in the work itself.

44. The fact that you, my beloved Hilary, have decided to return and join this community will profit both you and the community greatly, for now they are full of joy over your return. In their company please remember to pray for me and for my sins. I say 'in their company,' though I do not know whether you will be bringing or finding more joy there.

You are now the true Israel who gazes upon God in his heart, who has just been freed from the dark Egypt of this world, who has crossed the saving waters in which the enemy drowned, who follows the burning light of faith in the desert, who experiences things formerly bitter now made sweet by the wood of the cross, who draws from Christ waters welling up into eternal life,[90] who feeds his spirit from the bread from on high and who from the Gospel receives the divine word in thunder.[91] Because you keep company with Israel in the desert, you will certainly enter the promised land with Jesus.

In Christ Jesus our Lord, farewell.

---

[87] Pr *ambiunt? Habent* for Wo *volunt? iam habent.*

[88] Pr *Spiritu* for Wo *Christi Spiritu.*

[89] Pr *corde* for Wo *coram.*

[90] Jn 4:14. Pr *salientes in vitam aeternam aquas* for Wo *salientis in vitam aeternam aquae potum.*

[91] Ps 77:17–18; 104:7. Pr *tonitrui* for Wo *throni tui.*

BIBLIOGRAPhy

PRIMARY SOURCES

Athanasius. *Vita Beati Antonii Abbatis* (Latin trans. of the *Life of Antony*). *Patrologia Latina* 73, ed. J.-P. Migne. Turnholt: Brepols, 1977 (1846).

Bartelink, G. J. M. *Vie D'Antoine*. Sources Chrétiennes 400; Paris: Cerf, 1994.

Chevalier, Ulysse, ed. *Oeuvres complètes de Saint Avit, Évêque de Vienne*. Lyon: Librairie Générale Catholique et Classique, 1890.

Eucherius of Lyon. *De laude eremi*, ed. Salvatore Pricoco. Catania, 1965.

———. *Il Rifuto del Mondo: De contemptu mundi*, ed. Salvatore Pricoco. Firenze: Nardini, 1990.

———. 'Passio Agaunensium Martyrum: SS. Mauricii ac Sociorum Ejus', J.-P. Migne, ed., *Patrologia Latina* 50.827–832. Turnhout: Brepols, 1975 (1846).

———. *Sancti Evcherii Lvgdvnensis Formvlae spiritalis intellegentiae. Instrvctionvm libri duo. Passio agavnensivm martyrvm. Epistvla de lavde heremi. Accedvnt Epistvlae ab Salviano et Hilario et Rvstico* . . . . Vienna: F. Tempsky, 1894.

Fontaine, Jacques, ed. and trans. *Sulpice Sévère: Vie de Saint Martin*. Sources Chrétiennes 133–5; Paris: Cerf, 1967–9.

Frank, Karl Suso. 'Das Leben der Juraväter und die Magisterregel', *Regula Benedicti Studia* 13 (1984): 35–54.

Fry, Timothy, ed. *RB 1980: The Rule of Saint Benedict in Latin and English with Notes*. Collegeville, MN: The Liturgical Press, 1981.

Gregory of Tours. *Historia Francorum*, ed. B. Krusch. *Monumenta Germaniae Historica, Scriptores rerum merovingicarum*, vols. 1–2. Hannover, 1951.

Guy, Jean-Claude. *Jean Cassien: Institutions cénobitiques*. Sources Chrétiennes 109; Paris: Cerf, 1965.

Krusch, Bruno, ed. *Vita sanctorum abbatum acaunensium*, in *Passiones vitaeque sanctorum aevi Merovingici et antiquorum aliquot*. Monumenta Germaniae Historica, Scriptorum Rerum Merovingicarum, III. 125–66. Hannover: Impensis Bibliopolii Hahniani, 1896.

Martine, François. *Vie des pères du Jura.* Sources Chrétiennes 142; Paris: Cerf, 1988.

Petschenig, Michael, ed. *Iohannis Cassiani: De institutis coenobiorum* . . . . CSEL 17, Iohannis Cassiani Opera; Vienna: Tempsky, 1888.

Pichery, Eugène, ed. *Jean Cassien: Conférences.* Sources Chrétiennes 42, 54, & 64; Paris: Cerf, 1955–9.

Pieper, Rudolfus, ed. *Alcimi Ecdicii Aviti Viennensis Episcopi Opera Quae Supersunt.* Monumenta Germaniae Historica, Auctores antiquissimi, vol. 6; Berlin: Weidmannos, 1883.

Richardson, Ernest C., ed. *Hieronymous Liber de Viris Inlustribus; Gennadius Liber de Viris Inlustribus.* Texte und Untersuchungen 14.1; Leipzig: J. C. Hinrichs, 1896.

Vogüé, Adalbert de. *Les règles des saints pères.* Sources Chrétiennes 297–8; Paris: Cerf, 1982.

Vogüé, Adalbert de, and Joël Correau, eds. and trans. *Césaire d'Arles: Oeuvres monastiques;* vol. 1, *Oeuvres pour les moniales.* Sources Chrétiennes 345; Paris: Cerf, 1988.

Wotke, Carolus, ed. *Sancti Evcherii Lvgdvnensis Epistula de laude heremi.* CSEL 31; Prague: F. Tempsky, 1894.

PRIMARY SOURCES IN ENGLISH TRANSLATION

Brehaut, Ernest, trans. *History of the Franks.* New York: Octagon Books, 1973.

Cabaniss, Allen, trans. *The Emperor's Monk: Contemporary Life of Benedict of Aniane by Ardo.* Devon: Stockwell, 1979.

Dalton, O.M., trans. *The Letters of Sidonius.* Oxford: Clarendon, 1915.

———. *Life of the Fathers.* Oxford: Clarendon, 1927.

Deferrari, Roy Joseph, trans. 'St. Hilary: A Sermon on the Life of St. Honoratus', in Roy J. Deferrari, trans., et al., *Early Christian Biographies.* The Fathers of the Church 15; Washington, D. C.: The Catholic University of America Press, 1952.

———. *Early Christian Biographies.* Washington, D. C.: Catholic University of America Press, 1964.

Fry, Timothy, OSB. *RB 1980: The Rule of St. Benedict in English.* Collegeville, MN: The Liturgical Press, 1982.

Hoare, F. R., ed. and trans. 'St. Hilary: A Discourse on the Life of St. Honoratus', in F. R. Hoare, ed. and trans., *The Western Fathers.* New York: Sheed and Ward, 1954.

James, Edward, trans. *Gregory of Tours: Life of the Fathers*, Second Edition. Translated Texts for Historians, Latin Series 1; Liverpool: Liverpool UP, 1985.

McCarthy, Maria Caritas, trans. *The Rule for Nuns of St. Caesarius of Arles: A Translation with a Critical Introduction.* Washington, D.C.: Catholic University of America Press, 1960.

Noble, Thomas F. X. and Thomas Head. *Soldiers of Christ: Saints and Saints' Lives from Late Antiquity and the Early Middle Ages.* University Park, PA: The Pennsylvania State UP, 1995.

Palladius. *The Lausiac History*, trans. Robert T. Meyer. New York: Newman, 1964.

Peebles, Bernard M., trans. 'Sulpicius Severus: Writings', in Gerald G. Walsh, trans., et al., *Nicetas of Remesiana.* Fathers of the Church 7; New York: Fathers of the Church, 1949.

Ramsey, Boniface, OP. *John Cassian: The Conferences.* Ancient Christian Writers. Vol. 57. New York: Paulist, 1997.

Rose, Seraphim, trans. *Vita Patrum: The Life of the Fathers by St. Gregory of Tours.* Platina, CA: St. Herman of Alaska Brotherhood, 1988.

Severus, Sulpicius. 'The Life of Saint Martin', trans. by F. R. Hoare, in F. R. Hoare, ed. and trans., *The Western Fathers.* New York: Sheed and Ward, 1954.

———. 'The Life of Saint Martin of Tours', trans. by F. R. Hoare, in Thomas F. X. Noble and Thomas Head, eds., *Soldiers of Christ: Saints and Saints' Lives from Late Antoquity and the Early Middle Ages*, pp. 1–29. University Park, PA: The Pennsylvania State University Press, 1995.

———. 'Three Letters on St. Martin', trans. by F. R. Hoare, in F. R. Hoare, ed. and trans., *The Western Fathers.* New York: Sheed and Ward, 1954.

———. 'Two Dialogues', trans. by F. R. Hoare, in F. R. Hoare, ed. and trans., *The Western Fathers.* New York: Sheed and Ward, 1954.

Veilleux, Armand. *Pachomian KoinoniaI.* Three volumes. Kalamazoo:Cistercian Publications, 1980, 1981, 1982.

Vivian, Tim, and Apostolos N. Athanassakis, trans., *The Life of Antony*. Kalamazoo: Cistercian, forthcoming).

SECONDARY SOURCES

Baus, Karl, et al. *The Imperial Church from Constantine to the Early Middle Ages*, vol. II of *History of the Church* ed. by Hubert Jedin and John Dolan. London: Burns and Oates, 1980.

Beck, Henry G. J. *The Pastoral Care of Souls in South-East France During the Sixth Century*. Analecta Gregoriana 51, Series Facultatis Hist. Ecclesiasticae; Rome: Universitatis Gregoriana, 1950.

Benoit, D. P. *Histoire de l'abbaye de de la Terre de Saint-Claude*. Montreuil-sur-Mer: Imprimerie de la Chartreuse de Notre-Dame des Près, 1890.

Besse, Jean Martial Leon. *Les moines de l'ancienne France*. Paris, 1906.

Besson, Marius. *Recherces sur les origines des évêchés de Genève, Lausanne et Sion et leurs premiers titulaires jusqu'au déclin du VIe siècle*. Dissertation, Fribourg-Paris, 1906.

Brown, Peter. 'Relics and Social Status in the Age of Gregory of Tours', in Peter Brown, *Society and the Holy in Late Antiquity*, pp. 222–50. Berkeley & Los Angeles: University of California Press, 1982.

Chadwick, Nora K. *Poetry and Letters in Early Christian Gaul*. London: Bowes & Bowes, 1955.

Chaume, Maurice. 'Francs et Bourgondes aux cours du VIe siècle', in *Recherches d'histoire chrétienne et médiévale*, pp. 147–62. Dijon: Académie des sciences, arts, et belles-lettres, 1947.

Christin, Charles-Gabriel-Frédéric. *Dissertation sur l'établissement de l'abbaye de Saint-Claude, ses chroniques, ses légendes, ses chartes, ses usurpations et sur droits des habitants de cette terre*. Paris, 1772.

Clarke, H. B., and Mary Brennan, eds., *Columbanus and Merovingian Monasticism*. BAR Int. Ser. 113; Oxford: B.A.R., 1981.

Cottier, Jean-Pierre. *L'abbaye royale de Romainmôtier et le droit de sa terre du Ve au XIIIe siècle*. Lausanne, 1948.

Desprez, V. *Règles monastiques d'occident IVe-VIe siècle: D'Augustin à Ferréol*. Vie Monastique 9; Bégrolles-en-Mauges: Bellefontaine, 1980.

Dill, Samuel. *Law and Society in Early Medieval Europe: Studies in Legal History*. London: Variorum Reprints, 1988.

————. *Roman Society in Gaul in the Merovingian Age*. New York: Barnes & Noble, 1966 (1926).

Drinkwater, John, and Hugh Elton, eds. *Fifth-Century Gaul: A Crisis of Identity?* New York: Cambridge University Press, 1992.

Duchesne, L. 'La Vie des Pères du Jura', *Mélanges d'archéologie et d'histoire publiés par l'École française de Rome* 18 (1898): 1–16.

Dupraz, Louis. *Les Passions de S. Maurice d'Agaune: essai sur l'historicité de la tradition et contribution a l'étude de l'armée pré-dioclétienne (260–286) et des canonisations tardives de la fin du IVe siècle*. Fribourg: Éditions Universitaires, 1961.

Fisher, D. 'Liminality: The Vocation of the Church (I). The Desert Image in Early Christian Tradition'. *Cistercian Studies Quarterly* 24 (1989): 181–205.

Fontaine, Jacques. 'L'aristocratie occidentale devant le monachisme aux IVème et Vème siècles', *Rivista d'Istoria e Letteratura di Storia Religiosa* 15 (1979): 28–53.

————. 'L'ascétisme chrétien dans la littérature gallo-romaine d'Hilaire à Cassien', pp. 87–115 in *La Gallia romana*. Rome: Academia Nazionale dei Lincei, 1973.

————, and J.N. Hillgarth, eds. *The Seventh Century: Change and Continuity*. London: Warburg Institute–University of London, 1992.

Frank, Karl Suso. 'Das Leben der Juraväter und die Magisterregel', *Regula Benedicti Studia* 13 (1984): 35–54.

————. *Frühes Mönchtum im Abendland*. Zurich & Munich: Artemis, 1975.

Frend, W. H. C. *Martyrdom and Persecution in the Early Church: A Study of Conflict from the Maccabees to Donatus*. Grand Rapids, MI: Baker, repr. 1981 (1965).

————. 'Review of *Les passions de S. Maurice d'Agaune* by Louis Dupraz'. *Journal of Ecclesiastical History* 14 (1963): 85–6.

Gaudemet, J. 'Les aspects canoniques de la règle de saint Columban', in *Mélanges colombianiens: actes du Congrès international de Luxeuil, 20–23 juillet 1950*. Paris, 1951.

Geary, Patrick J. *Before France and Germany: The Creation and Transformation of the Merovingian World*. New York & Oxford: Oxford UP, 1988.

Goffart, Walter. *Barbarians and Romans, AD 418–585: The Technique of Accomodation*. Princeton: Princeton UP, 1980.

Grenier, Albert. 'Le Temple d'Izernore'. *Manuel d'Archéologie Gallo-romaine* 3.1, 403-6. Paris: Picard, 1931–60.

Griffe, E. *La Gaule chrétienne à l'époque romaine*. Three vols., rev. ed. Paris: Letouzey et Ané, 1964–6.

Heather, Peter J. *Goths and Romans*. Oxford: Oxford UP, 1992.

Heffernan, Thomas J. *Sacred Biography: Saints and their Biographers in the Middle Ages*. New York & Oxford: Oxford University Press, 1988.

Heinzelmann, Martin. 'L'Aristocratie et les évêches entre Loire et Rhin jusqu'a la fin du VIIe siècle'. *Revue d'histoire de l'église de France* 62 (1975): 75–90.

Heussi, Karl. *Der Ursprung des Mönchtums*. Tübingen, 1936.

Hillgarth, J.N. *The Conversion of Western Europe, 350–750*. Englewood Cliffs, NJ: Prentice-Hall, 1969.

Hoogterp, P.-W. 'Les Vies des Pères du Jura: Étude sur la langue'. *Bulletin du Cange: archivum latinitatis medii aevi* 9 (1934): 129–251.

Irsigler, Franz. 'On the Aristocratic Character of Early Frankish Society', in *The Medieval Nobility: Studies on the Ruling Classes of France and Germany from the Sixth to the Twelfth Century*. Amsterdam, NY: North-Holland Publishing Co., 1978.

James, Edward. 'Archaeology and the Merovingian Monastery', in H. B. Clarke and Mary Brennan, eds., *Columbanus and Merovingian Monasticism*, pp. 33–55. BAR Int. Ser. 113; Oxford: B.A.R., 1981.

———. *The Franks*. Oxford: Basil Blackwell, 1988.

———. *The Origins of France: From Clovis to the Capetians, 500–1000*. London: Macmillan, 1982.

Kempf, Friedrich, et al. *The Church in the Age of Feudalism*. Vol. III of *History of the Church* , ed. by Hubert Jedin and John Dolan. New York: Crossroad, 1987.

Jones, A. H. M. *The Later Roman Empire 284–602: A Social, Economic, and Administrative Survey*. Baltimore: Johns Hopkins, 1986.

Klingshirn, William E. *Caesarius of Arles: The Making of a Christian Community in Late Antique Gaul*. Cambridge Studies in Medieval Life and Thought; Cambridge: Cambridge UP, 1994.

König, D. *Amt und Askese: Priesteramt und Mönchtum bei den lateinischen Kirchenvätern in vorbenediktinscher Zeit*. Regulae Benedicti Studia, Supplementa 12; St. Otilien, 1985.

Lebecq, Stéphane, *Les Origines franques: Ve-IXe siècle. Nouvelle histoire de la France médiévale*, vol. 1. Paris: Èditions du Seuil, 1990.

Leclercq, Jean. ' "Eremus" et "Eremita" pour l'histoire du vocabulaire de la vie solitaire'. *Collectanea cisterciensia* 25 (1963): 8–30.

Longon, Auguste. *Géographie de la Gaule au VIe siècle*. Paris: Hachette, 1878.

Lorenz, R. 'Die Anfänge des abendländischen Mönchtums im 4. Jahrhundert'. *Zeitschrift für Kirchengeschichte* 77 (1966): 1–61.

Mâle, Émile. *La Fin du paganisme en Gaule et les plus anciennes basiliques chrétiennes*. Paris: Flammarion, 1950.

Markus, Robert. *The End of Ancient Christianity*. Cambridge: Cambridge UP, 1990.

——. 'From Caesarius to Boniface: Christianity and Paganism in Gaul', in Jacques Fontaine and J.N. Hillgarth, eds., *Le Septième siècle: Changements et continuités*, pp. 154–72. London: The Warburg Institute/University of London, 1992.

Masai, François. 'La "Vita patrum iurensium" et les débuts du monachisme à Saint-Maurice d'Agaune', in Johanne Autenrieth and Franz Brunhölzl, eds., *Festschrift Bernhard Bischoff zu seinem 65. Geburtstag*, pp. 43–69. Stuttgart: A. Hiersemann, 1971.

——. 'Recherches sur les Règles de S. Oyend et de S. Benoit'. *Regulae Benedicti Studia* 5 (1976): 43–73.

——. 'Review of *Vie des Pères du Jura* by François Martine'. *Revue d'histoire ecclésiastique* 65 (1970): 520–4.

Mathisen, Ralph W. *Ecclesiastical Factionalism and Religious Controversy in Fifth-Century Gaul*. Washington, D.C.: The Catholic University of America Press, 1989.

——. 'Episcopal Hierarchy and Tenure in Office in Late Roman Gaul: A Method for Establishing Dates of Ordination', *Francia* 17:1 (1990): 125–38.

——. *Roman Aristocrats in Barbarian Gaul: Strategies for Survival in an Age of Transition*. Austin: University of Texas Press, 1993.

Meinardus, Otto F. A. 'About the Translation of the Relics of the Theban Martyrs Sts. Cassius and Florentius from Bonn to Cairo', *Coptic Church Review* 13.2 (1992): 49–53.

Momigliano, Arnaldo, ed., *The Conflict between Paganism and Christianity in the Fourth Century*. Oxford: Clarendon, 1963.

Moyse, Gérard. 'Les origines du monachisme dans le diocèse de Besançon'. *Bibliothèque de l'École des Chartes* 13.1 (1973): 21–483.

Murray, Alexander Callander. *Germanic Kinship Structure: Studies in Law and Society in Antiquity and the Early Middle Ages*. Toronto: Pontifical Institute of Medieval Studies, 1983.

Nicholson, Jennifer, trans. *Caesar to Charlemagne: The Beginning of France*. New York: Barnes & Noble, 1968.

Périn, Patrick, and Laure-Charlotte Feffer. *Les Francs*. Vol. I, *A la conquête de la Gaule*; vol. II, *A l'origine de la France*. Paris: Colin, 1987.

Pietri, L. *La ville de Tours du IVe siècle au VIe siècle: Naissance d'une cité chrétienne*. Rome, 1983.

Pricoco, Salvatore. *L'isola dei santi : Il cenobio di Lerino e le origini del monachesimo gallico*. Rome: Edizioni dell'Ateneo & Bizzarri, 1978.

———. *Monaci filosofi e santi: Saggi di storia della cultura tardoantica*. Soveria Mannelli: Rubbettino Editore, 1992.

Prinz, Friedrich. 'Aristocracy and Christianity in Merovingian Gaul. An Essay', in Karl Bosl, ed., *Gesellschaft, Kultur, Literatur: Beiträge L. Wallach gewidmet*, pp. 153–65. Stuttgart: Anton Hiersemann, 1975.

———. *Frühes Mönchtum im Frankenreich: Kultur und Gesellschaft in Gallien, den Rheinlanden und Bayern am Beispiel der monastischen Entwicklung (4. bis 8. Jahrhundert)*. Munich & Vienna: R. Oldenbourg, 1965.

Reymond, Maurice. *Histoire de Romainmôtier*. Lausanne, 1928.

Riché, Pierre. 'Columbanus, his Followers and the Merovingian Church', in H. B. Clarke and Mary Brennan, eds., *Columbanus and Merovingian Monasticism*, pp. 59–72. BAR Int. Ser. 113; Oxford: B.A.R., 1981.

———. *Education and Culture in the Barbarian West, Sixth through Eighth Centuries*. Columbia, SC: South Carolina UP, 1976.

Robert, Ulysse. 'Chronique de Saint-Claude', *Bibliothèque de l'École des Chartes* 11 (1880): 561–9.

Rousseau, Philip. *Ascetics, Authority, and the Church in the Age of Jerome and Cassian*. Oxford: Oxford University Press, 1978.

———. *Pachomius: The Making of a Community in Fourth-Century Egypt*. Berkeley: University of California Press, 1985.

Russell, James C. *The Germanization of Early Medieval Christianity: A Sociohistorical Approach to Religious Transformation*. New York & Oxford: Oxford UP, 1994.

Stancliffe, Clare. 'From Town to Country: The Christianisation of the Toraine, 370–600', in Derek Baker, ed., *The Church in Town and Countryside*. Oxford: Blackwell, 1979.

————. *St. Martin and his Hagiographer*. Oxford: Clarendon, 1983.

Theurillat, J.-M. L'abbaye de Saint-Maurice d'Agaune des origines a la reforme canoniale, 515–830'. *Vallesia* 9 (1954): 1–128.

————. *Le Trésor de Saint-Maurice d'Agaune*. Saint-Maurice: Edition de l'Abbaye, 1956.

Thompson, E.A. 'Christianity and the Northern Barbarians', in Arnaldo Momigliano, ed., *The Confict between Paganism and Christianity in the Fourth Century*, pp. 56–78. Oxford: Clarendon, 1963.

van Bercham, Denis. 'Le Martyre de la légion thébaine: Essai sur la formation d'une legende'. *Schweizerische Beiträge zur Altertumswissenschaft*, fascicle 8. Basle, 1956.

Van Dam, Raymond. 'Images of Saint Martin in Late Roman and Early Merovingian Gaul'. *Viator* 19 (1988): 1–27.

————. *Leadership and Community in Late Antique Gaul*. Berkeley & Los Angeles: University of California Press, 1985.

————. *Saints and Their Miracles in Late Antique Gaul*. Princeton: Princeton UP, 1993.

Vergille, B. *Saint-Claude: Vie et présence*. Paris, 1960.

Vieillard-Troiekouroff, May. *Les Monuments réligieux de la Gaule d'après les œuvres de Grégoire de Tours*. Paris: H. Champion, 1976.

Vivian, Tim. *Histories of the Monks of Upper Egypt and the Life of Onnophrius*. Kalamazoo: Cistercian, 1993.

————. 'Words to Live By: A Conversation that the Elders Had with One Another Concerning Thoughts', *St. Vladimir's Theological Quarterly* 39.2 (1995): 127–41.

Vogüé, Adalbert de. 'Les débuts de la vie monastique à Lérins: Remarques sur un ouvrage récent'. *Revue d'Histoire Ecclésiastique* 88:1 (Jan.-March 1993): 5–53.

————. *Les Règles monastiques anciennes (400–700)*. Typologie des sources du moyen âge occidental; Turnhout: Brepols, 1985.

————. 'Monachisme et église dans la pensée de Cassien', in *Théologie de la vie monastique*, pp. 213–40. Théologie 49; Lyon, 1961. ET in 'Monasticism and the Church in the Writings of Cassian', *Monastic Studies* 3 (1965): 19–51.

————. 'La Vie de Pères du Jura et la datation de la Regula Orientalis'. *Revue d'Ascétique et d'Mystique* 47 (1971): 121–8.

Wallace-Hadrill, John M. *The Barbarian West: The Early Middle Ages A.D. 400–1000.* New York: Harper & Row, 1962.

————. *The Frankish Church.* Oxford: Clarendon, 1983.

————. *The Long-Haired Kings.* Toronto: University of Toronto Press, 1982 (1962).

Weidemann, Margarete. *Kulturgeschichte der Merowingerzeit nach den Werken Gregors von Tours.* Two vols.; Mainz: Verlag des römisch-germanischen Zentralmuseums, 1982.

Werner, Karl Ferdinand. 'La Place du VIIe siècle dans l'évolution politique et institionelle de la Gaule franque', in Jacques Fontaine and J.N. Hillgarth, eds., *The Seventh Century: Change and Continuity*, pp. 173–211. London: Warburg Institute–University of London, 1992.

Wood, Ian. 'A Prelude to Columbanus: The Monastic Achievement in the Burgundian Territories', in H.B. Clarke and Mary Brennan, eds., *Columbanus and Merovingian Monasticism*, pp. 3–32. BAR Int. Ser. 113; Oxford: B.A.R., 1981.

Woods, David. 'The Origin of the Legend of Maurice and the Theban Legion'. *Journal of Ecclesiastical History* 45:3 (1994): 385–95.

Young, Bailey K. 'Paganisme, christianisation et rites funéraires mérovingiens'. *Archéologie Médiévale* 7 (1977): 5–81.

Zöllner, Erich. *Geschichte der Franken, bis zur Mitte des sechsten Jahrhunderts.* Munich: C. H. Beck, 1970.

INDEX OF SCRIPTURE AND PATRISTIC REFERENCES

(Numbers Refer to Paragraph Numbers)

The Life of the Jura Fathers

OLD TESTAMENT

Genesis

3	29
5:22–24	30
8:8–12	2
15:5	121
28:12	123

Leviticus

12:2–8	12
12:8	12

1 Samuel

3:3	125
13:11–14	30
15:9–30	30

1 Kings

2:28	162
11:1–11	30
11:28	70
17:14, 16	69

2 Kings

2:11	30
4:43	70

1 Chronicles

12:28	70

Job

42:10	162

Psalms

76:11 (Vulgate)	15
131:6 (Vulgate)	3

Isaiah

52:1–2 (Vulgate)	84

Daniel

3:49–50	163

Wisdom

8:19	70

NEW TESTAMENT

Matthew

9:9	31
13:24–30	31

227

Avitus, Bishop of Vienne Letter XVIIII to Viventiolus

Eucherius of Lyon *The Passion of the Martyrs of Agaune*

Eucherius of Lyon *In Praise of the Desert*

in&ex of names

index of subjects

CISTERCIAN TEXTS

Bernard of Clairvaux

- Apologia to Abbot William
- Five Books on Consideration: Advice to a Pope
- Homilies in Praise of the Blessed Virgin Mary
- Letters of Bernard of Clairvaux / by B.S. James
- Life and Death of Saint Malachy the Irishman
- Love without Measure: Extracts from the Writings of St Bernard / by Paul Dimier
- On Grace and Free Choice
- On Loving God / Analysis by Emero Stiegman
- Parables and Sentences
- Sermons for the Summer Season
- Sermons on Conversion
- Sermons on the Song of Songs I–IV
- The Steps of Humility and Pride

William of Saint Thierry

- The Enigma of Faith
- Exposition on the Epistle to the Romans
- Exposition on the Song of Songs
- The Golden Epistle
- The Mirror of Faith
- The Nature and Dignity of Love
- On Contemplating God: Prayer & Meditations

Aelred of Rievaulx

- Dialogue on the Soul
- Liturgical Sermons, I
- The Mirror of Charity
- Spiritual Friendship
- Treatises I: On Jesus at the Age of Twelve, Rule for a Recluse, The Pastoral Prayer
- Walter Daniel: The Life of Aelred of Rievaulx

John of Ford

- Sermons on the Final Verses of the Songs of Songs I–VII

Gilbert of Hoyland

- Sermons on the Songs of Songs I–III
- Treatises, Sermons and Epistles

Other Early Cistercian Writers

- Adam of Perseigne, Letters of
- Alan of Lille: The Art of Preaching
- Amadeus of Lausanne: Homilies in Praise of Blessed Mary
- Baldwin of Ford: Spiritual Tractates I–II
- Geoffrey of Auxerre: On the Apocalypse
- Gertrud the Great: Spiritual Exercises
- Gertrud the Great: The Herald of God's Loving-Kindness (Books 1, 2)
- Gertrud the Great: The Herald of God's Loving-Kindness (Book 3)
- Guerric of Igny: Liturgical Sermons Vol. 1 & 2
- Helinand of Froidmont: Verses on Death
- Idung of Prüfening: Cistercians and Cluniacs: The Case for Cîteaux
- Isaac of Stella: Sermons on the Christian Year, I–[II]
- The Life of Beatrice of Nazareth
- Serlo of Wilton & Serlo of Savigny: Seven Unpublished Works
- Stephen of Lexington: Letters from Ireland
- Stephen of Sawley: Treatises

MONASTIC TEXTS

Eastern Monastic Tradition

- Besa: The Life of Shenoute
- Cyril of Scythopolis: Lives of the Monks of Palestine
- Dorotheos of Gaza: Discourses and Sayings
- Evagrius Ponticus: Praktikos and Chapters on Prayer
- Handmaids of the Lord: Lives of Holy Women in Late Antiquity & the Early Middle Ages / by Joan Petersen
- Harlots of the Desert / by Benedicta Ward
- John Moschos: The Spiritual Meadow
- Lives of the Desert Fathers
- Lives of Simeon Stylites / by Robert Doran
- The Luminous Eye / by Sebastian Brock
- Mena of Nikiou: Isaac of Alexandria & St Macrobius
- Pachomian Koinonia I–III (Armand Veilleux)
- Paphnutius: Histories/Monks of Upper Egypt
- The Sayings of the Desert Fathers / by Benedicta Ward
- Spiritual Direction in the Early Christian East / by Irénée Hausherr
- The Spiritually Beneficial Tales of Paul, Bishop of Monembasia / by John Wortley
- Symeon the New Theologian: TheTheological and Practical Treatises & The Three Theological Discourses / by Paul McGuckin
- Theodoret of Cyrrhus: A History of the Monks of Syria
- The Syriac Fathers on Prayer and the Spiritual Life / by Sebastian Brock

CISTERCIAN PUBLICATIONS

TITLES LISTING

Western Monastic Tradition

- Anselm of Canterbury: Letters I–III / by Walter Fröhlich
- Bede: Commentary...Acts of the Apostles
- Bede: Commentary...Seven Catholic Epistles
- Bede: Homilies on the Gospels I–II
- Bede: Excerpts from the Works of St Augustine on the Letters of the Blessed Apostle Paul
- The Celtic Monk / by U. Ó Maidín
- Life of the Jura Fathers
- Maxims of Stephen of Muret
- Peter of Celle: Selected Works
- Letters of Rancé I–II
- Rule of the Master
- Rule of Saint Augustine

Christian Spirituality

- The Cloud of Witnesses: The Development of Christian Doctrine / by David N. Bell
- The Call of Wild Geese / by Matthew Kelty
- The Cistercian Way / by André Louf
- The Contemplative Path
- Drinking From the Hidden Fountain / by Thomas Spidlík
- Eros and Allegory: Medieval Exegesis of the Song of Songs / by Denys Turner
- Fathers Talking / by Aelred Squire
- Friendship and Community / by Brian McGuire
- Gregory the Great: Forty Gospel Homilies
- High King of Heaven / by Benedicta Word
- The Hermitage Within / by a Monk
- Life of St Mary Magdalene and of Her Sister St Martha / by David Mycoff
- Many Mansions / by David N. Bell
- Mercy in Weakness / by André Louf
- The Name of Jesus / by Irénée Hausherr
- No Moment Too Small / by Norvene Vest
- Penthos: The Doctrine of Compunction in the Christian East / by Irénée Hausherr
- Praying the Word / by Enzo Bianchi
- Rancé and the Trappist Legacy / by A. J. Krailsheimer
- Russian Mystics / by Sergius Bolshakoff
- Sermons in a Monastery / by Matthew Kelty
- Silent Herald of Unity: The Life of Maria Gabrielle Sagheddu / by Martha Driscoll
- The Spirituality of the Christian East / by Thomas Spidlík
- The Spirituality of the Medieval West / by André Vauchez
- Tuning In To Grace / by André Louf
- Wholly Animals: A Book of Beastly Tales / by David N. Bell

MONASTIC STUDIES

- Community and Abbot in the Rule of St Benedict I–II / by Adalbert de Vogüé
- The Finances of the Cistercian Order in the Fourteenth Century / by Peter King
- Fountains Abbey and Its Benefactors / by Joan Wardrop
- The Hermit Monks of Grandmont / by Carole A. Hutchison
- In the Unity of the Holy Spirit / by Sighard Kleiner
- The Joy of Learning & the Love of God: Essays in Honor of Jean Leclercq
- Monastic Odyssey / by Marie Kervingant
- Monastic Practices / by Charles Cummings
- The Occupation of Celtic Sites in Ireland / by Geraldine Carville
- Reading St Benedict / by Adalbert de Vogüé
- Rule of St Benedict: A Doctrinal and Spiritual Commentary / by Adalbert de Vogüé
- The Rule of St Benedict / by Br. Pinocchio
- St Hugh of Lincoln / by David H. Farmer
- The Venerable Bede / by Benedicta Ward
- Western Monasticism / by Peter King
- What Nuns Read / by David N. Bell
- With Greater Liberty: A Short History of Christian Monasticism & Religious Orders / by Karl Frank

CISTERCIAN STUDIES

- Aelred of Rievaulx: A Study / by Aelred Squire
- Athirst for God: Spiritual Desire in Bernard of Clairvaux's Sermons on the Song of Songs / by Michael Casey
- Beatrice of Nazareth in Her Context / by Roger De Ganck
- Bernard of Clairvaux: Man, Monk, Mystic / by Michael Casey [tapes and readings]
- Bernardus Magister...Nonacentenary
- Catalogue of Manuscripts in the Obrecht Collection of the Institute of Cistercian Studies / by Anna Kirkwood
- Christ the Way: The Christology of Guerric of Igny / by John Morson
- The Cistercians in Denmark / by Brian McGuire
- The Cistercians in Scandinavia / by James France
- A Difficult Saint / by Brian McGuire
- A Gathering of Friends: Learning & Spirituality in John of Ford / by Costello and Holdsworth
- Image and Likeness: Augustinian Spirituality of William of St Thierry / by David Bell

- Index of Authors & Works in Cistercian Libraries in Great Britain I / by David Bell
- Index of Cistercian Authors and Works in Medieval Library Catalogues in Great Britian / by David Bell
- The Mystical Theology of St Bernard / by Étienne Gilson
- The New Monastery: Texts & Studies on the Earliest Cistercians
- Nicolas Cotheret's Annals of Cîteaux / by Louis J. Lekai
- Pater Bernhardus: Martin Luther and Saint Bernard / by Franz Posset
- Pathway of Peace / by Charles Dumont
- A Second Look at Saint Bernard / by Jean Leclercq
- The Spiritual Teachings of St Bernard of Clairvaux / by John R. Sommerfeldt
- Studies in Medieval Cistercian History
- Studiosorum Speculum / by Louis J. Lekai
- Three Founders of Cîteaux / by Jean-Baptiste Van Damme
- Towards Unification with God (Beatrice of Nazareth in Her Context, 2)
- William, Abbot of St Thierry
- Women and St Bernard of Clairvaux / by Jean Leclercq

MEDIEVAL RELIGIOUS WOMEN

edited by Lillian Thomas Shank and John A. Nichols:
- Distant Echoes
- Hidden Springs: Cistercian Monastic Women (2 volumes)
- Peace Weavers

CARTHUSIAN TRADITION

- The Call of Silent Love / by A Carthusian
- The Freedom of Obedience / by A Carthusian
- From Advent to Pentecost
- Guigo II: The Ladder of Monks & Twelve Meditations / by Colledge & Walsh
- Halfway to Heaven / by R.B. Lockhart
- Interior Prayer / by A Carthusian
- Meditations of Guigo II / by A. Gordon Mursall
- The Prayer of Love and Silence / by A Carthusian
- Poor, Therefore Rich / by A Carthusian
- They Speak by Silences / by A Carthusian
- The Way of Silent Love (A Carthusian Miscellany)
- Where Silence is Praise / by A Carthusian
- The Wound of Love (A Carthusian Miscellany)

CISTERCIAN ART, ARCHITECTURE & MUSIC

- Cistercian Abbeys of Britain
- Cistercians in Medieval Art / by James France
- Studies in Medieval Art and Architecture / edited by Meredith Parsons Lillich
  (Volumes II–V are now available)
- Stones Laid Before the Lord / by Anselme Dimier
- Treasures Old and New: Nine Centuries of Cistercian Music (compact disc and cassette)

THOMAS MERTON

- The Climate of Monastic Prayer / by T. Merton
- Legacy of Thomas Merton / by P. Hart
- Message of Thomas Merton / by P. Hart
- Monastic Journey of Thomas Merton / by P. Hart
- Thomas Merton/Monk / by P. Hart
- Thomas Merton on St Bernard
- Toward an Integrated Humanity / edited by M. Basil Pennington

CISTERCIAN LITURGICAL DOCUMENTS SERIES

- Cistercian Liturgical Documents Series / edited by Chrysogonus Waddell, ocso
- Hymn Collection of the...Paraclete
- *Institutiones nostrae:* The Paraclete Statutes
- Molesme Summer-Season Breviary (4 volumes)
- Old French Ordinary & Breviary of the Abbey of the Paraclete (2 volumes)
- Twelfth-century Cistercian Hymnal (2 volumes)
- The Twelfth-century Cistercian Psalter
- Two Early Cistercian *Libelli Missarum*

STUDIA PATRISTICA

- Studia Patristica XVIII, Volumes 1, 2 and 3

CISTERCIAN PUBLICATIONS

HOW TO CONTACT US

Editorial Queries

Editorial queries & advance book information should be directed to the Editorial Offices:

- Cistercian Publications
  WMU Station
  1201 Oliver Street
  Kalamazoo, Michigan 49008

- Telephone 616 387 8920
- Fax 616 387 8390
- e-mail mcdougall@wmich.edu

How to Order in the United States

Customers may order these books through booksellers, from the editorial office, or directly from the warehouse:

- Cistercian Publications
  Saint Joseph's Abbey
  167 North Spencer Road
  Spencer, Massachusetts 01562-1233

- Telephone 508 885 8730
- Fax 508 885 4687
- e-mail cistpub@spencerabbey.org
- Web Site www.spencerabbey.org/cistpub

How to Order from Canada

- Novalis
  49 Front Street East, Second Floor
  Toronto, Ontario M5E 1B3

- Telephone 416 363 3303
            1 800 387 7164
- Fax 416 363 9409

How to Order from Europe

- Cistercian Publications
  97 Loughborough Road
  Thringstone, Coalville, Leicester LE67 8LQ

- Fax 44 1530 45 02 10
- e-mail MsbcistP@aol.com

Cistercian Publications is a non-profit corporat-ion. Its publishing program is restricted to mo-nastic texts in translation and books on the monastic tradition.

A complete catalogue of texts in translation and studies on early, medieval, and modern monas-ticism is available, free of charge, from any of the addresses above.